D1161553

FLORIDA STATE
UNIVERSITY LIBRARIES

JUL 10 1997

TALLAHASSEE, FLORIDA

BUILDING A PALESTINIAN STATE

INDIANA SERIES IN ARAB AND ISLAMIC STUDIES

Salih J. Altoma, Iliya Harik, and Mark Tessler, general editors

Building a Palestinian State

THE INCOMPLETE REVOLUTION

Glenn E. Robinson

INDIANA UNIVERSITY PRESS

Bloomington and Indianapolis

HN
660
Z9
E46
1997

© 1997 by Glenn E. Robinson

All rights reserved

No part of this book may be reproduced or utilized in any
form or by any means, electronic or mechanical, including
photocopying and recording, or by any information storage and
retrieval system, without permission in writing from the publisher.
The Association of American University Presses' Resolution on
Permissions constitutes the only exception to this prohibition.

The paper used in this publication meets the minimum
requirements of American National Standard for Information
Sciences—Permanence of Paper for Printed Library
Materials, ANSI Z39.48-1984.

Manufactured in the United States of America

Library of Congress Cataloging-in-Publication Data

Robinson, Glenn E., date
Building a Palestinian state : the incomplete revolution / Glenn E. Robinson.
p.   cm. — (Indiana series in Arab and Islamic studies)
Includes bibliographical references and index.
ISBN 0–253–33217–6 (cl : alk. paper). — ISBN 0–253–21082–8 (pa : alk. paper)
1. Elite (Social sciences)—Palestine. 2. Palestine—Politics and
government. 3. Intifada, 1987– 4. Palestinian Arabs—Political
activity. 5. Nationalism—Palestine. I. Title. II. Series.
HN660.Z9E46   1997
305.52'095694—dc20   96–24708

1   2   3   4   5   02   01   00   99   98   97

For Elizabeth

CONTENTS

PREFACE

This book is about issues of collective action as well as about the Palestinians. That is, while it is a case study of the Intifada and its aftermath, the book also focuses on three central questions of revolutionary collective action.

The first question I ask is fundamental: Why do people rebel? More precisely, since grievances are always present in any society, what makes an aggrieved people turn from individual acts of rebellion to sustained collective action? I take up this question in the Palestinian case by asking what made the Intifada, the 1987–93 uprising, possible, given that Palestinians in the West Bank and Gaza had lived under Israeli military occupation for twenty years before the Intifada began without engaging in anything approaching this level of action. The question is not really what were the causes of the Intifada, since any people would chafe under military occupation, but rather what happened to transform individual anger into a revolutionary process.

The second question has to do with the revolutionary process itself. How is revolutionary collective action sustained in the face of overwhelming counterforce (as states almost always have over rebellious societies)? In this case, how could the Palestinians sustain collective action for years in the face of harsh Israeli measures meant to deter such action?

Third, and perhaps most interesting, is this question: How does the revolutionary process shape the political outcome in an emerging state? That is, when revolutions come to power, what can the dynamics of the revolution itself tell us about how the new state will look? What are the relationships between revolutionary causes, processes, and political outcomes? In the Palestinian case, the question is the same: How do the dynamics of the Intifada impact the state-building process of the Palestine Liberation Organization (PLO) in the West Bank and Gaza? What is the "logic" of Palestinian state-building?

In answer to the first question, I argue that the Intifada became possible only with the rise of a new and distinctive political elite in the West Bank and Gaza. Palestinian politics had long been dominated by an urban, landowning elite, which had its roots in nineteenth-century Ottoman policies. Ruling states had used this class, known as the notables, to maintain effective social control. The two bases on which the notables' authority rested were a web of traditional patron-client relations and ownership of land. Each pillar was undermined by the unintended consequences of Israeli policies: opening Israel's labor markets to mostly agrarian Palestinians weakened patron-client networks, and land confiscations attacked that which brought the notable class social power—control over land.

The new elite which rose to prominence in the 1980s came from a different social class than its notable counterpart. The new elite was not a landowning class, and its members were more likely to be from villages, refugee camps, and small towns than from urban centers. Because it came from a lower social class, the new elite was much more extensive than the old one. It largely coalesced at Palestinian universities—institutions that did not exist prior to 1972.

In large measure because it came from a different social class, the new elite promulgated an ideology different from that of the old elite. While the notables ultimately espoused political transformation—independence from Israel—the new elite sought not just political but also social transformation: to remake Palestinian society, thus undermining the social bases of notable power. It was this new elite that undertook a policy of popular mobilization in the 1980s. Grassroots organizations forged in this period—student blocs, labor unions, women's committees, agricultural relief committees, medical relief committees, voluntary works organizations—were the institutional expression of the new elite. Grassroots mobilization provided a means to both oppose notable power and build the social and political relations necessary to sustain the Intifada.

Structural change made the policy of mobilization possible. In this case, structural change—primarily changing patterns of employment, land tenure, and higher education—not only helped to eclipse the power of an old elite and create a counterelite but also produced a society in which the possibility of mobilization existed. In short, the changing labor market made peasants into Palestinians.

The Intifada thus was made possible by the emergence of a new political elite, itself the by-product of structural transformations in Palestinian society. Sustained collective action could not be undertaken in the absence of the institutions and ideology of the new elite (in contradistinction to the nonmobilizational ideology of, and the absence of institutions built by, the notable elite). While the Palestinians always had a surplus of grievances living under military occupation, revolutionary collective action had to wait for a counterelite that could organize it. Not surprisingly, while the Intifada was primarily about confronting the occupation, it also contained a strong antinotable, transformative flavor.

In terms of the second question—sustaining collective action in the face of overwhelming force—I argue that central to understanding the Palestinians' ability to sustain the Intifada is the notion of devolved authority. With the rise of a new elite, authority had spread downward in society and become much more diffused within it than before. This was of critical importance. Earlier attempts to confront the occupation had largely failed because authority in Palestinian society was concentrated in a small stratum at the top of society. Israel could cut off the metaphorical head of the beast, and the nascent rebellion would collapse. In the Intifada, when one group of leaders was arrested another would immediately spring up.

The institutions of devolved authority numbered in the thousands. They included not only the extant grassroots organizations but also the popular committees (*lijan sha'biya*), which virtually ran Palestinian society during the Intifada. Such popular organizations ranged from the ever-changing leadership of the Intifada (*al-qiyada al-wataniyya al-muwahida l'il-intifada,* or the Unified National Leadership of the Uprising, UNLU) to local branches of the UNLU to ad hoc committees that distributed food during curfews or taught neighborhood students when schools were closed. They included militant groups, which would enforce strikes, attack collaborators, and organize confrontations with Israeli forces. Such groups sustained collective action in spite of harsh Israeli measures to stop it—and in spite of attempts by the PLO in Tunis to undermine autonomous political actions outside its control.

In sum, the revolutionary process was directly linked to the structural changes which preceded it. In this case, structural changes had weakened an old elite and brought a counterelite to the fore. This new elite mobilized a transformed society in order to better confront the occupation. By so doing, authority was pushed downward in society away from the notable elite and toward a much broader spectrum of individuals. The devolution of authority was seen directly in the Intifada by the emergence of thousands of popular institutions which organized Palestinian society under emergency conditions and which Israel found to be impossible to eliminate. Sustained collective action, then, was directly linked to the reorganization of authority in Palestinian society by the mobilization efforts of the new elite.

While the Intifada was a social revolution, it remained incomplete. It was a social revolution precisely because of its social transformative element. In other words, it was not only an anticolonial political revolution but also a movement that sought to remake internal Palestinian society. The promise of social transformation was never entirely fulfilled. The new elite was never able to fully consolidate its position of power, largely because the Intifada was never able to throw off the yoke of Israeli occupation. Only by actually coming to power in a new polity would the new elite be able to consolidate not only the political changes but also the social changes of the Intifada.

The new elite, however, would not have the chance to consolidate its position, because political power in the post-Intifada polity was captured by an outside political force, one geographically and politically removed from the West Bank and Gaza: the PLO in Tunis. In answering the third question posed at the outset—the relationship between revolutionary process and political outcome—the Palestinian case can be seen to be exceptional in two significant ways. First, while all successful social revolutions create their own states, the Intifada produced its own polity without first enjoying success. Only after it was contained and largely defeated did the Intifada produce the political outcome of a new polity. Second, the political elite that came to power in the new "state" was not the same political elite that produced the revolution.

The new Palestinian polity shares the major problem of all revolutions brought to power: the devolved authority necessary for sustaining the revolution is directly at odds with the impulse to centralize authority in the new state. This problem was multiplied in the Palestinian case because the "outside" PLO which came to power in Palestine—epitomized by Yasir Arafat—did not have practical political experience with Palestinian society in the West Bank and Gaza. Put bluntly, the new "regime" did not trust its own society because it had so few connections with it. In particular, it did not trust the political elite which produced the Intifada—a political elite largely consisting of PLO members from inside Gaza and the West Bank. In fact, given the unusual circumstances under which it came to power in Palestine, the first political task of the outside PLO was to undermine the new elite through co-optation, coercion, and marginalization. The authoritarianism and the anti-institutional personalization of politics currently practiced by the Palestinian regime— the antithesis of the politics of the new elite—are largely aimed at consolidating the power of the Palestinian Authority.

The order of the chapters reflects the cause-process-outcome dynamic just outlined. The first three chapters focus on elite conflict prior to the Intifada, including the structural changes in Palestinian society which framed the struggle. The first chapter is an overview of the rise and politics of the Palestinian notable class which has so dominated Palestinian politics. In chapter 2, I discuss the rise of a counterelite by focusing on the student movement at Palestinian universities after 1972. Chapter 3 examines the mobilization campaign of the new elite before and during the Intifada by providing case studies of medical and agricultural relief committees.

The next three chapters deal specifically with the Intifada, concentrating on the issues of devolved authority and sustained collective action. Chapter 4, a case study of one town in the West Bank, Bayt Sahur, examines in detail how elite conflict and popular organization played out locally during the Intifada. The title of the chapter, "Abu Barbur," comes from a less-than-complimentary name members of the new elite in Bayt Sahur used for their mayor; it can be seen as a metaphor for the notable social class. In chapter 5, I expand the argument on devolved authority by examining the issue of popular committees more broadly throughout the West Bank and Gaza during the Intifada. Chapter 6 deals with Islamist mobilization and collective action during the Intifada as a competitor to the "inside" PLO.

The last chapter deals with the political outcome of the Intifada—the state-building process born of the Oslo Accords. It is in this chapter that I discuss the "disconnect" between the extant distribution of authority in Palestine and an outside elite trying to centralize and consolidate its authority after it had captured the revolution. This contradiction has been the primary source of instability in Palestine under self-rule.

While relevant secondary sources have been consulted, the vast bulk of information in this book comes from primary research, principally interviews and documentary material. Interviews were conducted and materials gathered during seven months of fieldwork in 1989–90; this initial research was followed by further fieldwork in 1992, 1994, and 1995.

A Note on Transliteration and Translation

The system of transliteration adopted in this book is intended to balance the interests of both readers and nonreaders of Arabic. *Ayns* and *hamzas* are the only diacritics included in the text, and both are indicated by a vertical prime ('). Well-known names are transliterated as they are found in the Western press (e.g., Gaza instead of Ghazza). Where multiple English spellings are commonly found for a single name, the more correct transliteration has been employed (e.g., Yasir instead of Yasser). Unless otherwise noted, all translations are by the author.

ACKNOWLEDGMENTS

I gratefully acknowledge the institutions and individuals who made this book possible. Fieldwork, undertaken in 1989–90, 1992, 1994, and 1995, was variously sponsored by the University of California at Berkeley, the Naval Postgraduate School, and the United States Institute of Peace. The Truman Institute at the Hebrew University of Jerusalem kindly hosted me during the original fieldwork.

Whatever merit this book has is largely due to the people who have read part or all of it in its various manifestations. They include Ken Jowitt, Ira Lapidus, Chalmers Johnson, Robert Springborg, Ghassan Andoni, Elias Rishmawi, Majid Nassar, Salim Tamari, Ziad Abu-Amr, Manuel Hassassian, Efrach Zilberman, Janet Rabinowitch, and David Waldner. David has been a constant source of intellectual inspiration and a good friend. I would also like to thank Ann Lesch and Mark Tessler, who reviewed the manuscript for Indiana University Press and provided many helpful comments. Their enthusiastic response to the work was particularly gratifying.

Thanks go also to the hundreds of Palestinians who spent thousands of hours indulging my questions. Their openness and hospitality in the midst of trying circumstances were remarkable.

An earlier version of chapter 3 appeared in the *International Journal of Middle East Studies* 25:2 (May 1993) and is reprinted here with the permission of Cambridge University Press.

Elizabeth Keeler Robinson has lived with this project for years. She has been my greatest source of support, a wonderful companion, and a terrific editor throughout. It is to her that this book is dedicated.

BUILDING A PALESTINIAN STATE

1

The Traditional Notable Elite in Palestine

The dominant political group within the Palestinian community in the nineteenth and twentieth centuries was the social class referred to as notables. The formation of this notable class can be traced to the mid-nineteenth century, when the Ottoman Empire, as part of its general administrative restructuring, used prominent local figures in Palestine as intermediaries to the larger population in the area. As intermediaries between the Porte (the Ottoman seat of power, in Istanbul) and the population, the notables, or *a'yan*, were generally charged with the collection and transmission of tax revenues. Over time, notables coalesced politically into a class and were able to translate their intermediary position into significant wealth, generally in the form of landowning. In turn, their wealth was translated into political prominence, especially after the demise of the Ottoman Empire following the First World War.

The politics of notables was not unique to Palestine.[1] In fact, the same process could be seen throughout the Levant, where the Ottomans relied on partially autonomous local intermediaries to carry out state policy. As in Palestine, this social class came to dominate politics in the twentieth century in much of the Arab world. In most Arab countries the notable class was not displaced until the 1950s and 1960s, when military coups brought historically less-privileged groups to power.

While the notable class was overthrown generally in the Arab world in the postindependence period, in Palestine it retained its superior position.[2] The reason was quite simple: all dominant states continued to utilize Palestinian notables as useful intermediaries to the local population. Mimicking Ottoman policy, successor states all sought to bolster notable hegemony as a means of enhancing social control under their rule. For example, Ian Lustick has shown conclusively that Israel maintained social control among Palestinians who remained in Israel after 1948 in part by co-opting the remaining elite and distributing resources through them instead of through state offices. In this way, the local Palestinian population remained dependent on a class of intermediaries who had an interest in political tranquillity.[3]

Nor was this larger pattern of intermediary social control unique to the Middle East. Studies in other Third World areas have shown this pattern of indirect rule to be common, particularly in British colonial areas. In a case strikingly similar to the Palestinian one, David Laitin has shown how British policy in Yorubaland sought to enhance social control by strengthening the "chiefs" of ancestral homelands, leaders whose political role was negligible but who had a degree of social legitimacy. By shifting resource distribution patterns to the advantage of these chiefs, the British created a strong intermediary group with an interest in preserving the social and political status quo. In time, the ideological structures which underpinned this system—in particular, projecting ancestral homelands as the primary locus of identity—became hegemonic.[4] Joel Migdal has shown a similar pattern of social control in British-ruled Sierra Leone.[5]

None of this is to suggest that Palestinian notables as a class have been without internal dissension. One of the striking features of notable politics, particularly under the British mandate, was an exceptionally high level of elite factionalism. This factionalism has usually been described as between Palestinian notable families (e.g., the Husaynis versus the Nashashibis) or between alliances of notable families (the *majlisiya* versus the *mu'arada*). A more fruitful understanding of the primary political and historical cleavages among notables comes from the distinction between nationalist and status notables. Nationalist notables have sought to gain political power through the use of nationalist ideologies but without concomitant social change. Status notables have sought to maintain the prevailing political and social orders. It was only through the rise of a counterelite in the 1980s that political transformation and social transformation were seen as dual objectives.

What follows is a brief interpretive overview of the development and political prominence of the notable social class in Palestinian society. I argue that state policy in Palestine not only created and maintained the notable elite for purposes of social control but did so decades after the notables had been overthrown elsewhere in the Arab world. In this regard, there was little difference between Ottoman, British, Jordanian, Egyptian, and Israeli policies: each ruler adopted and continued the policy of its predecessor. For each, the notables proved to be an indispensable asset, an intermediary without which states could not effectively rule. It was the collective genius of the notable class to be politically useful to successive and very different powers, and thereby to preserve their own privileged position.

An understanding of the role and history of Palestinian notables as presented in this chapter is necessary to comprehend both the challenge posed to this class by the rise of a new counterelite in the 1980s and the antinotable flavor which permeated the Intifada; it is also essential to understand the politics of the post-Oslo period, when the Palestinian Authority under Yasir Arafat tried to resuscitate the notables once more as a reliable intermediary to a politically skeptical population.

The Rise of Palestinian Notables under Late Ottoman Rule

The rise of the notables was an unintended consequence of Ottoman policies in the nineteenth century. As part of their defensive modernization campaign to ward off European power, the Ottomans engaged in numerous administrative, educational, and military reforms throughout their territory. In order to implement these reforms—and, in particular, to enhance tax revenues to the Porte—Istanbul attempted to amplify and centralize its power. Prior to the rise of the European threat, Istanbul was content to rule its vast empire in an indirect, decentralized fashion. So decentralized was Ottoman rule that, in the early nineteenth century, it lost power altogether in some places. For example, Egypt under Muhammad Ali was part of the Ottoman Empire in name only. Where possible, as in Anatolia, Istanbul reasserted direct control and implemented far-reaching reforms. Elsewhere, including in the Levant, Istanbul was unable to systematically assert direct authority. Instead, the Ottomans utilized the services of prominent, usually urban, individuals as intermediaries between the state and its subjects. Often these intermediaries had already served the empire in some modest official capacity prior to assuming their new roles. It was these intermediaries who were ultimately charged with overseeing Ottoman rule in the provinces and, in particular, with the collection of local taxes. So was born the politics of notables.

Albert Hourani has identified three types of notables, or *a'yan,* in the Ottoman Middle East. First were the religious leaders, the *'ulama,* who gained prominence owing both to the nature of their positions and to the large tracts of *waqf,* or religiously endowed, lands that they controlled. Second were military leaders of local garrisons who had gained a certain stature owing to the arms and soldiers they commanded. Third were the "secular notables," the elite who derived their wealth from land and trade.[6] The a'yan were, in Haim Gerber's analysis, the "strata of provincial leaders and rulers that virtually monopolized control of the countryside in many provinces" of the Ottoman Empire.[7]

In Palestine, as throughout the Ottoman Empire, *iltizam,* or tax-farming, was employed by Istanbul to secure revenues for military and economic development and other political requirements. During the *tanzimat,* or restructuring period, the Ottomans abolished the system of iltizam (1839) only to discover that they were unable to collect taxes directly.[8] Thus, Istanbul was obliged to reinstitute tax-farming three years later. However, the Ottomans did abolish the hereditary nature of assigning tax-farmers, or *multazims*, and instead opted for awarding the positions to the highest bidders in an attempt to enhance state revenues. The nascent urban notable class was strengthened the most by this policy change, as its members were the most capable of bidding for the various concessions that Istanbul offered.[9]

A central event in the making of the notable class was the Ottoman Land Law of 1858. Prior to promulgation of this law, *de jure* private property did not exist in the Ottoman Empire, although many rural tracts constituted *de facto* private property. The 1858 Land Law changed the formal standing of property, so that "land could, for the first time in Ottoman history, be owned on paper."[10] This law was intended to help the peasantry purchase small parcels of land; this would, it was believed, produce increased tax revenues. However, the law instead eventually resulted in the creation of vast estates. Ironically, the peasants themselves participated in forming these holdings: fearing a greater tax burden, they often registered their land in the name of dead relatives or local notables.[11] The enormous size of these landholdings was again a first in Ottoman history.[12] Given the kind of autonomy local notables enjoyed in the Levant, it was not surprising that they were able to turn this law to their advantage, in time becoming a landed elite. The single largest private estate ever established in Ottoman Palestine was held by Alfred Sursoq, when he purchased from Istanbul a 200,000-dunum tract along the coastal plain. Like many notables, Sursoq was an absentee landlord, living in Beirut.

In general, urban notables were able to manipulate a variety of Ottoman policies in such a way as to enhance their own position, often at the expense of Istanbul. Even policies designed to curb the notables' power often had the opposite effect.[13] However, it is important not to overstress the rivalry aspect of the relationship between Istanbul and local notables. Notables often served the empire loyally in various official capacities, sometimes working in Istanbul itself. In other words, the notables, as a whole, saw no contradiction between their increasing power at the expense of Istanbul and their positions within the Ottoman administration.

More important, the notables served a useful purpose to Istanbul, first and foremost by increasing tax revenues to the Porte. While the Ottomans did not intend to create the notable class, neither did they object too loudly to notable activities. Whatever their degree of local power, the notables remained intermediaries between the Ottoman state and Levantine society; they were not renegades or rivals for state power. It was not until the First World War that some notables' thoughts turned to sedition, to actually trying to replace Ottoman rule with their own. Until that time, the relationship between Istanbul and the notables was mutually beneficial. Istanbul occasionally expressed concerns about its slipping provincial authority, but such concerns were always mitigated by the larger service the notables provided the state.

By the turn of the century one could identify the important notable families of Palestine. For example, in Jerusalem the Khalidis, Jarallahs, Khatibs, and Alamis still were part of the a'yan stratum but of diminishing import, while the Husaynis, Nashashibis, Nusaybas, and Dajanis were increasingly important; in Hebron, the notable families included the Ja'baris, Tamimis, and 'Amrs; in Nablus, the Tuqan, Abd al-Hadi, Nabulsi, and Shaq'a clans were prominent; while in the Gaza-Jaffa coastal strip the Abu Khadras, Shawwas, and Baytars were the primary patron families. Some families, like the Husaynis and Tamimis, held prominence in more than one city.

As in Damascus, the early ideological core of notable politics centered on emerging nationalisms, both Arabist and particularist. But unlike the notables in Damascus, Palestinian notables also focused on anti-Zionism. The Jewish presence in Palestine had doubled between 1880 and 1914, increasing from 35,000 (6 percent of Palestine's population) to 75,000 (12 percent).[14] The notables were clearly worried about Zionist immigration, and as early as 1891 some notables had pressed the Ottoman Sultan to end Jewish immigration and land purchases in Palestine. Just as Syrian notables were the earliest backers of Arab nationalism, Palestinian notables were the earliest anti-Zionists.

Intranotable Conflict during the British Mandate

If Ottoman state policies were, in large part, responsible for the rise of the notables' power, British policy contributed significantly to the maintenance of this power and the intensity of intranotable conflict, two characteristics of Palestinian society during the Mandate period. In general, British policy sought to subdue and control Palestinian society by distributing posts, privileges, and resources through notable families. By co-opting these families and their patronage networks and using them as intermediaries to the local population, the British were able to control the Palestinian population more easily. Notable patronage networks—which reached deep into even the most rural areas—and, by extension, notable power, were deliberately strengthened by British policy. Even the high rate of urbanization that marked the Mandate years—a process which often undermined other traditional patronage networks—did not greatly affect local power structures. As Migdal notes, "Arab political leadership for the most part remained the bailiwick of the notable families until the end of the Mandate."[15]

The preeminent notable rivalry of the Mandate period was the well-known Husayni-Nashashibi split. Each clan's wealth was based on ownership of land, each family had considerable influence throughout the Palestinian community, and both worked rather closely with the British, especially in the first decade of British rule. Even the infamous Haj Amin al-Husayni, so demonized in his later years as an anti-British, anti-Zionist zealot, was a willing partner to British rule for the better part of two decades.[16]

The British were initially careful in balancing their appointments between competing notable families, naming at the outset of their rule one member of the Nashashibi family to be mayor of Jerusalem and Haj Amin al-Husayni to be the mufti, or leading cleric, of Jerusalem. Husayni was subsequently elected president of the British-created Supreme Muslim Council in 1922. The council had complete jurisdiction over waqf funds, with annual revenues of approximately 50,000 British pounds.[17] The Supreme Muslim Council and its resources soon became the focal point of notable rivalry, pitting the Nashashibis and their allied clans (known as the *mu'arada,* the opposition) against the Husayni alliance (the *majlisiya,* or council supporters). The notable rivalry continued to intensify in the 1920s until virtually every group in the country was lined up on one side or the other.[18]

While such notable rivalry was a natural by-product of the British pattern of resource distribution in Palestine, antagonism on the part of the Husaynis later prompted the British to back the more cooperative Nashashibi clan and its allies. In fact, the Nashashibis proved crucial to the British in suppressing the 1935–39 Arab revolt. The rebellion was led by rural elements and had an antinotable flavor, in addition to the more pronounced anti-Zionist and anti-British sentiments. It was initiated in November 1935 when Shaykh Iz al-Din al-Qassam, a Haifa-based preacher, led a band of followers into a *jihad,* or religious war, against British colonialism and Zionist settlement.[19] Qassam had invited Haj Amin al-Husayni to join in the jihad, but Husayni declined. Although Qassam was killed early on, his legacy continued, and a four-year revolt ensued.[20]

Forced to react to events they did not control, the notables briefly put aside their differences. In an attempt to capture the revolt and portray it as their own, the Nashashibi, Husayni, and allied notable clans formed the Arab Higher Committee (AHC) in April 1936. The most significant action undertaken by the AHC was to coordinate a six-month commercial strike as its part in the revolt. Still, notable rivalry was so intense in the 1930s that not even the revolt could unify the notables' ranks. The Husaynis actively supported the rebellion, while the Nashashibis, after their withdrawal from the Arab Higher Committee in 1937, worked in cooperation with the British to quash the revolt, to the point of attacking Palestinian rebels.[21] When the rebellion's symbolic end came in March 1939 with the killing of a leading rebel, Abd al-Rahim al-Haj Muhammad, it was a Nashashibi follower, Farid al-Irshayd, who supplied the British with the information on Haj Muhammad's where-abouts and who fought with the British in the subsequent ambush.[22]

While the enmity between rival notables was intense and clearly weakened Palestinian capacity to confront the Zionist movement, there was an underlying basis of shared interest. Although the Husaynis and Nashashibis had bitterly different political agendas, they both viewed overall notable hegemony as natural and not to be challenged. In addition, neither family promoted any sort of social transformation which might undermine its position over the long term. This was truly an intraelite conflict, not a struggle between socially distinctive rival groups or classes.

The famous rivalry between the Husaynis and Nashashibis should be understood in the context of a more lasting conflict within the notable elite which pitted status notables against nationalist notables. The schism between these two sets of notables had its roots in an earlier divide between Ottomanists and Arabists. Philip Khoury and C. Ernest Dawn have convincingly shown that rival political leaders in the battle between Ottomanism and Arabism in the first quarter of this century came from the same social class, often from the same notable families. Those who advocated the new ideology of Arabism often had failed to secure public office and were generally younger, better educated, and somewhat less wealthy. But, as Khoury stresses, these were relatively minor differences within the same socioeconomic class.[23]

A similar distinction characterized status notables and nationalist notables. Status notables were somewhat wealthier, more closely tied to the state administration, more oriented to the status quo in their political outlook, more dependent on clan (*hamula*) ties, and often less educated than their nationalist notable counterparts. Both types of notables came from the same social class, however, and often from the same families; thus, their rivalry cannot be considered class-based. It should be noted that nationalist notables came not only from Ottoman tax-farming families but also from families that garnered wealth from commercial success in the early decades of the twentieth century. Often, a generational difference was important, with nationalist notables usually younger than status notables.

All of the various parties and institutions inhabited by Palestinians during the Mandate years were simply facades, or fronts, for notable families. For example, the Arab Executive of 1920, the Supreme Muslim Council, the National Party, Palestine Arab Party, Reform Party, National Bloc, Youth Congress, and Arab Higher Committee were all institutional facades for clan politics or, in the case of the Arab Higher Committee, were a facile show of unity in the face of external exigencies. More specifically, these institutions were fronts for status notables, by far the dominant group of notables during this period. Only the Istiqlal Party represented an ideological break from the status notables, and its formation nicely captured the distinction between status notables and nationalist notables.

The Istiqlal Party was created in 1932 and had its strongest support in Haifa. The fact that its locus of support was in Haifa is significant because it was the coast of Palestine which was furthest removed from notable control. The coast was an area where the sons of status notables could mingle with nonnotable professionals, intelligentsia, bureaucrats, and technocrats, and could more readily formulate ideological positions that were removed from the conservative politics of their inland kin. The Istiqlal Party was supported by a number of social elements created or transformed by the rapid socioeconomic changes which marked the Mandate years.[24] The coast of Palestine was also the area of the most concentrated Zionist presence, which explains, in part, why the ideology of Istiqlal was more nationalist and militant than the usual notable politics. Istiqlal notables pushed for independence from Britain, for an end to Zionist settlement, for pan-Arabism, and for greater democratization within Palestinian politics.

Despite its often hostile rhetoric vis-à-vis the politics of Palestinian notables, the Istiqlal was, at base, also a notable party. The professionals who made up its membership were generally from notable families. The founder of and principal power behind the Istiqlal Party was a lawyer, 'Awn Abd al-Hadi. The Abd al-Hadi family, perhaps the most prominent notable clan in the Nablus area, owned 15,000 acres in Palestine.[25] The Istiqlal's distinctiveness was that it was the only significant institutional expression of nationalist notables during the Mandate. Palestinian society would have to wait until the late 1960s to again witness prominent nationalist notable institutions; then, in contrast to the 1930s, nationalist notable politics would predominate.

In sum, the notables maintained their positions of power within the Palestinian community owing in large part to British policies enabling the a'yan families to strengthen their patronage networks. Rivalry, often bitter, plagued notable politics during the Mandate and undermined the Palestinian community's ability to resist British colonialism and Zionist encroachment. In spite of their bitter political feuds, both nationalist and status notables opposed significant social change. There was no question of a true counterelite in this period.

The Revival of Status Notables under Israeli, Jordanian, and Egyptian Rule

Israel, Jordan, and Egypt largely replicated Ottoman and British policies of social control by strengthening the notable elite through the allocation of resources. These policies met with considerable success in spite of the fact that conflict among notables had helped lead to the loss of Palestine in 1948. In what amounted to a tacit understanding between notables and their respective rulers, these families were able to maintain the bases of their power (through land, business dealings, political patronage, etc.) in exchange for relative political quiescence. Because both Israel and the Arab states sought to prevent significant political turmoil from their respective Palestinian communities, their policies sought to prop up the most conservative elements within Palestinian society, thereby making sedition more difficult.

Lustick has shown how Israeli co-optation of notables was neither formalized in any institutional sense nor grounded in any expressed ideology which the notables embraced.[26] Instead, co-optation was "rooted in the regime's belief that material inducements, threats of material deprivation, and individual self-interest [were] the keys to successful manipulation of Arab elites." The kinds of day-to-day favors which Israel provided to the notables in order to induce cooperation included removing potentially serious "rumors" concerning certain individuals from military files, making farm machinery available at half the market rate, giving medical priorities to relatives of notables, providing favors regarding visitations and marriages, giving special permits for store licenses, setting up travel and work priorities, and granting religious concessions. In addition, reflecting their continued rivalry, notables often "feared that refusal to cooperate [with the state] would result in the ascendance of antagonistic clans or personal enemies." In fact, a "clear pattern of patron-client relationships between the regime and traditional Arab elites" had become visible as early as 1951. Based in part on the "careful distribution of favors, privileges, and special dispensations," including an occasional seat in the Knesset, notable co-optation proved to be an effective way to keep the Palestinian community politically quiet.

Jordan annexed the West Bank in April 1950 and quickly moved to undermine any independent political leadership among the Palestinians. King Abdallah's notable strategy rested, in part, on playing off the Husayni-Nashashibi rivalry. Because the Husaynis were more powerful than the Nashashibis and less amenable to the king's political designs, Abdallah (like his British patrons before him) favored the Nashashibis. The alliance between the king and the status notables, especially the Nashashibis, was formed early, as many of these notables supported Abdallah's incorporation of the West Bank into Jordan.[27] It seems clear that the a'yan strategy of relinquishing leadership over the issue of Palestine to Abdallah was done in order to guarantee the notables' leadership over the local Palestinian community. In other words, for the a'yan, the larger national question was secondary to continued control by the notables over more local, parochial, interests.

While Israel and Egypt prevented Palestinian notables from having decision-making positions in government, King Abdallah was forthcoming in appointing status notables, especially those in the Nashashibi circle, to high positions in the Jordanian administration. For example, in the first cabinet after the annexation of the West Bank there were a number of West Bank ministers from the Nashashibi alliance, including Raghib al-Nashashibi as the minister of agriculture, Ruhi Abd al-Hadi as the minister of justice, Ahmad Tuqan as the minister of public works and rehabilitation, Sa'id Ala al-Din as the minister of trade and customs, and Anastas Hananya as the minister of transport and posts.[28]

However diminished the notables were as Palestinian national leaders, they generally maintained their local constituencies in the West Bank. It was precisely those notables who had tacitly renounced their national Palestinian aspirations who were chosen for positions in the Jordanian state. Like the Ottomans and the British before them, the Hashemites of Jordan used the a'yan as go-betweens with the West Bank population, giving notables local power as intermediaries. Patronage networks were thereby maintained or increased, as access to state resources was to be had only through local notables. It is therefore no surprise that "there was no strong separatist current on the West Bank for most of the years of Jordanian rule [because] Palestinian leaders in the West Bank were willing to work economically and politically with the regime in Amman."[29]

Thus, the combination of Jordanian state policies regarding West Bank notables and notable acceptance of—and arguably preference for—more locally based influence prevented the emergence of an autonomous and powerful Palestinian national movement in Jordan.

Egyptian state policies in Gaza likewise relied on the co-optation of status notables and the manipulation of the Palestinian movement for Egypt's own ends. Always able to find Palestinian notables to fill organizations controlled by Egypt, both King Faruq and Gamal Abd al-Nasir refused to permit an autonomous Palestinian leadership to emerge. Throughout its nineteen-year rule in Gaza, Egypt utilized status notable families as intermediaries to the local population. Both the Rayyes and Shawwa clans were used by the Egyptians to maintain political calm in Gaza, and both families continued to prosper as a result.

Egyptian-controlled Palestinian politics after the emergence of Israel appeared first in the form of the All Palestine Government, which was inaugurated in Gaza on September 22, 1948, under the leadership of Haj Amin al-Husayni. Created as a sort of government-in-exile, the All Palestine Government quickly lost any autonomy it might have enjoyed. Tightly controlled by Cairo, it was used as an Egyptian weapon in its wider rivalry with Jordan. In fact, Egypt controlled Gaza and its borders with an iron hand; in the years immediately following the loss of Palestine, Egypt either prevented Palestinians from crossing the Gaza border into Israel or allowed it for their own reasons at specific times.[30]

Even the Palestine Liberation Organization was, in its origins, an Egyptian creation. Formed in 1964, it was designed to take pressure off Nasir for his inaction on the Israeli front. For Nasir, it was a way "to keep the Palestinian problem under his own supervision."[31] Ahmad al-Shuqayri headed the PLO and appointed an executive committee, which consisted of fifteen relatively conservative middle-aged professionals. Probably under pressure from Nasir, who feared Israeli retaliation, the PLO forbade any commando actions against Israel.[32] Because of its complete dependence on Cairo and its inaction against Israel, the PLO did not gain widespread Palestinian support until after the 1967 war, when it was taken over by guerrilla factions, principally Fatah.

The Politics of Notables under Israeli Occupation

In the years that followed the 1967 Israeli conquest of the West Bank and Gaza, status notables continued to benefit from state policies which sought to utilize them as intermediaries. The long-time mayor of Hebron, Shaykh Ja'bari, for example, "passed easily from being the vital link of the Jordanians to the population to playing the same role for the Israelis."[33] To a lesser degree, the growing popularity of the *feda'yin* guerrillas in the first years after the war prompted notables to consolidate their political position, a policy that the Israelis encouraged. The ascendancy of the usually Jerusalem-based status notables in the West Bank in the 1967–73 period came about in part because of their previous positions in the Jordanian regime and in part because of the PLO's "lack of interest in West Bank politics."[34] The economic wealth of the notables, both in land and in capital, their religious and social preeminence in West Bank society, and their monopoly of higher education were valuable assets that worked to preserve the authority and influence of these pro-Jordanian politicians under early Israeli occupation.[35]

Perhaps the most important reason for the persistence of the status notables in the years following the 1967 war was the impressive economic boom that occurred in the occupied territories. Figures vary, but there is wide agreement that both the West Bank–Gaza economy and the per capita gross national product rose dramatically between 1968 and 1973. The Bank of Israel estimates that GNP growth averaged 18 percent per year, while per capita GNP rose 15 percent per year. Others calculate these figures as 9 percent and 6 to 7 percent, respectively.[36]

The crushing of the Palestinian military infrastructure in Jordan by the Hashemites in 1970—"Black September"—undermined the feda'yin's position within the Palestinian national movement and, after a time, also helped to discredit the status notables, who were intimately tied to the Jordanian monarchy. Even the 1972 municipal elections, which constituted a victory for the status notables, proved to be a short-lived reprieve.

In the 1970s, nationalist notables increasingly replaced status notables as leaders on the ground in the West Bank and Gaza. There were a number of institutional expressions of nationalist notable power in the 1970s, including the opening of the nationalist *al-Fajr* and *al-Sha'b* newspapers in 1972 and the creation of the Palestine National Front (1973–77 and 1979) and the National Guidance Committee (1978–82). However, the single most important event in nationalist politics in the occupied territories in the 1970s was the April 1976 municipal elections.

These elections were welcomed by most concerned parties. The Israelis allowed them in order to find local substitutes for the increasingly popular PLO, while Jordan and Fatah pushed their supporters to participate. Fearing an eclipse of power, the status notables opposed the elections and only reluctantly campaigned, and then primarily along clan lines.[37] Nine former mayors, including Hebron's Shaykh Ja'bari, refused to participate, even after Israeli inducements to do so. In all, 205 council members were elected, including twenty-four mayors (of whom ten were incumbents).

Members of the nationalist elite who came to the fore as a result of these elections were younger, better educated, and more ideological than their status notable counterparts.[38] Two-thirds of the elected councilors were under age fifty, while 10 percent were younger than thirty, compared to 40 percent and 3 percent, respectively, in the 1972 municipal elections. In addition, 28 percent of those elected had a university education, while only 10 percent of those elected in the 1972 elections did. Moreover, 40 percent of the new council members and one-third of the new mayors were openly nationalistic or leftist, while the 1972 results were 20 percent and 8 percent, respectively.[39]

It is important to note, however, that these nationalist notables were sociologically similar to the status notables they replaced. In the words of Emile Sahliyeh, the nationalist notables came from "well-to-do and socially prominent families. They had no economic and social agenda that differentiated them from the older generation. Their distinctiveness stemmed from their ideological orientation and political rhetoric."[40]

Even the most "radical nationalist" of the mayors, Karim Khalaf of Ramallah and Bassam al-Shaq'a of Nablus, came from well-to-do families whose wealth derived from commercial success. Fahd al-Qawasma of Hebron likewise came from a local notable family. Two status notables remained as mayors: Elias Freij of Bethlehem and Rashad al-Shawwa of Gaza.

The greater nationalist ideology that characterized many of the winning candidates in 1976 did not initially bother the Israeli government, which saw the new mayors as "young members of the big and wealthy West Bank veteran *hamulas,* or the traditional big families which adjusted to the new political climate and dispatched their younger and politically more radical sons to run for municipal office, in order to maintain their socio-political power intact."[41]

External parties likewise were pleased with the outcome. Jordan did not see the results of the 1976 elections as contrary to its interests. Jordanian overtures to the various municipalities were generally well received, while many mayors visited Amman or applied for funds from Jordan, or both, soon after the elections were concluded. Even the two most hardline mayors, al-Shaq'a and Khalaf, sent "positive signals" to Jordan.[42] The conservative wing in Fatah was also pleased with the results. Having encouraged the candidates to run, Fatah correctly viewed the new municipal leadership as sympathetic to the thinking of its branch of the PLO.

Far from signaling the birth of political radicalism in the occupied territories, the 1976 elections and their aftermath marked the beginning of an alliance between Fatah, the nationalist notables in the occupied territories, and, to a lesser degree, Jordan. Fatah was always an amalgam of quite divergent political views. Its rhetoric aside, Fatah was constituted in large part by nonrevolutionary elements. So pronounced was its conservative tilt that, beginning in the mid-1970s, Palestinian communists routinely accused Fatah of being a part of the "Arab reactionary and Western imperialist camp."[43] Further, Fatah was often blasted by various Palestinian elements, including some mayors, for being too closely tied to Saudi Arabia and Jordan, two of the most conservative states in the Arab world.[44] Fatah was viewed as a basically conservative movement which reflected the traditional clan politics of Palestinian society. For example, an overwhelming majority of the Fatah feda'yin were members either of the Husayni family or of clans linked to the Husayni patronage network.[45] Additionally, Yasir Arafat was linked to the Husayni family via his mother, and for a time he was the personal secretary to Abd al-Qadir al-Husayni, a Palestinian hero during the 1947–48 war.[46]

Thus, as notable leadership in the territories became more nationalistic, both Jordan and Fatah saw their interests being served: Jordan because the leaders were still from the notable hamulas and therefore had shared family and economic interests with the Hashemite kingdom, and Fatah because the new leaders promised a more nationalist—and pro-PLO—ideology at a time when Fatah was shifting its primary attention to the West Bank and Gaza and away from the conquest of Israel.

In the first decade of occupation, Israel in effect exported its own policy of Arab social control to the West Bank and Gaza. While this policy was not as effective as it had been in Israel itself, it was not without success. Notables continued to enjoy a relatively privileged position and were allowed benefits—such as fewer travel restrictions and more easily obtained permits for a variety of activities—not extended to most Palestinians. In addition, the military government made Palestinian municipalities the central administrative unit for all Palestinians. All permits, applications, and official requests had to be made through municipal offices. As already noted, the municipalities were themselves the domain of notable families in this period. Again, a discernible pattern of indirect rule via the funneling of favors and resources through the notable social class was visible. Even though the dominant notables used increasingly nationalistic, anti-Zionist rhetoric, Israel's policy of social control was not seriously threatened—until the 1980s.

Structural Change and the Eclipse of Notable Hegemony

The prominent political position that notables had enjoyed in Palestine for over a century was increasingly diminished throughout the 1980s, particularly during the Intifada. What happened in this period that led to the eclipse of the notables' power? This marginalization was the byproduct of three structural changes that occurred under Israeli rule: the virtual elimination of the Palestinian peasantry, land confiscation, and the establishment of a Palestinian university system. Each of these changes undermined the position of notables and helped create a truly new counterelite to challenge the notables' influence.

In the aftermath of the 1967 war, Israel opened its labor markets to Palestinians from the West Bank and Gaza. This policy was mutually beneficial to Israeli employers (primarily in the construction and agricultural sectors) and Palestinian workers. For Israel, the West Bank and Gaza represented a source of cheap labor. Not only would Palestinians do work Israelis shied away from, but they would do it for wages far lower than their Jewish counterparts. In addition, the various benefits that would need to be paid for Israeli workers, increasing the total cost of labor, would rarely be paid for Palestinians. With such obvious incentives, Israeli employers actively exploited the Palestinian labor market. For most of the period of occupation, jobs in Israel were by far the largest source of employment in the West Bank and Gaza. During the 1980s, fully 40 percent of the total Palestinian labor force (about 120,000 workers) worked daily in Israel.

In spite of obvious exploitation, Palestinians were eager to take the jobs. There are a number of reasons for this, the most important being the lack of jobs in the West Bank and Gaza. Moreover, while the wages were low compared to the wages of Israelis, they were high compared to what—if anything—could be earned in the occupied territories. This was particularly true for unskilled Palestinian peasants, or subsistence farmers, who could earn very little money by staying in agriculture. It was primarily this section of the population, in addition to camp residents, that took jobs in Israel. Villages throughout the western half of the West Bank were virtually depopulated of male labor during the day.

The cumulative effect of Israel's opening its labor markets to Palestinians was to eliminate the Palestinian peasantry—still a majority of the West Bank population under Jordanian rule—and replace it with wage laborers. The political ramifications of such a social transformation were significant, as they have been everywhere in the world where this change has taken place. It created a working class of people less tied to village life; it exposed these workers not only to exploitative relations but also to a much more advanced industrial society; it diminished rural reliance on notable patronage, damaging long-standing patron-client networks; and it made the workers more open to recruitment into political action. In short, it turned peasants into Palestinians.

The second structural change which undermined the notables' power could be found in the shift in the pattern of landholding in the occupied territories. In particular, Israel's confiscation and other takings of land in the West Bank and Gaza constituted an attack on the original pillar of the notables' power: control over land. While the Labor Party in Israel confiscated lands for settlements and other purposes, this process accelerated rapidly after the Likud Party came to power in 1977. Like land reform everywhere, Likud's version of Palestinian "land reform" had familiar political ramifications: it undermined landowners both by directly confiscating their lands and by eliminating the influence of patrons over land they may not have owned but over which they had considerable sway. On the eve of the Intifada, over half of the West Bank and one-third of Gaza had been confiscated or otherwise made unavailable for Palestinian use.

Land takings came in a variety of forms. Some land would be directly confiscated, with the state recognizing the legal owners (often notables) and seizing the property in any case for building Jewish settlements and the like. More often, the military government would declare certain lands to be "state lands"—sometimes using the 1858 Ottoman Land Law as justification. Fallow lands or parcels used for livestock grazing were the most vulnerable to being declared state lands. Such land remained technically in the possession of the state, and even when settlements were built on the land it did not revert to private property. The most common form of seizure was for "security reasons," where little explanation had to be given to justify the move. Again, more often than not "security" confiscations would ultimately be used for Jewish settlements. Finally, relatively small amounts of land were confiscated in the name of natural preserves, scenic areas, forest lands, and the like.[47]

Needless to say, for Palestinians this was all Palestinian land to which Israel had no right. But once the military government had decided to take a parcel of land, the burden of proof of ownership or use was on the Palestinians. Even in cases where Palestinians produced the required documentation, the land was often still taken. The end result of such massive—and illegal—confiscations was, of course, tremendous bitterness on the part of the Palestinians. This bitterness was keenly felt by notables, often victims of the confiscations. Additionally, the inability of the notables to stop the seizures was not lost on other Palestinians.

The third important structural change was the development of the Palestinian university system, beginning in 1972. This process is discussed in detail in the following chapter. Briefly, prior to 1972 no Palestinian university existed in the West Bank or Gaza, although there were a small number of teacher training schools and vocational institutes. Those few Palestinians who acquired university degrees prior to 1972 were almost exclusively the sons of the notable elite, who were sent to study elsewhere in the Arab world or abroad. The growth of the Palestinian university system in the 1970s and 1980s meant that tens of thousands of Palestinians who otherwise would not have gone to a university now did. Moreover, the student body more closely resembled the larger Palestinian population, with about 70 percent of the university students coming from refugee camps, villages, and small towns. It was from this stratum that the new Palestinian counterelite was drawn. And it was this new elite that posed a direct political challenge to the notables.

This new elite began a process of political mobilization in the 1980s which undermined both Israel's social control in the West Bank and the power of the notable social class. Such political mobilization was in part a response to the Camp David Accords, and would not have been possible without the three structural changes: the rise of wage labor produced a social stratum open to recruitment in the mobilization campaign; land confiscations weakened the ability and desire of the notables to vitiate the mobilization; and the university system produced a counterelite to undertake the mobilization.

Political mobilization occurred in several sectors of the Palestinian population. Joost Hiltermann has produced a valuable history of the mobilization of labor and women in the years preceding the Intifada.[48] Nonnotable urban professionals in the medical and agricultural sectors likewise built organizations that linked the provision of social services with political activism, cementing ties between urban and rural Palestinians.[49] The student movement and the related Voluntary Works Program constituted perhaps the most significant of all the mobilization campaigns.[50] The ideology which permeated these campaigns reflected not only the activist, antioccupation nature of the new elite but also the antinotable sentiments this elite shared.

A final observation pertaining to the eclipse of the notable elite in the 1980s is necessary. The principal argument throughout this chapter has concerned the centrality of state policies to the maintenance of the notables' power for purposes of social control. It is ironic that the Israeli state under the Likud Party rejected a century of evidence—including that produced in Israel proper after 1948—about the necessity of supporting the notable social class in order to ensure political quiescence. Instead, Likud engaged in a frontal assault on the notables, believing them to be too nationalistic. First, it outlawed the Palestine National Front and the National Guidance Council, then dismissed and, in some cases, deported the mayors elected in the 1976 municipal elections. Moreover, the money flow from the PLO into the West Bank, much of it to institutions controlled by notables, was stopped.[51] As already mentioned, land confiscation accelerated after 1977. In a further attempt to fragment Palestinian leadership, the Likud, under the direction of Menachem Milson (1981–82), established the Village Leagues as its preferred Palestinian intermediary. The Village Leagues was a coalition of rural thugs and other marginal personalities who, unlike the notables, had no standing in the Palestinian community and therefore little chance to enhance social control.

Even the 1982 Israeli invasion of Lebanon had the unintended consequence of bolstering the counterelite. Israel's objective during the invasion was to destroy the PLO and, by so doing, to sever the Palestinian community in the occupied territories from the "outside" PLO. It was assumed that the occupied territories would be completely leaderless as a result, thus making the Likud's goal of permanent Israeli control of the West Bank more feasible. Instead, the destruction of the PLO in Lebanon focused Palestinian attention and resources exclusively on developments in the West Bank and Gaza. The counterelite was also part of the PLO but was largely autonomous. The invasion demonstrated to members of the new elite that they would have to go it alone in resisting Israel's occupation—that the burden of resistance was on them. Thus, instead of politically decapitating the Palestinians, the invasion actually energized the mobilization campaign, further hurting notable power.

State policies to ensure social control in Palestine relied on the creation and maintenance of the notable social class. For over a century, each sovereign power that ruled Palestine used this class as an intermediary to the larger Palestinian population in order to maximize political quiescence. Ottoman, British, Jordanian, Egyptian, and Israeli patterns of resource distribution were all largely the same: resources (broadly defined) which flowed from the state to society went through the notable social class, strengthening patron-client networks and, as a result, social control. The persistence of the notable elite in Palestine was in contrast to the downfall of notables as the foremost political class in most Arab countries in the 1950s and 1960s. Structural changes in the post-1967 period, shortsighted Israeli policies, and a political mobilization campaign undertaken by an emerging counterelite all helped to eclipse the position notables had enjoyed for so long. The Intifada was the culmination of the changing elite structure in the West Bank and Gaza.

2

The Rise of a New Political Elite in the West Bank and Gaza

While Israeli policies in the West Bank and Gaza after 1967 largely sought to bolster the traditional leadership of the Palestinian notables, the exigencies of the Israeli occupation helped to undermine this very stratum. In the 1970s and 1980s a new Palestinian political elite made up of nonnotables emerged in the occupied territories. While the formation of this new elite had several causes, including changing labor requirements and shared prison experiences, it was primarily grounded in the powerful student movements at the new Palestinian universities. As a whole, this new elite was larger, younger, better educated, from more modest class origins, and less urban than its notable counterpart. In addition, women constituted a significant portion of this new stratum. This elite fully embraced the cause of Palestinian nationalism, something to which the notables had largely paid only lip service, and took an activist stance against the military occupation. The new elite was central to the process of mass mobilization in the 1980s as its members took leadership positions in the emerging Palestinian grassroots organizations in the occupied territories.

This chapter examines the process of elite formation in the West Bank and Gaza by focusing on the Palestinian student movement: its political background, the rise of student blocs, recruitment, the method of solidifying social relations through the Voluntary Works Program, and the social origins of the student population. It was this new elite which laid the foundations for the Intifada through the program of mass mobilization in the 1980s and then emerged as the dominant political force in the occupied territories during the Palestinian uprising.

The Early Years

For nearly a decade after the beginning of the Israeli occupation of the West Bank in June 1967, the Communist-affiliated Jordanian Student Union (JSU) was the primary student political organization in the occupied territories.[1] JSU's only rival was the General Federation of the Students of Palestine (GFSP), founded in 1959. After 1967, the GFSP increasingly was associated with George Habash's Popular Front for the Liberation of Palestine (PFLP), and was crushed in 1969 by Israel because of its militancy.

The JSU was generally unrivaled as the dominant student political organization in the West Bank in the late 1960s and 1970s for two reasons. First, throughout this period the PLO's efforts, and in particular Fatah's, concentrated on the liberation of the whole of Palestine and not on seeking a rump state in the West Bank. As a result of the PLO's general lack of interest in political organizations in the West Bank, the Communist Party—which at that time was not a full member of the PLO[2]—had no significant competitors.[3] Second, Israel allowed the Communist Party, unlike the PLO, to operate relatively openly in the occupied territories, most likely because the Communists had long since accepted the notion of a two-state solution in Palestine, implicitly accepting the permanence of Israel. Furthermore, the Communists had renounced armed struggle as an unproductive tactic considering the imbalance of power in the area. Rather, they had traditionally viewed class struggle and anti-imperialism as more important than nationalist disputes.

However, it was Palestinian nationalism, embodied in the PLO, that increasingly engaged the student population in the 1970s. Concurrent with the upsurge in Palestinian nationalism was the founding of new universities in the occupied territories and the subsequent vast expansion of the student population. The first and still most prestigious Palestinian university, Bir Zeit, was officially founded in 1972, although it had roots as a secondary school dating back to 1924. What had been a two-year college in the 1960s was transformed into a four-year university after the 1967 war because of a compelling need for the establishment of an Arab university in the occupied territory.

A second Palestinian university, Bethlehem, was established in 1973–74 by the Christian Brothers and is affiliated with the Vatican. In 1977, a teachers' training institute that had been established in Nablus in 1963 was converted into al-Najah National University. An Islamic college founded in 1971 added colleges of liberal arts (1980) and science (1986) to become Hebron University. During this same period, the Islamic University of Gaza was established in conjunction with al-Azhar University in Cairo, one of the oldest and most prestigious institutes of Islamic learning in the world. Moreover, an umbrella university was constituted in Jerusalem.[4] In addition, smaller technical and training schools were either established or upgraded during this period.

While Israel did little to assist and much to hinder this proliferation in Palestinian higher education, it did allow the process to go forward. By doing so, Israel unwittingly helped midwife the very elite which most dramatically sought to overthrow Israel's military occupation in the form of the Intifada.

Student enrollment in the newly opened Palestinian universities expanded sharply in the 1970s and 1980s. In 1977–78, 2,601 Palestinians were enrolled in higher education. In just four years, the number more than tripled.[5] By 1987–88, nearly 16,000 students were enrolled at the major Palestinian universities (see table 1). The number swells to nearly 20,000 if community colleges and shari'a schools are included.

TABLE 1

Enrollment at Major Palestinian Universities, 1987–88

University	Number of Students
Najah	3,045
Bir Zeit	2,653
Hebron	1,423
Hebron Polytechnic	986
Bethlehem	1,596
Islamic - Gaza	4,438
Jerusalem	1,562
Total	*15,703*

Does not include community colleges and shari'a schools.
Source: Council for Higher Education, *Statistical Guidebook to Palestinian Universities, 1987/88–1988/ 89* (in Arabic) (Jerusalem, n.d.), p. 33.

The importance of the fact that, for the first time, tens of thousands of Palestinians participated in university life in the 1970s and 1980s cannot be overestimated. The pivotal role of students in politics, especially in the Third World, is well known. In the Palestinian case, political socialization and recruitment were staples of the educational experience, even for the unenthusiastic. According to a Bir Zeit University professor, "university life was so infused by political activity that reluctant students often felt compelled to participate in protests to avoid criticism of their fellow students."[6]

The Formation of Political Blocs and Student Elections in the 1980s

Students associated with the PFLP established the first student bloc, the Progressive Student Action Front, at Bethlehem University in 1980.

Within two years the three other major PLO factions had also established political blocs at the universities: Student Unity (associated with the Democratic Front for the Liberation of Palestine, or DFLP, which had earlier split from the PFLP), Progressive Student Union (Palestine Communist Party [PCP]), and Shabiba (Fatah). As was the case for all Palestinian mobilizing organizations, Fatah's entry in the student blocs was the last to form and the least organized, but it was the best funded and had the most participants.

The leadership of the political blocs came principally from Palestinians who had spent time in Israeli prisons and had been released in the late 1970s.[7] The political socialization among Palestinian prisoners in Israeli jails—the "people's schools," in the words of Palestinian novelist Sahar Khalifeh[8]—was crucial to the coalescence of this new elite. Prisoners from all over the West Bank and Gaza were often held in the same detention centers, enabling relationships to form, political strategy to be discussed, and skills to be honed.[9] The centrality of the prison experience to the development of a Palestinian activist elite seemingly was lost on the Israelis. During the Intifada, for example, Israel held most Palestinian political prisoners in the same compound, Ketziot/Ansar III in the Negev desert. The list of those imprisoned in the Negev read like a Who's Who of Palestinian political life: student activists, labor leaders, university professors, doctors, journalists, and the like. The point to be made here is that years before the Intifada broke out, prison was seen within the Palestinian community as a principal training ground for future activists. And it was the graduates of these "people's schools" who often assumed leadership roles in the Palestinian student movement.

In the early 1980s, the student blocs associated with the PLO banded together in various alliances at Palestinian universities, principally to offset the growth of Islamist groups. The Iranian revolution of 1978–79 had lifted the fortunes of the Islamist movement in Palestine, as it had elsewhere in the Muslim world, as people saw the potential power of utilizing Islam to overthrow an oppressive secular state supported by the West. With the exception of the Islamic University in Gaza, where Islamists routinely swept student elections, the secular PLO blocs were able to hold off the Islamist challenge to their political hegemony in the occupied territories.

PLO hegemony in the student movement in the West Bank and Gaza in the years preceding the Intifada could be seen in the results of student body elections at nearly all Palestinian universities, as representative data demonstrate.

At Bir Zeit University in the years preceding the Intifada, for example, PLO groups dominated elections, with the nationalists (Fatah) and the leftists receiving about the same support. The Islamists generally won between a quarter and a third of the total vote.

The 1984–85 Bir Zeit elections were won by Shabiba (Fatah), which had allied itself with the small DFLP bloc (see table 2). The Islamist bloc fared well, as did a leftist coalition of the PCP and PFLP. The split in the PLO after the 1982 Lebanon war was still reflected in the small number of votes that the Abu Musa faction received. Abu Musa, backed by Syria, had led a renegade faction of Fatah in an attempt to overthrow Yasir Arafat following the defeat of the PLO in Lebanon. While Abu Musa was never very popular in the occupied territories, 1984–85 represented this faction's last attempt to win votes in student body elections at Bir Zeit.

TABLE 2

Bir Zeit University Student Body Elections, 1984–85

Bloc	Votes	Percentage
Fatah/DFLP	800	39
Islamist	612	30
PFLP/PCP	560	27
Abu Musa	90	4
Total	2,062	100

Source: Office of Student Affairs, Bir Zeit University.

The following year, Shabiba broke off its alliance with the DFLP and ran—and won—alone (see table 3). The three leftist factions in the PLO formed a "progressive" (*taqadduma*) front and ran a close second, while the Islamist bloc slipped slightly.

TABLE 3

Bir Zeit University Student Body Elections, 1985–86

Bloc	Votes	Percentage
Fatah	787	38
PFLP/DFLP/PCP	725	35
Islamist	563	27
Total	2,075	100

Source: Office of Student Affairs, Bir Zeit University.

In the last election held at Bir Zeit prior to the Intifada and the closing of the university (1986–87), Fatah allied with the DFLP and PCP at the expense of the PFLP. The growing isolation of PFLP from the other PLO factions was a trend that continued during the Intifada, as the PFLP often found itself more closely aligned with Hamas, the primary Islamist movement during the uprising, than with the rest of the PLO. The Islamist bloc, meanwhile, improved its standing. (See table 4.)

TABLE 4

Bir Zeit University Student Body Elections, 1986–87

Bloc	Votes	Percentage
Fatah/PCP/DFLP	830	42
Islamist	651	33
PFLP	482	25
Total	1,963	100

Source: Office of Student Affairs, Bir Zeit University.

PLO hegemony was also seen at al-Najah University in Nablus on the eve of the Intifada, but with two caveats. First, Fatah was far more powerful vis-à-vis its leftist challengers within the PLO at al-Najah than at Bir Zeit. Second, a much stronger Islamist movement was Fatah's principal rival in the student population. In fact, in the early 1980s, the Islamist movement dominated elections, winning outright in 1980–81 and splitting the vote the following year. In response to the Islamist challenge, all factions of the PLO joined forces the following two years to win the student council elections. No student elections were held in 1984–85 because of a policy disagreement between the student council and the university administration.

Fatah and Islamist strength was seen clearly in the two al-Najah University elections which preceded the Intifada. In the 1985–86 elections, Fatah's Shabiba ran without benefit of a coalition and won a strong plurality (see table 5). The PFLP allied with Abu Musa to form a rejectionist bloc hostile to Fatah, while the DFLP fared poorly running alone. Turnout was 87 percent.

The 1986–87 election results at al-Najah University saw virtually no change from the year before (table 6). The Islamist bloc fared somewhat better and the PFLP—without the now defunct Abu Musa faction— slightly worse. Turnout was down, but still strong at 82 percent.

Bethlehem University, by virtue of its strong institutional ties to the Vatican, has a disproportionately high Christian representation, even

TABLE 5

Al-Najah University Student Body Elections, 1985–86

Bloc	Votes	Percentage
Fatah	1,511	49
Islamist	1,154	38
PFLP/Abu Musa	309	10
DFLP	98	3
Total	3,072	100

Source: *Observations on the Student Elections at al-Najah National University in Nablus* (in Arabic), Office of Public Relations, al-Najah University.

TABLE 6

Al-Najah University Student Body Elections, 1986–87

Bloc	Votes	Percentage
Fatah	1,253	48
Islamist	1,063	41
PFLP	190	7
DFLP	87	3
Total	2,593	99

Source: *Observations on the Student Elections at al-Najah National University in Nablus* (in Arabic), Office of Public Relations, al-Najah University.

though Christians constitute less than 3 percent of the Palestinian population in the West Bank and Gaza. In recent years, one third of its student body and 85 percent of its faculty have come from Christian families.[10] As a result of the relatively high percentage of Christian students at Bethlehem University, the PFLP and PCP—the political factions with which Palestinian Christians have been most closely associated—did very well in the various student body elections held in the 1980s. Conversely, while two-thirds of the student body is Muslim, very few of its students have been Islamists. Rather, the Muslims who enroll at Bethlehem have tended to be secular, with strong nationalist or leftist political sentiments. The overwhelming strength of the three leftist factions of the PLO at Bethlehem in the years preceding the Intifada can be seen in the results of the student body elections, shown in table 7.

TABLE 7

Party Affiliation of Student Council Officers, Bethlehem University, 1980–87

	1980/81	1981/82	1982/83	1983/84	1984/85	1985/86	1986/87
President	PCP	PCP	PFLP	PFLP	PFLP	PFLP	Fatah
V.P.	PCP	PFLP	PFLP	PFLP	PCP	PCP	PFLP
Secretary	DFLP	DFLP	PFLP	PCP	PCP	PCP	PCP
Treasurer	PFLP	PFLP	PFLP	DFLP	DFLP	PFLP	DFLP

Source: Office of Student Affairs, Bethlehem University.

Student Council elections were held at Bethlehem University in the fall of 1989, in spite of the university's extended closure by the military government. Since covert"illegal"classes were being conducted during this period, clandestine student council elections were also held. The elections were split, with Fatah winning the presidency and treasury, the Communists taking the vice-presidency, and the PFLP winning the secretary's position.[11]

The political situation in Gaza on the eve of the Intifada was different from that in the West Bank. There the Islamists had benefited greatly from the highly charged political atmosphere in the mid-1980s, enhanced by a series of dramatic attacks on Israeli forces by the Islamic Jihad, and from the deportation of rival PLO leaders. This trend was reflected in the fall 1987 elections at the Islamic University in Gaza (dual elections were held for women and men; see table 8). Turnout was nearly 80 percent.

TABLE 8

1987 Student Body Elections at the Islamic University in Gaza

Bloc	Percentage (female)	Percentage (male)
Muslim Brethren	75	60
Fatah	17	29
PFLP/DFLP/PCP	2	*
Islamic Jihad	4	11
Total	98†	100

*Did not enter candidates.
†Missing 2 percent unaccounted for.
Sources: Ann M. Lesch,"Prelude to the Uprising in the Gaza Strip,"*Journal of Palestine Studies* no. 77 (Autumn 1990), p. 15, and *al-Fajr* (weekly), December 6, 1987.

Throughout the 1980s there was a clear pattern of heavy politicization at Palestinian universities; it centered primarily on the PLO factions but had, at most universities, a strong Islamist current. While pro-Jordanian sympathies during the 1980s were marginal in Palestinian society as a whole, they were nonexistent at Palestinian universities.[12] Student body elections regularly had turnouts in excess of 80 percent and were often occasions for nationalist, anti-Israeli demonstrations. Politicized Palestinians coming out of local universities constituted the core of the new Palestinian elite and provided the catalyst for social and political change in the occupied territories, from the building of mass organizations to the Intifada.

Political Recruitment at Palestinian Universities

Incoming students at Palestinian universities prior to the Intifada were actively recruited to one or another political faction.[13] Given the intensely politicized atmosphere of Palestinian society in the 1980s, such factional activity could be expected. However, the reasons that people joined various factions had more to do with social utility and self-identity than with competing political platforms. The process of recruitment took a number of forms, but in the early stages it was often based on social activities, such as helping new students to register and choose classes, and perhaps inviting the new student to an informal gathering or party. If things went smoothly, the student would be asked to join that faction. One Bir Zeit graduate described her experience when she began her university career:

> I had an older brother who belonged to Fatah, so I was first approached by them. A person approached me, was very sweet, and helped me register for classes. She spent a great deal of time with me and invited me to various activities. After a while it became clear that I was not interested in Fatah, so they backed off. A member of the Communist Party then approached me and did pretty much the same thing. Because their ideology was more meaningful to me, I joined the PCP.[14]

Recruitment was often done on the basis of family ties or on the recommendation of friends. Students who had family or other ties to a particular faction, as the student just quoted did through her brother, were known to have been politically active in high school, or showed themselves to be politically involved once they arrived on campus were particularly targeted for recruitment. However, caution was always employed in the evaluation of any new recruit—a screening or probationary period was standard—owing to the Israeli penchant for trying to place collaborators within the factions on campus.

The political factionalism which marked Palestinian campuses in the

1980s often spilled over the university walls and could be seen in the formation of political space in the adjoining town. For example, each faction at Bir Zeit University had a particular restaurant which members frequented. This practice continued even after the universities were closed during the Intifada. In one instance, in November 1991, Israeli troops sought to arrest a number of PFLP activists in the Ramallah area and so commandeered two civilian vehicles and drove to the "PFLP coffeehouse." As it turned out, "those who knew they were wanted slipped away and those who did not escape were people who were not wanted."[15] The nonpolitical students would routinely avoid factional restaurants in nearby Ramallah and dined at the Kit-Kat restaurant instead. Many of these students would ultimately vote for Fatah in the student elections but would not be active members of that umbrella faction.

The style of social gatherings varied between the factions on campus. While gatherings of the three leftist PLO factions would often be rather somber affairs, Fatah parties would include dancing and other light entertainment that the other factions disdained. In addition, Fatah excursions to destinations outside Ramallah would generally be free of charge and buses would be provided, while Fatah's more financially strapped counterparts would generally require a pay-as-you-go approach. Fatah organizations in the occupied territories were almost always better funded than the parallel organizations run by other factions in the PLO. This was due in large part to the political priorities of the Fatah-dominated Joint Committee, which provided Arab funds to Palestinian organizations.

It is important to remember that recruitment into factions was taken very seriously by all involved, and was not viewed as a part-time commitment. Factional life at Palestinian universities was all-consuming: it dictated in large measure the people with whom time was spent, the stores and restaurants patronized, the quality and type of resistance undertaken, the parties attended, and the personal ties which would persist after one left the university. As noted, factional participation went far beyond political programs; after all, few Palestinians could speak to the doctrinal differences separating the PFLP and DFLP in the 1980s. Rather, recruitment into the factions included strong social considerations of family and friends, as well as the related questions of identity politics.

Expanding National Ties: The Voluntary Works Program

Student activism was not limited to campus life. During the 1970s and increasingly in the 1980s, students were involved in a plethora of activities which created and strengthened their ties to the wider Palestinian community. Various projects undertaken in rural areas helped to politicize villagers often removed from nationalist life, and helped to cement relations that were then employed in the expansion of mass organizations. The factional grassroots organizations which were established in the 1980s by university graduates and which promoted health care, agricultural relief, and women's rights used the contacts made through these extracurricular university projects to help mobilize a broad national constituency. The strength of this growing web of alliances and relations was seen clearly during the Intifada, when Israeli attempts to isolate rural areas from their urban counterparts and to set one against the other largely failed.

The most important and widespread of these university projects was the Voluntary Works Program. Begun in 1972 as a literacy project by Bir Zeit students of middle-class origins, the program quickly gained popularity, particularly but not exclusively among university students in the East Jerusalem and Ramallah areas. Like all Palestinian populist organizations in the 1970s, the program was initially dominated by the Communist Party as a means to mobilize mass support.[16]

By 1980 the program had grown large enough that a Higher Committee for Voluntary Work in the West Bank and Gaza was formed to coordinate the voluntary activities of dispersed committees. While Bir Zeit remained the focal point of the movement—the announcement of the formation of the Higher Committee was made on the university grounds—the program had branched out by 1980 to include 37 local committees and 1,200 active members. In just two years, from 1980 to 1982, the now 6,500 volunteers from 96 local branches had reclaimed 6,000 dunums of uncultivated land, had planted 34,000 olive and fig trees, and had repaired numerous roads, sewage lines, and water pipes.

Although literacy campaigns in the refugee camps and villages constituted an important feature of the Voluntary Works Program, its central aim throughout the 1980s was to strengthen Palestinian agriculture in order to make land confiscation by Israel more difficult.[17] In particular, the student volunteers worked in rural areas during harvest season (especially during the olive harvest) in order to replace the thousands of agricultural workers who had taken better-paying jobs in Israel. By generating greater farm income, the students also tried to stem the flow of emigration of often rural Palestinians to Gulf oil countries, Jordan, and elsewhere in search of prosperity. Well over half a million Palestinians emigrated from the West Bank and Gaza in the period between the 1967 war and the Intifada.[18]

On a strictly economic basis the impact of the Voluntary Works Program on agricultural production was minimal. What the volunteers did succeed in doing, however, was to bridge the gap between urban and rural Palestine. In one significant example, volunteers from Bir Zeit and Ramallah conducted a two-week work camp in the Hebron area in order to build a road which, for the first time, connected the remote village of Udaysa with Hebron and, by extension, the rest of the West Bank.[19]

The ideological underpinnings of the Voluntary Works Program reflected the glorification by middle-class urbanites of rural life and the attributes of working the land. In the words of Palestinian scholar Lisa Taraki,

> It is not coincidental that manual labor was the dominant form of work; it was a deliberate decision, taken with the aim of breaking down the barrier between intellectual and physical labor, and of spanning the gulf separating the town from the countryside. This outlook is naturally a reflection of the fact that the idea of voluntary work originated in the towns, and in particular among middle-class intellectuals, professionals, and students with little contact with workers or peasants.[20]

The Voluntary Works Program faced a number of obstacles. Israeli authorities correctly saw the dangers inherent in this grassroots process of nation-building. By minimizing urban-rural and class divides, Palestinians were actively engaged in constructing and consolidating a national Palestinian consciousness which would deny Israel's claim that, in the words of former Israeli prime minister Golda Meir, "a Palestinian people does not exist." As a result, the Israeli government sought to undermine the movement, first by trying to turn the village heads, or *mukhtars*, against various projects. This was often done by reminding the mukhtars of the communist—i.e., atheist—origins of the Voluntary Works Program. When such appeals failed to stop projects from being undertaken, more direct methods were employed. A favored technique was to set up military checkpoints not far from project work sites and deny entrance to volunteers.

A second problem—one that plagued all mass organization in the 1980s—was the increasing factionalization of the Voluntary Works Program. Local committees were usually associated with one of the major PLO factions. This was not surprising, given the student participation in the program and the factionalized nature of student politics during this period. However, political competition between the factions hindered greater coordination among the local program branches while, paradoxically, it increased the number and scope of local branches.

Student leaders at the universities often either gained their political initiation working for the Voluntary Works Program, went on from their student experiences to organize new volunteers, or helped lead other mass organizations. The program became such a central ingredient in student life that several universities mandated participation. Bir Zeit University, for example, required all students to volunteer 120 hours in the program in order to graduate. Through such work, not only did an emerging political elite consolidate its ties internally, but it also built relations with the wider, mostly rural and refugee camp Palestinian populations. Increasingly, the crux of the student movement itself came from just those strata of Palestinian society that were traditionally underrepresented in the political elite: villagers and refugees.

The Social Origins of Palestinian University Students

The creation of Palestinian universities in the 1970s meant that, for the first time, significant numbers of Palestinians who were not members of elite notable families could gain a university education. This represented a consequential break from earlier periods, when only the sons (and occasionally daughters) of urban notable families had access to higher education, often at the American University of Beirut, or in Egypt, Jordan, Europe, or the United States. In the 1970s and 1980s, while the children of notable families often continued to be educated abroad, Palestinian universities were attended by more and more students from villages and refugee camps, as well as from middle- and lower-class urban quarters.[21] The changing class and demographic nature of the educated stratum of Palestinian society led, in large measure, to the radicalization of the student movement in the 1980s. This new elite—an elite based on educational achievement, not class origins—was more interested in confrontation and social change than in accommodation and social inertia.

Part of the difficulty in arguing for a shift from urban to rural politics lies in making the distinction between what is urban and what is rural in a place as small as the occupied territories. Only the refugee camp population is relatively distinctive.[22] Certainly, the three largest Palestinian towns in the West Bank—East Jerusalem, Nablus, and Hebron—can be viewed as fundamentally urban, each with over 100,000 residents. However, as they have expanded, these towns have approached and often engulfed neighboring villages, thus diluting their urban character. Modestly populated towns such as Jenin (26,000), Tulkarim (30,000), Qalqilya (20,000), Bethlehem (34,000), Ramallah (25,000), al-Bira (23,000), Yatta (20,000), and Jericho (13,000) have both urban and rural characteristics. Some, such as Ramallah and al-Bira, have expanded toward each other to the point where they are indistinguishable. None of the more than 350 remaining villages in the West Bank is far removed from an urban locale.

In spite of the fact that the distinctiveness—and therefore the importance—of the urban/rural dichotomy in the occupied Palestinian territories is not as rigorously defined as it may be in larger countries, the available evidence suggests that there was a clear nonurban majority attending Palestinian universities. In fact, approximately 70 percent of the Palestinian university population during the 1980s came from refugee camps, villages, and small towns. In other words, student enrollment at Palestinian universities broadly reflected Palestinian demographics, where over two-thirds of West Bank and Gaza Palestinians live in nonurban areas. Consider the figures from al-Najah University in Nablus, shown in table 9.

TABLE 9

Regional Origins of Students at al-Najah University, Fall 1986

District	Males	%	Females	%	Total	%
Jerusalem	3	<1	1	<1	4	<1
Nablus	592	17	717	21	1,309	38
Hebron	95	3	13	<1	108	3
Ramallah	24	<1	5	<1	29	1
Tulkarim	652	19	489	14	1,141	33
Jenin	302	9	166	5	468	14
Bethlehem	8	<1	2	<1	10	<1
Gaza	282	8	65	2	347	10
Total	1,958	57	1,458	43	3,416	100

Source: *Geographical Distribution of Students* (in Arabic), al-Najah University.

The figures for al-Najah University are insightful on several points. First, the percentage of female students (43 percent) compares favorably to many universities in the Arab world, where female representation has been rather low. Such figures are reflective of the role Palestinian women took in the general mobilization campaign in the 1980s. However, the fact that half of all the women attending al-Najah came from the Nablus district, compared with only 30 percent for males, and 94 percent of the female students came from the Nablus-Jenin-Tulkarim triangle, as opposed to 79 percent of the males, suggests that Palestinian families were more willing to have their sons than their daughters either commute greater distances to school or live in student housing at school.

More interesting, perhaps, is what can be gleaned from these data about the rural flavor of the student population. Assuming that all of the students from the Jerusalem, Nablus, and Hebron regions actually came from those cities and not from outlying villages and camps, their combined total is only 42 percent of the total student population and only 35 percent of the male student population. If a more reasonable assumption—that half of the students from the Jerusalem, Nablus, and Hebron districts actually came from villages and camps—is made, then only 21 percent of the student population at al-Najah University came from cities. Thus, it seems reasonable to assume that upwards of three-quarters of the students at al-Najah University actually came from villages, refugee camps, and small provincial towns such as Qalqilya and Jenin. This figure corresponds to what I was told by an official from the Office of Public Affairs at al-Najah University: that 75 percent of the students there come from villages and refugee camps.[23]

Bethlehem University saw a similar pattern, as shown in table 10. The data date from the 1988–89 academic year, when the university was officially closed but continued to provide "underground" classes. Because of the circumstances surrounding the 1988–89 year, it is reasonable to assume that more students than usual came from areas in the immediate vicinity of Bethlehem.

TABLE 10

Regional Origins of Students at Bethlehem University, 1988–89

District	Males	%	Females	%	Total	%
Jerusalem	187	12	255	16	442	28
Nablus	30	2	11	<1	41	3
Hebron	212	13	73	5	285	18
Ramallah	84	5	26	2	110	7
Tulkarim	35	2	8	<1	43	3
Jenin	34	2	14	<1	48	3
Bethlehem	240	15	302	19	542	34
Gaza	35	2	26	2	61	4
Jericho	3	<1	9	<1	12	<1
Israel	0	0	2	<1	2	<1
Total	*860*	*54*	*726*	*46*	*1,586*	*100*

Source: *College Totals* (in Arabic), Office of Student Affairs, Bethlehem University.

Once again, female representation, at 46 percent of the total student body, is impressive. As at al-Najah University, virtually all (87 percent) of the female students came from the immediate area (Bethlehem, East Jerusalem, and Hebron), and most likely lived at home with their families. Moreover, if the same somewhat circuitous route noted earlier is used to gauge the urban/rural split at Bethlehem University, then the three largest urban areas in the West Bank provided 49 percent of Bethlehem's students. If, again, half of the students in the Jerusalem,

Nablus, and Hebron districts actually came from outlying villages and refugee camps and not from the cities themselves, then the urban share drops to about a quarter of the student population. Thus, as at al-Najah University, about three quarters of the students at Bethlehem University came from villages, refugee camps, and small towns.

Bir Zeit, as befits its position as the premier Palestinian university, has had a greater diversity in the origins of its students. That is, students from all over the occupied territories have sought to enroll at Bir Zeit. Figures in table 11 bear this out.

TABLE 11

Regional Origins of Students at Bir Zeit University, 1987–88

District	Fall 1987	Percentage	Fall 1988	Percentage
Jerusalem	276	11	147	13
Nablus	275	11	116	10
Hebron	168	7	73	7
Ramallah	702	27	383	34
Bethlehem	75	3	31	3
Jenin	292	11	86	8
Tulkarim	283	11	117	10
Qalqilya	36	1	17	2
Gaza	428	17	142	13
Jericho	5	<1	1	<1
Other	14	1	4	<1
Total	2,554	100	1,117	100

Source: *Geographical Distribution of Students* (in Arabic) Office of the Registrar, Bir Zeit University.

In 1987 and 1988 the districts of Jerusalem, Nablus, and Hebron provided a combined 29 percent and 30 percent, respectively, of all Bir Zeit students. The urban student representation at Bir Zeit, then, was even lower than at other Palestinian universities. Other points can be made from these data. For example, Bir Zeit had a far larger contingent of students from Gaza than did either al-Najah or Bethlehem. Clearly, Bir Zeit was the university of choice for those Gazans who did not wish to attend the Islamic University in Gaza. Often it was Bir Zeit–educated activists in Gaza who built the political infrastructure which spread a nationalist, rather than Islamist, interpretation of the Palestinian condition. This goes a long way toward explaining why the PLO was able to hold its own in Gaza in terms of popular loyalty vis-à-vis Hamas and other Islamist groups both during and after the Intifada.

These figures also point to the sharp drop in student enrollment during the period of underground education.[24] From a normal enrollment in 1987 of 2,554 students, enrollment dropped by more than 50 percent to 1,117, as the university was formally closed by Israeli military authorities. Those who continued to enroll generally did so to complete their degrees by taking "illegal" classes held off-campus. As could be expected, most of the decline came from students farthest removed from the Ramallah campus. In particular, Gazan enrollment fell to one-third of its pre-Intifada levels, while similar drops were seen from the Jenin and Tulkarim areas. The percentage of students who hailed from Ramallah and East Jerusalem increased during the Intifada from 38 percent to 47 percent, although their total numbers declined by nearly half.

Aggregate figures further bolster the argument presented here. For example, of the 16,001 students enrolled in Palestinian universities for the 1987–88 year, only 5,567 students, or 35 percent, came from the Jerusalem, Hebron, and Nablus districts.[25] Even if one discounts the Islamic University in Gaza (where all 4,438 students enrolled that year came from Gaza) and only considers the West Bank universities, the Jerusalem, Hebron, and Nablus districts provided fewer than half—48 percent—of all students.[26] Again, assuming that half of those students actually came from areas outside the city boundaries, then about three-quarters of all students during the 1987–88 school year came from camps, villages, and provincial towns.

One must use these data with some caution. While the student enrollment figures and the regional origins of students are accurate, the assumption about the breakdown of student origins within each district is just that: an assumption. Thus one cannot say with precision the number of university students who came from villages, camps, and provincial towns. However, the general pattern is clear, and one can say with a degree of confidence that between two-thirds and three-quarters of Palestinian university students in the mid-1980s did hail from areas other than the major urban centers of Jerusalem, Hebron, and Nablus. Not coincidentally, the disproportionate representation of camp dwellers and villagers at Palestinian universities was replicated in the large Ketziot/Ansar III prison for political prisoners during the Intifada, where 71 percent of the inmates came from rural areas and refugee camps.[27]

While the student population at Palestinian universities overwhelmingly had modest social origins, even the sons and daughters of the socially privileged classes who attended these universities often underwent an ideological conversion. A former Bir Zeit student who has been active in the Palestinian women's movement and who was a Marxist in spite of—or perhaps because of—the fact that she comes from one of the most prominent Palestinian notable families told me in an interview:

> I joined the Palestine Communist Party in part as a revolt against the label of [my family name]. The university was key in my ideological transformation. Ideas of resistance, identity, and state were formulated there. My extended family still does not understand. They consider me arrogant, and say that I don't mix well. This gave me a conflict in self-perception: where do I belong? the values of my family or the values of my beliefs? This made me insecure. But I needed to rid myself of this baggage of family labels. My extended family still believes that this is just a fad that I am going through. My actually joining the PCP started out as peer pressure. Clearly my friends around me affected my choice of political parties and philosophies. But I knew I was a Marxist at school. I was never oppressed class-wise because of my family's income. After all, I went to a private school before Bir Zeit. But the philosophy—class struggle, distribution of wealth—appealed to me. Also the realistic political platform of the PCP [i.e., the longtime party platform of a two-state solution to the Palestine problem] gave me something I could really do that was possible. I could find a place in the struggle that was more concrete. Sure, there was a difference between what I wanted emotionally [i.e., all of Palestine] and what I thought was realistic. I knew there was more to the struggle than just what I wanted or what the Palestinians as a whole wanted. We are part of a larger set of forces. I knew there were some things that were possible and some things that were not possible to do. I needed a place for myself.[28]

As university education expanded dramatically in the 1970s and 1980s, new Palestinian social classes—principally villagers and refugee camp residents from middle- and lower-income groups—not only experienced university student life for the first time but also came to dominate it. As a result of the changing class character of the Palestinian student population, the student movement was radicalized. The activists in the student movement employed strategies to more directly confront the Israeli military occupation as well as to bring about social change within Palestinian society. It was this ideological imperative which led to the establishment of grassroots organizations in the 1980s—women's committees, labor blocs, medical and agricultural relief committees, the Voluntary Works Program—whose explicit purposes were to mobilize Palestinian society against Israel's occupation and to marginalize the traditional Palestinian elite.

The experiences garnered at the Palestinian universities were essential in the political maturation of an emerging elite. Not only did university life partially remove students from the often constricting social milieu in which their families lived, but it also allowed members of disparate social classes to interact and establish new sociopolitical ties.

Both in prison and in college, members of the new elite came to know each other on a personal basis. These ties were crucial, both in the formation of mass organizations in the 1980s and in the establishment and leadership of the popular committees in the occupied territories during the Intifada. Such committees were the principal organizational structures and sources of authority in the uprising. In addition, members of the Unified National Leadership of the Uprising were often former activists for one or another PLO faction in the student movement.

Israel, by grudgingly allowing Palestinian universities to open and expand, ironically assisted in the formation of a new political elite drawn from a far broader stratum of Palestinians than the narrowly based notable elite of earlier generations. Because of the very size of this new elite, Israeli attempts to vanquish it—through deportations, encouraged emigration, imprisonment, extended closures of universities, and the like—proved futile.

3

The Professional Middle Class

I have argued thus far that the political mobilization of Palestinians in the occupied territories in the 1980s was closely tied to the rise of a new elite and the marginalization of the traditional notable leadership. Such mobilization was necessary in order to overcome, at least in part, the class, kin, and regional cleavages that had long fragmented Palestinian society and that had been used by occupying powers to undermine collective national action. Mobilization often parallels economic development, although in the Palestinian case, it took place despite Israeli policies which sought, especially after 1977, to deliberately underdevelop the Palestinian economy.[1] A new elite—itself the by-product of post-1967 developments—took advantage of the dramatic changes in Palestinian society at the grassroots level by recruiting large numbers of Palestinians into new forms of social organization. These new institutions were responsible for the forging of new identities which made possible sustained collective action in the form of the Intifada.

I suggested in chapter 2 that the new elite was more village- and camp-based than the notable social class. However, the increasing importance of nonurban areas as centers of Palestinian political leadership in the 1980s did not lead to the total exclusion of Palestinian cities, particularly East Jerusalem, from the mobilization process. What was different was that the political lead in East Jerusalem was taken by nonlanded urban professionals, not members of the notable social class, and found expression in the creation of urban-based, rural-oriented relief committees.

This chapter focuses on the rise of medical and agricultural relief committees in the occupied territories during the 1980s and their subsequent roles in the Intifada. A number of themes are common to these committees. First, each of the medical and agricultural relief committees was loosely tied to one of the four major factions of the Palestine Liberation Organization: Fatah, Popular Front for the Liberation of Palestine (PFLP), Democratic Front for the Liberation of Palestine

(DFLP), and the Palestine Communist Party (PCP).[2] Second, the competition between the various committees both encouraged greater productive activity and, at the same time, led to wasteful duplications of effort because of political considerations. Third, all were created by members of a new elite fully cognizant that their efforts were aimed in part at superseding the activities of an older, more conservative elite. Fourth, the end result of their efforts was the bolstering of independent medical and agricultural infrastructures in the occupied territories. Fifth, these committees helped to build ties between the urban professional classes and the rural and refugee-camp populations, which comprise about two-thirds of the total population of the occupied territories. Previously, the educated urban elite rarely ventured into the hundreds of villages and camps in the West Bank and Gaza.

The Medical Relief Committees in the Occupied Territories

By virtually any measure, the standards of health care in the Israeli-occupied West Bank and Gaza Strip from 1967 to 1987 lagged well behind those in both Israel and Jordan. For example, in 1985 infant mortality in the occupied territories was reported to be as high as 70 per 1,000 live births, while it was 55 in Jordan and 14 in Israel. In the occupied territories there were between 6 and 8 doctors for every 10,000 Palestinian inhabitants in 1986, while Israel had 28 and Jordan 22. From 1974 to 1985 the ratio of the number of hospital beds to population in the occupied territories actually decreased from 2.2 to 1.6 per 1,000 individuals; by 1992 the figure had declined further to 1.1 per 1,000. By comparison, in Israel in 1985 there were 6.1 hospital beds per 1,000 people. Palestinian life expectancy was the lowest in the region. Other problems included the virtual absence of adequate health care in rural areas, lack of coordination between health care providers, and low levels of health insurance.[3]

Naturally, health problems intensified dramatically during the Intifada. In addition to the hundreds of Palestinians killed by Israeli soldiers and settlers during the uprising, tens of thousands of Palestinians were injured. The Save the Children organization estimates that 50,000 to 63,000 children under the age of sixteen were injured and needed medical attention during the first two years of the Intifada.[4] Over the course of the Intifada, nearly 10 percent of the Palestinian population was killed or wounded. In addition, curfews, closed military zones, detentions of wounded Palestinians prior to medical treatment, denials of referrals to Israeli hospitals, periodic cut-offs of running water to Palestinian camps and villages, routine beatings, and other similar developments meant that the state of Palestinian health care had become precarious and that demands on overburdened facilities had multiplied.

The Palestinian reaction to the poor state of health care under military occupation went from accommodation to disengagement. Mustafa Barghouti and Rita Giacaman argue that there have been three distinct phases in the Palestinian health care response to the occupation.[5] The first phase, which lasted until the mid-1970s, was dominated by "the old medical establishment" comprised of well-to-do doctors, from prominent families, who had graduated in the 1940s and 1950s. These doctors "understood health, disease, and medical care as simple and pure biological phenomena, divorced from social, economic, and political contexts, and within a strict biomedical framework. Consequently, they equated health development with technical and mechanical development of premises, instruments, and procedures." The policy was to push for centralized hospitals and up-to-date equipment, and to do this within the parameters of Israeli law. The end result was relatively good care for a small and privileged stratum of society while primary health care was nonexistent in many areas.

The second phase, which dominated the middle and late 1970s, emphasized greater autonomy from the military government in the field of health care, while still operating within the military's laws and regulations. This period was still dominated by "urban-based monied individuals," but they were more closely tied to the nationalist movement. These years were marked by struggles between Palestinian charitable societies, in particular Jerusalem's Maqassad hospital and the Red Crescent societies, and the military administration over permits for health facilities. Although this period saw a degree of success in expanding health care for Palestinians, the health care leadership remained wedded to the notions of urban biomedical care and the necessity to be bound by Israeli law. The difference in leadership in health care in the first and second phases paralleled the broader rivalry during this time between status notables and nationalist notables.

The third phase began in 1979, and was marked by decentralism, volunteerism, and noncompliance with Israeli regulations. Primary health care and prevention, with an emphasis on providing services to rural areas through education, mobile clinics, and small permanent clinics, were the bases of this new movement. It was led by urban-based young professionals in their twenties and thirties, many of whom had strong ties to the grassroots organizations that flourished in the occupied territories in the 1970s and 1980s. There were particularly strong ties between the new health committees and women's committees. Female doctors were especially active in the health committees, making up as much as one third of all health committee doctors, while they made up less than a tenth of all Palestinian doctors nationwide. Health committees were one of the few areas where Palestinian professional women were allowed to excel.

The Union of Palestinian Medical Relief Committees

Responding to the need to disengage from both Israeli control and notable dominance of Palestinian health care, a segment of the urban professional establishment loosely affiliated with the Palestine Communist Party founded the Union of Palestinian Medical Relief Committees (UPMRC) in 1979. The goals of the UPMRC were to bring primary health care and health education to rural areas, and to do so without seeking Israeli permission first. During the first few years of its operation, the UPMRC was dismissed by the existing health community as "Communists" and "leftists" who sought to "cheapen medicine by going to the villages."[6] The organization was not taken seriously by the Israeli military administration, which paid it virtually no attention.

Women played a key role in both the founding and the operations of the UPMRC. There was a significant overlap between the PCP-affiliated women's committee, the Union of Palestinian Working Women's Committees (UPWWC), established in 1978, and the UPMRC. According to both groups, members of the UPWWC were at the center of the establishment of the medical committee. In addition, according to figures provided by the UPMRC, 6 percent of all Palestinian doctors in the occupied territories in 1989 were women, while 32 percent of UPMRC doctors were women. Moreover, fully 70 percent of UPMRC employees were women.

Between 1979 and 1987, the UPMRC established seventeen permanent clinics in the occupied territories. Barghouti claims that these were not just clinics but "health centers" which emphasized "prevention, education, and first aid training, not just curative medicine."

The exigencies of the Intifada compelled the UPMRC to respond creatively. In the initial twenty-two months of the uprising, the UPMRC established five first-aid centers. These centers not only treated patients for a whole range of problems—from bullet wounds to brucellosis—but also engaged in training villagers in first aid. Training villagers to treat the great majority of medical problems they encountered meant that only a small number of cases needed to be brought to urban areas. In addition to these first-aid stations, the UPMRC stressed education about first-aid treatment. In the same twenty-two-month period, the UPMRC gave in excess of 1,000 sessions, teaching 22,000 people the basic principles of first aid. Moreover, during this same period they distributed over 19,000 first-aid kits.

The most intriguing activity of the UPMRC during the uprising was the creation of a national blood donor system. Prior to the Intifada, the UPMRC had tried to institute a computerized donor system, much like those in Western countries, but had had little success. Many Palestinians viewed the procedure as potentially harmful to themselves. Such a fear of blood contamination by unknown outsiders is not unusual in traditional societies. Overcoming ungrounded fears of social contamination or pollution is one indication of a transition away from a strictly traditional social ontology. What is unusual about this case was the rapidity with which this fear was overcome during the crisis period of the Intifada. Beginning in February 1988, the UPMRC restarted a blood grouping campaign where relevant data—blood type and Rh factor—were listed on a card carried by donors. By October 1989, 24,000 Palestinians were catalogued on the computerized donor list. According to Barghouti,

> the card system is organized through popular committees in camps, villages, and towns. Now a hospital can contact us and we can give them a list of names and locations of individuals in a given area who have the needed blood type. This system has saved hundreds of lives. Often the shabab [young activists] will match cards of the wounded with theirs and those with matching blood types will accompany the wounded to the hospital so that blood can be given on the spot.

The system met with such initial success that blood was often used for non-Intifada patients. While the response to calls for blood donations eased after the Intifada, the system remained. By 1994, the UPMRC data base for blood donors numbered approximately 40,000; three-quarters of the donors were in the West Bank. Although the overall response weakened with time, emergency situations, such as the Ibrahimi mosque massacre in 1994, still prompted significant blood donations.

The financial health of the UPMRC, like that of similar nongovernmental organizations (NGOs) in the West Bank and Gaza, was always precarious. The UPMRC recovered only about a quarter of its operating budget from fees. The rest had to be raised from Palestinian benefactors and foreign sources. Two-thirds of the UPMRC's Intifada-period activities were done gratis by about 800 volunteers, nearly half of whom were doctors. Although the UPMRC is not a charitable organization, about 6 percent of the pre-Intifada patients were treated free of charge. With the pauperization of the Palestinian community during the Intifada, the percentage of "social patients" rose to about one-fifth of the total. The reliance on Western donors was necessary, according to UPMRC officials, because Arab sources "prefer to fund big projects like large hospitals and fancy machines instead of primary health care."

By 1994, the UPMRC had founded 31 permanent clinics, 9 mobile clinics serving 200 villages and camps, 11 rehabilitation programs serving 80 communities, and 7 mobile dental clinics serving 50 communities.

It continued to stress the role of women in primary health care, establishing the only Women's Health Program in the occupied territories, as well as working directly with local women's committees in twenty-three villages. It served 370,000 people in 1993. The end of the Intifada led the UPMRC to close four emergency clinics in Nablus, and convert three underground clinics in Jenin and Gaza into permanent clinics. Ironically, the Oslo Accords brought greater financial difficulties to the UPMRC—and other NGOs—as donors diverted their resources to the Palestinian Authority (PA), and the PA sought to squeeze "opposition"-affiliated NGOs for their own political purposes.

Union of Health Work Committees

The Union of Health Work Committees (UHWC), a PFLP-affiliated health committee, was established in 1985.[7] The reasons for launching the UHWC closely paralleled those for the UPMRC, and were centered both on the poor health facilities available to most Palestinians and the notable-dominated health profession. As one of the founders of UHWC explained,

> In the 1970s Palestinian health care was in the hands of either reactionary elements in the Palestinian community [i.e., notables] or well-meaning but naive international organizations. For example, U.N. organizations dealt with Israelis when providing for Palestinians. Clearly, Israelis and Palestinians have different views of the needs of Palestinian health care. Besides, by dealing with the enemy, even these well-meaning organizations became suspicious in the eyes of many Palestinians. Also during the 1970s, about 70 percent of all health care personnel were in private practices. This was a problem because it meant that the overwhelming majority of doctors were either politically reactionary or too expensive for most Palestinians to afford, or both. As a result, Palestinians often would either not get proper care or would go broke getting it.[8]

Even prior to the UHWC's founding in 1985, members worked on a part-time basis, visiting villages on weekends or holidays. The first committee of doctors, based at Maqassad hospital, would plan the visits and would work with any individuals or groups that could arrange them, including women's committees, charitable organizations, village leaders, clubs, and the like. As doctors were recruited and more committees formed, residents of a greater number of villages received vaccinations, hygiene education, physical examinations, and other primary health care. Still, most villages were removed from any regular care. UHWC estimates that prior to the Intifada, only 55 percent of the 480 West Bank villages were covered medically, meaning that a clinic was located in the village or a nearby village, or that a mobile clinic made regular stops there.[9]

In the years preceding the Intifada, the UHWC established thirteen permanent clinics in rural areas of the occupied territories, and conducted dozens of visits to villages through their "mobile clinic" service. Besides helping to better the health conditions of rural Palestinians, these activities helped to create and strengthen ties between urban professionals based in the East Jerusalem/Ramallah area, Nablus, Hebron, and Gaza, and village-based Palestinians. These relations were critical in the early months of the Intifada as the medical emergency created by the uprising became apparent.

In the first month of the Intifada, UHWC distributed 5,000 first-aid kits. In addition, an urgent effort was undertaken to build more clinics and involve more people in the mobilization efforts. As one official noted, "we have thousands of people 'working' for us but only 2 percent of them are paid." By the end of 1989, UHWC had established thirty-three permanent clinics in nine administrative districts. During 1989, these clinics treated 70,325 patients, of whom over 17,000 were not charged. During this same year, over 140 mobile clinic visits treated more than 15,000 Palestinians, more than half of whom were Intifada patients or "social cases" and thus were not charged.[10] A number of other activities were similarly upgraded, in particular educational programs.

Unlike the other health committees, UHWC gave significant attention to the health needs in Gaza during the Intifada. This was due in part to the Popular Front's significant political strength in Gaza, principally in Rafah.[11] In fact, UHWC officials claimed that by 1989 they provided health care to 15 percent of the Gazan population, through nine medical and dental clinics.[12]

While the UHWC has loose ties to the PFLP, recruitment of doctors into its clinics has not followed strict political lines. As one leader said,

> We recruit mostly through personal ties. For example, one of us may know a prospective doctor through our work in the mobile clinics. We would then pay him a social visit. We might refer patients to him and then invite him to be more involved in our work. There are no political obstacles. He has to be a nationalist, but not necessarily from one particular faction, and he has to be a humanitarian. But most of all, he has to be clean—to have a spotless reputation.

In actual fact, many—probably most—doctors who joined the UHWC had political leanings similar to the leftist PFLP. As health committees tied to other political factions also existed, it was common for doctors and staff to work with that health group which reflected their politics. Both the providers and, to a lesser degree, the recipients of these medical services were aware of the larger political agenda. The ability to translate medical—and other social—services into a particular political vision was the key to the struggle within the Palestinian community for ideological hegemony.

The process of institutional consolidation—many clinics had been established precipitously under emergency conditions—gradually led to fewer clinics, but those that remained were of a generally higher quality. The end of the Intifada, of course, decreased the demand for medical outposts "at any cost." By 1995, over one-third of all UHWC clinics had been closed, leaving twenty-six to continue UHWC's work.[13] The single best clinic established anywhere in the occupied territories during the Intifada, in Bayt Sahur, remained in the UHWC network (see chapter 4 for a more in-depth discussion of this clinic).

A more pressing problem for the UHWC in the aftermath of the Oslo Accords was the virtual cessation of funding assistance by Western aid donors. The Palestinian Authority pressed all donors to direct money through the PA itself, and not distribute resources directly to Palestinian NGOs. While the PA's attempt—and general Western compliance with the PA's directive—was a problem for all Palestinian NGOs, it was particularly problematic for groups associated with the oppositional PFLP. Representatives from the UHWC were told orally and in writing on a number of occasions by foreign aid donors that they would not receive assistance until the PFLP relaxed its opposition to the Oslo Accords. The fact that assistance in the post-Oslo period was so closely tied to the larger political structure and not to the level of professionalism and effectiveness of institutions did not bode well for the development of Palestinian civil society.

Union of Health Care Committees

In response to the poor state of health care under Israeli occupation, spurred on by competition from other political factions, and assisted by the Women's Action Committee,[14] medical professionals loosely affiliated with the DFLP began providing informal health care in the early 1980s, which became formalized in 1985 as the Union of Health Care Committees (UHCC). The thinking which went into building the UHCC paralleled that of the other health committees:

> In the early 1980s there was a lot of thinking about general problems, especially medical problems, in Palestinian society. UNRWA and the government hospitals were only providing limited services, and, in a sense, were improper [i.e., politically]. The costs of private practices were very high in relation to Palestinian living standards, so people just could not really afford them. The end result of this situation was that people were paying a very high price: their health. Some Palestinians were saying that big was better—that big machines and big hospitals were the solution. Others maintained that "only the end of occupation could bring about a solution to our problems. In the meantime, there is nothing we can or should do." We said that there is no end in sight to the occupation and

to wait that long would be irresponsible. We have to do it ourselves. The problems we face—high mortality rate, family planning, hygiene, over-crowding, gastroenteritis, dehydration, infectious diseases, skin diseases, etc.—cannot wait for the end of occupation.[15]

The DFLP-affiliated Women's Action Committee was central to the building of the UHCC, and would take the initiative for organizing medical visits to West Bank villages. Women's health, primarily that of rural women, was part of the Women's Action Committee's platform owing principally to the high level of medical problems associated with childbearing in agricultural areas. During village visits, UHCC doctors would give check-ups, provide medicine free of charge, and give "mini-lectures on health and the spacing of children. The latter was a delicate subject for social reasons. Often there is competition between, say, sisters-in-law as to who can have the most babies. If the first had six, the next in line would try to have more than six."[16]

Over the course of the 1980s, mobile clinics and periodic visits were gradually superseded by permanent clinics. As the leader of UHCC put it,

> There was a strong relationship between the women's committee and the village women, but we were more like outsiders. This is why we decided to change our policy from occasional visits to establishing permanent clinics. In this way we can cement the relationship between our union and the local population. Now, we are part of the community, can learn their needs and provide care appropriate for their situation.[17]

As with the other health committees, UHCC was important prior to the uprising but became critical with the Intifada. On the eve of the Intifada, UHCC had established a dozen permanent clinics. In the first two years of the uprising, fourteen more clinics of widely varying size and quality were built. Consistent with the general policies of all the Palestinian grassroots organizations, the UHCC neither registered its twenty-six clinics nor coordinated its activities with Israeli military authorities.

By January 1990, UHCC employed fifty-eight people on a full-time basis and had 450 unpaid volunteers who had been given medical or paramedical training. Drugs were provided at cost, while each visit to a clinic cost the equivalent of $1.50. Still, 40 percent of the patients in the first two years of the uprising were treated free of charge because they were either Intifada patients (i.e., wounded during a protest) or hardship cases. General funding for clinic operations came from fees, membership dues, and international donations from Europe and the United States. Funding was occasionally quite specific, with a foreign donor sponsoring a particular clinic, instead of the larger union.

While the Women's Action Committee was central to UHCC's early work, acting as an intermediary between the doctors and thousands of village women, its role became marginalized as UHCC grew and created permanent structures in the village areas, particularly in the Nablus region. For its part, the women's committee turned its attention to other areas during the Intifada, in particular establishing and strengthening women's cooperatives and home production.

The growing division in the DFLP after 1988 became an irreparable rupture with the 1991 Madrid conference. The split in the DFLP was reflected in its grassroots institutions, including the UHCC, as some organizations remained tied to the major Hawatmeh faction of the DFLP and others switched to the Abd-Rabbu faction (later Fida). In the case of the DFLP health committee, ideology and family overlapped: the breakaway doctors were led by the brother-in-law of Zuhara Kamal, a political leader of the Abd-Rabbu "rebels," and a leader of the Women's Action Committee (which likewise split). Such division decimated the UHCC, and led to the closure of all but twelve clinics in 1992. In subsequent years, the UHCC rebuilt some of its institutions, but it was not able to regain its earlier status. It was likewise hurt by the post-Oslo reluctance of foreign donors to direct resources to Palestinian NGOs associated with the opposition.

Health Services Council

As with all other Palestinian grassroots organizations, the Fatah-affiliated health committee was the last to be established, and then somewhat reluctantly. As Fatah has been an umbrella organization representing many elements of the Palestinian nationalist movement, it has lacked a coherent core or vanguard which can implement and sustain certain policies. In addition, Fatah has been the party of nationalist notables who, like other socially conservative strata of the population, have not fully embraced a policy of political mobilization. Patronage continued to be one means of policy implementation for all the Fatah-affiliated bodies, although organizational imperative was not absent.

Begun in 1986 as the Health Services Committees, the Health Services Council was formally established in 1990 following a 1989 internal reorganization. HSC was formed as a response both to the pressing health care needs of Palestinian society and to the creation of the other three health committees. However, HSC differed from the other health committees in several important ways. First, HSC had no overt political agenda. The charters of the other committees all had explicitly political contents, such as that of the Union of Health Care Committees: "The UHCC is part of the national movement of our people fighting for their national rights, at the forefront of which are the right to return, to self-determination, and the establishment of an independent state."[18] HSC did not make a similar claim. Second, unlike the other health care committees, HSC viewed itself as a charitable society, not a grassroots organization. In fact, it officially registered with the Israeli government as a nonprofit association, breaking an unwritten rule against coordinating activities with the Israeli authorities. Third, although there is a Fatah-affiliated women's committee (Women's Committees for Social Work), it was not involved in the establishment or maintenance of HSC. Fourth, HSC did not rely on volunteers in the provision of health care, believing that a volunteer system would be disrupted by high turnover rates.[19]

By far the best-funded Palestinian health NGO, HSC was able to establish or affiliate with numerous clinics in a short period. In fact, by 1992, eighty-four clinics—many of rather dubious quality—were tied to the HSC. Over half of these clinics were located in the Nablus-Jenin-Tulkarim triangle in the northern section of the West Bank, a Fatah stronghold. The July 1989 reorganization led to greater centralization and an emphasis on building larger and more geographically centralized medical centers. For example, HSC closed fourteen clinics in the Ramallah area, opting to serve patients through three larger centers instead. The drift toward fewer centralized facilities with more doctors and better available equipment—i.e., away from primary health care—paralleled the kind of care earlier associated with doctors from urban notable families, many of whom had been tied to Fatah for some time.

Although HSC officials maintained that 80 percent to 90 percent of costs were recovered by the clinics themselves, it seems clear that high rates of outside funding contributed to their success. Fatah and its constituent organizations had by far the largest number of followers but also the least developed human and institutional infrastructure in the occupied territories. It was probable that the rapid development of HSC services came into being primarily through money and only secondarily through political activism. Throughout the 1980s, the Joint Jordanian-Palestinian Committee for the Steadfastness of the Palestinian People in the Occupied Homeland, a distributive organization funded by members of the Arab League and controlled by the PLO (principally Fatah) in conjunction with Jordan, funneled money into the occupied territories. Fatah organizations were always the best-funded, sometimes to the total exclusion of others.

Not surprisingly, among the health NGOs, HSC had the fewest qualms about the post-Oslo autonomy dominated by Fatah. In fact, HSC was the only one of the NGOs which talked openly of being absorbed by the interim authority, and did not see the necessity of an autonomous civil society for democratic development. In the words of the head of the HSC, Anis al-Qaq:

> HSC has always viewed the national interest above its organizational interest. The Intifada created a vacuum that needed to be filled, and we did so. But autonomy has no vacuum of central authority, so it raises the

question of our existence. Are we permanent? Temporary? We will do what the Palestinian Authority wants us to do. If it wants to absorb us into the government structure, that's fine. If it wants us to stay as an independent NGO, that's fine too. If we stay as an NGO, we expect the government to support us. The other groups have built their empires, and think they must remain as empires under autonomy. The times are changing—we need to build our own state more than have empires. Show me where these types of organizations elsewhere remain independent. If NGOs don't fit with the master national plan, then we are going against the national interest. It is one thing to act against the Israeli occupation, but this is *our* government and we must cooperate. All the popular organizations that arose under occupation must make the transition to building our own state. The reasons for our existence are becoming less or are disappearing.[20]

In sum, in the years prior to and during the Intifada, a network of primarily provincial and rural clinics was established by Palestinian health NGOs which brought together on a full-time basis urban medical professionals and rural Palestinians. The establishment of a national health infrastructure diminished dependence on outsiders by increasing the capability of Palestinians to furnish basic health care to far more of their own people. A 1992 survey of the West Bank found, for example, that Palestinian health NGOs had established 132 clinics in 118 communities, concentrated in the poorest communities and serving nearly half of the population.[21]

Problems with Health Care during the Intifada

Although the establishment of a medical infrastructure with an emphasis on primary care proved to be one of the principal successes of the Intifada, the process was not without problems. First, the rapidity with which many of these clinics were established—well over 100 in the first two years of the Intifada—led to great unevenness in quality. This was especially true for makeshift clinics undertaken without help from one of the four health committees, although even many of the committee clinics were of dubious quality. Some new clinics, like one in the town of Bayt Sahur, were first-rate operations, while others were "little more than a doctor and some drugs—not nearly sufficient for the needs."[22]

Second, while political rivalry helped create a medical infrastructure, it also led to wasteful duplications of resources. Since a decision to set up a clinic in one village instead of another was done not only in terms of objective criteria (need-based) but also for subjective, often political, reasons two clinics might be found in one village and none in another. On the subject of "duplication clinics," health committee officials were particularly sensitive. For example, UPMRC had a clinic in the village of

Bayt 'Anan in the Ramallah area when UHCC established a second one, claiming that UPMRC's facility "was not a full clinic. After we set up our clinic, they upgraded theirs to a clinic level and then told us that we were on their turf."[23] When asked about similar incidents, the head of the UPMRC responded:

> Why do some of these organizations insist upon opening clinics in villages where there is already one present? Especially in light of the fact that there are dozens or hundreds of villages with none. The duplication is done for political reasons or perhaps for other nonprofessional reasons, such as relatives of the decision-maker are located in that village. After we raise these criticisms, the other committees say that we should forget the past. We categorically reject this and tell them if duplication exists, then move your clinic![24]

A related problem was the lack of coordination between health care committees during the Intifada, when the appearance of unity had been strongly encouraged in all quarters. Although efforts were made by both women's committees and unions (each having four factionalized committees) to create larger bodies to formally coordinate activities during the Intifada, no similar undertaking occurred in the field of health. However, there was some degree of informal or *ad hoc* cooperation. For example, a unified committee of three of the health committees was formed in Nablus during the uprising to better coordinate the health community's response to the Intifada. The UPMRC generally rejected any moves toward institutionalized unity because it viewed the other committees as more explicitly political: "There is no framework for overarching cooperation and there shouldn't be. Any cooperation should be local and specific, not systematic. Any platform for cooperation needs to be done on a professional basis, not a political one."[25] It should be noted that each committee decried the political factionalization of all the other health committees while denying any such motivation for itself.

In a controversial opinion piece in the newspaper *al-Quds*, the respected Palestinian economist Hisham Awartani blasted the "power centers" (*marakiz al-quwa*) in the health committees whose activities too often were designed "in order to realize personal gain."[26] While appreciating the difficulties of providing health care during an uprising, Awartani was very critical of the establishment of factionalized health committees, believing that too often politics was placed ahead of good health. Awartani pulled no punches:

> The doctors in the West Bank are a mafia. People are intimidated by them. They are taking advantage of the Intifada and buying huge unneeded equipment, and making fortunes for themselves. Embezzlement is not uncommon. The competition among the factions for each to be the most successful is a case of personal ambitions outweighing national interests.

At the least there is mismanagement. At worst, there is outright corruption. Ideological factionalism alone is not a problem, as elsewhere such factions are known simply as political parties. But if we are trying to build our own state and it is based on the structures of four or five different groups, then what?[27]

Finally, Israeli harassment and repression made their mark on the health committees as they did on all areas of Palestinian life during the Intifada. A number of clinics were closed, had equipment destroyed, or had personnel arrested by Israeli authorities. For example, a clinic run by the UHWC near Nablus was closed and its equipment confiscated by the army, while another UHWC clinic in the Ramallah area was demolished because it lacked a construction permit. (Construction permits for any new Palestinian building, difficult to acquire prior to the uprising, were nearly impossible to obtain during the Intifada.) In addition, a large number of doctors were either arrested or harassed for doing their work.

In spite of the problems created both by political factionalism and by the realities of life under military occupation, the health committees established a structure of health care that was a great improvement over what had existed before the 1980s. The political competition and the emergency of the Intifada energized the health committees to build more facilities to provide more—if often uneven—care. In the absence of a state with its concomitant control over factors essential to good health—proper sewage disposal and clean water, for example—the Palestinian health committees could never be expected to dramatically improve primary health care in the West Bank and Gaza. As one observer noted, "The committees can talk all day about primary health care and hygiene—but how much hygiene can one have in Nablus when the city's raw sewage is still dumped in the fields, and spreads northward with the rains?"[28] While primary health care can be expected to improve under autonomy, the lack of Palestinian control over its own water resources does not bode well for this sector.

The relations forged between urban medical professionals and rural populations during the 1980s helped to overcome social fragmentation and to intensify national mobilization during this period. Throughout the 1980s, hundreds of health care professionals treated thousands of rural patients in the countryside, and, in doing so, created a network of contacts in hundreds of villages. The fact that women's committees often initiated and mediated this interaction helped to encourage more village women to associate with those professionals most involved in the effort to recruit and mobilize Palestinians into the nationalist movement toward self-help and self-empowerment. Such efforts helped to extend the ideological message of the new elite to other strata of the Palestinian population.

The Agricultural Relief Committees and the Intifada's
Back-to-the-Land Movement

A development parallel to that occurring in the area of health care was taking place in the agricultural arena. Once again, urban-based professional agronomists and engineers initiated widespread contact with thousands of farmers during the 1980s in an effort to both improve a declining agricultural sector and to encourage Palestinian self-sufficiency. The hope was to diminish agricultural dependency on Israel and thereby to enhance national disengagement from the occupying power.

Well before the Intifada began, Palestinian farmers faced a number of severe problems, many of which were political in nature. These difficulties included restricted water use, loss of labor, flooded markets, restricted exports, lack of credit, limited land availability, and poor education.[29]

Since Israeli permits for digging new wells or expanding existing wells were rarely given, irrigation farming was virtually impossible. In fact, only about 4 to 5 percent of all cultivated areas in the West Bank were irrigated.[30] As a result, Palestinian farmers were limited to rain-fed agriculture, curbing profits and employment opportunities. The consequence was a long decline in agriculture as a percentage of the gross domestic product in the occupied territories. To make matters worse, annually approximately 80 to 85 percent of the West Bank water supply was either diverted to Israel or used by Jewish settlers in the occupied territory.

As agricultural profits stagnated, rural Palestinians increasingly left the farms to work in better-paying jobs in Israel, or found work in Jordan or the Gulf oil countries. Agricultural laborers comprised 45 percent of the total West Bank labor force in 1969 but just 19 percent in 1984. In absolute numbers, the agricultural labor force plunged 42 percent in the West Bank from 1969 to 1985, while it shrank by 39 percent in Gaza.[31] These numbers alone indicate the extent to which rural patron-client ties were disrupted, as tens of thousands of Palestinians left traditional farming pursuits and were thus more available for recruitment into new forms of social organization.

Subsidized Israeli agricultural products had unhindered access to Palestinian markets, leading to a loss of market share by Palestinian farmers not entitled to similar state subsidies. Also, while Israeli farmers had free access to the markets in the occupied territories, Palestinian farmers had to get permits from Agrexco or Citrusboard, both Israeli concerns, to sell products in Israel. As a rule, any product that was also grown in Israel was forbidden to be imported from the occupied territories. Furthermore, as agricultural production increased in other Arab countries, Palestinian exports diminished.

All Palestinian lending institutions were closed by Israel following 1967, leading to a lack of credit for Palestinian farmers. A handful of small lending institutions were later established, but they operated under severe restrictions.

Land use had virtually peaked, so that there was little chance of increasing productivity on already cultivated land (because of restrictions on water use) or expanding cultivation on large plots of contiguous virgin lands. Waves of land confiscations by Israel decreased the already-limited farmlands.

Finally, prior to 1986, Israel did not permit Palestinian universities to have agricultural programs. The result was a poorly educated labor force.

The Formation of the Agricultural Relief Committees

The seeming intent of the military government's policies toward the Palestinian agricultural sector was to gradually discourage the productive use of the land, thereby facilitating its confiscation. In addition to the problems just listed, monies allocated for agricultural research dropped precipitously in the 1970s and 1980s, as did the number of Palestinians working on agricultural extension for the Military Government. In 1977, there were 550 employees working in the agricultural departments in the West Bank; by 1989, that number had dropped to 141.[32] The lack of agricultural extension services was evidenced by a 1986 survey conducted by the Palestinian Agricultural Relief Committee (PARC), which found that 50 percent of Palestinian farmers had never met a government extension official while another 40 percent had had only limited contact.

Funding for the agricultural sector came in part from the Joint Committee. Of the approximately $400 million distributed by the Joint Committee in the West Bank and Gaza between 1979 and 1985, about $30 million went to the agricultural sector via the Jordan Cooperative Organization (JCO). The funds, especially after 1982, tended to be distributed to and therefore benefit the notable class (often individuals with ties to Jordan) and those associated with the conservative wing of Fatah. While agricultural development was the stated goal, monies were often distributed with a view toward patronage and political loyalty. In the view of PARC officials,

> The use of JCO funds in the occupied territories is now infamous: the funds were widely seen as being channeled to the large landowning class in the territories rather than supporting the small peasant sector. Most of the large cooperatives are controlled by the large landowners. The channeling of funds was seen as a form of patronage payment, rather than serving any developmental purpose.[33]

Motivated explicitly by a desire to halt the downward spiral of Palestinian agricultural production and implicitly by ideological and class concerns, a number of agricultural engineers in Jericho began to conduct gratis extension visits to small farmers in the Jordan Valley in 1983. A year later, this small program was broadened and formalized into the Palestinian Agricultural Relief Committee, and was loosely affiliated with the Palestine Communist Party. Its goal was to give "priority to helping small peasant farmers, and [work] as an agricultural extension network in cooperation with local farmers' committees. [The] overall strategy is to promote the formation and consolidation of local farmers' committees through which to promote various aspects of self-help and agricultural development."[34] By the end of 1984, PARC had sixty volunteers working regularly throughout the West Bank offering technical advice.[35] A year later PARC expanded its agenda beyond technical advising, and emphasized the expansion of local agricultural groups to more efficiently organize agricultural resources. By 1990, PARC employed forty-five engineers in the occupied territories, in addition to having a wide network of volunteers and working with dozens of local committees.[36] By 1994, the number of full-time PARC employees had increased to eighty, working out of seven centers.[37]

While PARC was the first and biggest agricultural relief committee, it did not long remain the only one. In 1986, Majdi Muhtasib broke away from PARC and helped establish the Technical Center for Agricultural Services (TCAS). The split had political overtones. While PARC maintained its PCP ties, TCAS quickly turned into a loose coalition of DFLP and Fatah elements. Not to be outdone, agronomists loosely affiliated with the PFLP established a similar organization, the Union of Agricultural Work Committees (UAWC), in 1986. Both of these groups remained quite small; two other agricultural committees were stillborn.

Each of these committees outwardly professed interest only in agricultural development while criticizing the others for being too political. For example, a leading PARC official maintained that "the other relief committees were established in order to compete with us so they could be seen as a political power. Hence, they are much more overtly political than we are."[38] TCAS officials responded that "we are fully prepared to enter into a joint committee with them. The problem is that the others are too ideological."[39] Although they explicitly denied or downplayed the political content of their own work, it was clear that the members of the agricultural committees were fully cognizant of the intensely political nature of their projects: self-help, self-empowerment, disengagement, and social change.

What is important to remember in this maze of acronyms is that in the years immediately preceding the outbreak of the Intifada, a framework was constructed by urban professionals with two goals: to diminish dependence on Israel by encouraging agricultural self-sufficiency and to create a network of people throughout the occupied territories who shared the idea that, in effect, vegetables and politics were closely intertwined. The Intifada provided the opportunity for this nascent configuration to be developed rapidly.

Strengthening the Infrastructure during the Intifada

Agricultural self-sufficiency was a goal of the Intifada leadership, and was repeatedly encouraged in a number of *bayanat*, or leaflets, issued periodically by the Unified National Leadership of the Uprising (UNLU). There were three primary reasons for promoting such self-sufficiency. First, by consuming products raised locally, Palestinians denied capital to Israeli interests, deepening the economic crisis in Israel. Second, growing their own food, or at least some of it, enabled Palestinians to stretch their savings in economically difficult times. Third, and most important, by producing backyard crops Palestinians experienced a sense of self-empowerment—a feeling that they were able, as individuals, to help throw off the military occupation.

As early as bayan 4, issued in mid-January 1988, the UNLU called for "concentrating all energy on cultivating the land, achieving maximum self-sufficiency." A second call for boycotting Israeli products and practicing self-sufficiency was made two weeks later in bayan 6. The most explicit imperative was made in bayan 8, dated February 20, 1988:

> It is a long and hard road, but it is the only sure path. Let the uprising escalate toward civil disobedience. Let us deny the occupation its monopoly on authority. Let the authority of the UNLU and the heroes of stones and Molotovs be the true foundation. Let us boycott the enemy's departments, its projects, and its goods as much as we can. Let us multiply its economic, political, human, and morale losses. Only by making our enemy's losses greater than its gains will it depart from our land. Let us return to our soil and till it, for it is a blessed resource for all. Many of our basic needs can be provided through a small plot of land adjacent to our houses. Frugality will make your income last longer; it supports your steadfastness and reduces the heavy burden of life under occupation. Vegetable gardening and animal husbandry can be easily done. Let us remember that the Vietnamese defeated U.S. tyranny not only by the gun but also by the wise use of their land.

Such calls became frequent in subsequent leaflets. In response to these calls and in line with their general ideology, agricultural relief committees, in conjunction with local agricultural popular committees, led what turned out to be a surprisingly successful attempt at agricultural disengagement from Israel.

In the early months of the Intifada, the agricultural relief committees helped to form and work with agricultural popular committees in villages, camps, and towns. In the first six months of the Intifada, hundreds of grassroots voluntary associations were formed which dealt with local agricultural production. As popular committees were not outlawed by Israel until August 1988, involvement in these alternative structures of authority prior to that time was done openly and with great enthusiasm. The local committees usually consisted of current and recently graduated university students and day laborers who were no longer working in Israel. In fact, figures compiled by the government of Israel indicate that over 7,500 more agricultural workers were employed in the West Bank in 1988—the first full year of the Intifada—than in 1987.[40] Even this conservative figure (it would not include backyard farmers) suggests a significant return to agriculture by those who formerly worked in Israel. According to one NGO employee who regularly worked with agricultural popular committees, local committee members were generally the "newly involved," often former wage laborers in Israel, as older Palestinians were "far more skeptical of cooperatives and other new developments."[41] By all accounts, the newcomers were the biggest risk-takers in agricultural production.

Even though, after August 1988, participation in popular committees of any kind carried a ten-year prison term under Israeli law, such committees continued to proliferate. In 1989, for example, PARC engineers worked with sixty popular committees in 122 villages throughout the occupied territories.[42] Both TCAS and the UAWC likewise worked with local popular committees in their assistance projects.

With the establishment of a wide network of popular committees and women's committees with which to work, the distribution of seedlings as well as follow-up extension visits became easier. In 1989, for example, PARC distributed 500,000 vegetable seedlings which it had produced in its own nursery. In the same year, over 2,500 extension visits dealing with crop production were made by PARC officials to 122 villages.[43] UAWC distributed 615,000 vegetable seedlings during the first two years of the Intifada.[44]

In addition to assisting both regular farmers and the newly engaged backyard farmers, the agricultural relief committees assisted in promoting small-scale local animal husbandry during the Intifada. PARC established rabbit farms in Bayt Jala and Ramallah, worked with twenty-three chicken-egg, twelve rabbit, and two goat cooperatives, and maintained that it made over 500 related extension visits in the northern half of the West Bank in 1989.[45] UAWC claimed to have distributed 7,200 egg-laying chickens and 28,500 gamehens during 1988–89.[46] The committees usually would buy the chickens and cows from Israel, while sheep and goats were purchased from local Palestinian concerns. Realizing the extent of the self-sufficiency movement, Israeli officials began urging Jewish farmers not to sell cows and other animals to Palestinians. In some ways it was too late, as overall animal husbandry increased by about 30 percent during the first two years of the Intifada, while the increase in chickens was much higher.[47] In fact, TCAS estimates that in the Hebron area alone—where the self-sufficiency movement was always the weakest—there was an increase of 700 percent in the number of egg-producing chickens in the first two years of the Intifada.[48]

The level of success of the self-sufficiency movement varied across the West Bank. The Nablus area, for example, overcame considerable difficulties to register some success in this movement. The area has a reputation for political activism, reflected in Nablus's nickname *jabal al-nar,* Fire Mountain. During the Intifada, Nablus was rewarded for its resistance with an especially high number of days under curfew. Such hardship in the downtown area helped to mobilize the surrounding communities to produce and distribute foodstuffs for its residents. By 1989, Nablus had thirty-nine popular committees which basically ran municipal affairs.[49] Included in this number were several popular committees which dealt with backyard farming. In addition, each of the agricultural relief committees was active in the Nablus area, both prior to and during the Intifada.

The back-to-the-land movement in Nablus had some startling successes during the Intifada. According to the Nablus office of Israel's Ministry of Agriculture, most of the gains were made in the areas of animal husbandry and vegetable production, while citrus production lagged behind, primarily because of the length of time needed for the plants to bear fruit. Still, an additional 200 to 300 dunums of land in the Nablus area came under citrus cultivation during the first two years of the Intifada.[50]

Table 12 shows significant changes which occurred in the Nablus area during the first two years of the Intifada as a result of the self-sufficiency movement. The addition of nearly 500 cows in the region reflects only small-scale operations (usually two to four cows) and not large dairy farms. Conversely, the figures for sheep, goats, and chickens include changes only in commercial farms and exclude the often considerable increases in "backyard" animals. Thus, the enhanced levels of animal husbandry depicted in the table may well understate the actual changes. Note should be made of the near doubling of lands cultivated for vegetable production, which led to an increase of more than 30 percent in total vegetable production in the Nablus area in the first two years of the Intifada.

The village of Salfit, southwest of Nablus on the West Bank, had an

TABLE 12

Animal Husbandry and Cultivation in the Nablus Area during the Intifada

	1987	December 1989
Cows*	715	1,200
Sheep†	22,000	24,800
Goats†	12,600	12,600
Chickens (eggs)‡	9,000	13,000
Chickens (meat)‡	465,000	663,000
Dunums under vegetable cultivation	2,500	4,800
Irrigated dunums under cultivation	1,400	1,600
Unirrigated dunums under cultivation	185,000	190,000

*Does not reflect changes in large farms.
†Includes only changes in commercial farms, not private homes.
‡Only groupings of 500 or more are counted.
Source: Israeli Ministry of Agriculture, Nablus office.

even greater agricultural turnaround. Long a stronghold of the Palestine Communist Party, Salfit was chosen by PARC to be a regional center. This village of 4,500 Palestinians is close enough to both the Jewish settlement of Ariel and Israel proper that it had an unusually large wage-labor population who worked as manual laborers in these areas instead of in local businesses or farms. Wages earned in Israel or Ariel were substantially higher than those in the West Bank.

When the Intifada broke out, employment in Israel or on the settlements was strongly discouraged by the leadership of the uprising; this prompted hundreds of local workers to take up work near their homes, often in the farming sector. Initially, virtually all of the 600 or so Salfitis who were employed by Israelis boycotted their jobs. Even by the end of the second year of the Intifada, when many Palestinians had returned to their former jobs in Israel, about 300 Salfitis who had formerly worked in Israel refused to return.[51] The combination of available workers, agricultural expertise, and high levels of enthusiasm for the back-to-the-land movement produced a virtual green revolution in Salfit during the Intifada. Before the Intifada, most of Salfit's vegetables came from the Nablus area and Israel. During the first two years of the Intifada, Salfit became completely self-sufficient in tomatoes (it had grown none previously) and virtually self-sufficient in cucumbers. No Israeli fruits and vegetables were sold in Salfit's markets in this period; Israeli-grown bananas had been replaced by bananas grown by Palestinians in the Jordan Valley. In addition, potatoes, peas, beans, eggplant, cauliflower, and peppers were also grown, often in newly erected greenhouses. Similar strides were made in animal husbandry. In fact, the movement to increase local agricultural production was so successful that excess Salfiti vegetables were often bought by local popular committees for distribution to residents of Nablus when that city was under curfew—a reversal of the pre-Intifada situation.

To accomplish this significant increase in agricultural production, Salfitis not only employed basic technologies such as greenhouses but also brought under cultivation marginal lands which had not previously been considered cultivable, usually in small plots. Some of the newly cultivated land—about 100 dunums in all—had been left unplanted for several years as its owners worked in Israel, while a number of smaller plots had never been cultivated.

Hebron is a more socially and politically conservative city than Nablus, as is generally the case when the southern half of the West Bank is compared to the northern half. As a result, the three leftist factions of the PLO have never been able to gain a solid foothold in the area. Instead, Fatah and the Muslim Brethren (now Hamas) have dominated the local scene. Because of such social conservatism, alternative structures of authority in the Intifada—the popular committees—were neither as abundant nor as powerful in Hebron as they were elsewhere in the West Bank.

TCAS established its headquarters in Hebron in part because PARC had very little impact there. The coalition which makes up TCAS was well suited for the Hebron environment as it was the Fatah members of the organization who were more active politically, while the DFLP-leaning members concentrated much more on purely agricultural concerns. This informal division of labor helps explain why TCAS worked with the Women's Committee for Social Work (the Fatah-aligned women's committee) and not with the Women's Action Committees (DFLP) when distributing seedlings to village popular committees or making extension visits.

Through the work of the agricultural committees as well as politically unaffiliated Palestinians, significant steps were taken in the Hebron area to strengthen food independence from Israel, as figures for the first two years of the Intifada indicate: a 700 percent increase in the number of chickens raised for eggs, an increase of 800 dairy cows (from 400 to 1,200), a drop in vegetable imports from Israel as a percentage of total consumption from 70 percent to about 10 percent, and a decline in fruit imports from Israel as a percentage of total consumption from 60 percent to about 10 percent.[52]

Although these cases highlight the self-sufficiency movement during the Intifada, they were by no means the only examples. Many towns and villages throughout the West Bank engaged in similar activities, with varying degrees of success.

Israeli Responses to the Self-Sufficiency Movement

Faced with a movement that not only threatened structural changes to the dependent relationship of the occupied territories with Israel but also was quickly becoming the symbolic center of the Intifada, Israel responded forcefully. The greatest harm to Palestinian agriculture was caused by Israel's imposition of extended curfews on a large number of villages. A few examples will suffice to make the point.[53]

The village of Idna was under twenty-four-hour curfew between May 15 and June 6, 1988, during the harvest season for a variety of vegetables. Ninety-five percent of the crop rotted in the fields. The town of Qabatiya was placed under curfew from July 4 to July 24, 1988, leading to the loss of over 90 percent of the vegetable crop, 80 percent of the grape harvest, and one million vegetable seedlings being raised in three local nurseries. The village of Til, near Nablus, was placed under curfew for forty continuous days in August and September 1988, the first twenty-seven days of which were around-the-clock curfew. Seventy-five percent of the fig crop was lost. The village of Bani Na'im was placed under curfew for fifteen continuous days in December 1989, during which time the Israeli authorities refused to allow in chicken feed. As a result, as many as 50,000 chickens perished.[54]

In addition to curfews, Israel imposed a number of measures which undermined Palestinian agriculture, including uprooting tens of thousands of trees, confiscating land, impeding the transport of agricultural products, and destroying farm machinery. In some cases, there was outright sabotage. In December 1989, Israeli settlers sprayed chemicals on 540 dunums of grapes in Halhul, near Hebron, ruining the crop and resulting in damages in excess of $100,000.[55] One shipment of agricultural produce on its way to France was ruined when the refrigeration system was tampered with. A Palestinian official working for Israel's Ministry of Agriculture accused Agrexco, Israel's agricultural export company through which all Palestinian agricultural exports had to pass, of systematic legal sabotage: "Agrexco used to inspect boxes [of produce] randomly before we could export them. Now, every single box is opened and searched. This damages the goods by bruising them—especially the vegetables—and, as a result, lowers their value."[56]

Government restrictions were placed on the sale of the prolific egg-producing F-1 hybrid chickens to the occupied territories, leading to both an expensive black market in the hybrid and a shift to the less-productive local (*baladi*) scavenger chickens. When Salfit's agricultural boom was recognized, Israeli authorities in the summer of 1989 slashed the village's water allocation by 50 percent to fifteen cubic meters a day. In addition, during the first two years of the Intifada, the price of barley (the primary feed crop for livestock) increased 250 percent, becoming more expensive, at one point, than wheat. According to Hisham Awartani, this dramatic price increase was only partly due to market forces:

> Clearly the decision was taken to hurt the Palestinian agricultural movement by making inputs for Palestinian farmers very high. It was another tactic in the farming war. Remember, the only seller of corn and barley in Israel is Dagon, an Israeli company based in Haifa. They can set prices as they wish, as there is no competition. The net impact for livestock owners in the West Bank was disastrous.[57]

Finally, certain factors beyond the control of both protagonists conspired to undermine the self-sufficiency movement. In particular, the collapse of the Jordanian dinar during this period drove up relative prices for Palestinians who kept their savings in that currency, as most did. Moreover, when Jordan formally severed its administrative ties to the West Bank in July 1988, it also closed its markets to virtually all West Bank agricultural exports. Whereas 50,000 to 60,000 tons of fruits and vegetables were previously exported annually to and through Jordan, suddenly almost none was allowed to enter.

The Balance Sheet

Determining with any precision the overall numbers of the self-sufficiency movement and the effect of the boycott of Israeli agricultural products is difficult. One small example of the problem in gauging these figures is the fact that, in light of the boycott, a number of Israeli companies disguised the Israeli origins of their products. For example, juice made at the Israeli settlement of Neveh Ya'kov was labeled in Arabic as having been made in the nearby Palestinian town of al-Ram, so that it might be more readily marketed in the West Bank. Still, some rough numbers can be compiled.

Three trends were particularly important in this sector during the Intifada: agricultural and animal husbandry rose markedly, the agricultural labor force expanded by one-third, and imports from Israel declined. As for the first trend, statistics compiled by both Israel and the World Bank demonstrate that the self-sufficiency movement clearly resulted in greater local production. Israeli figures compiled in the annual *Statistical Abstract* reflect these changes. During the first year of the Intifada, the value of all crops, livestock and livestock products in the West Bank increased 51 percent over the previous year. Although a significant increase in the value of the crops (up 75 percent) was due to a rebound of the olive harvest from a particularly bad previous year, other crops were also up. The vegetable harvest in the West Bank jumped by 14 percent and fruit by 29 percent. The 22 percent rise in the value of livestock products in the West Bank during (roughly) the first year of the Intifada included increases in milk by 26 percent and eggs by 20 percent. Figures for Gaza showed a similar pattern. Overall, the value of agricultural and livestock output in Gaza rose 14 percent during the first year of the Intifada, including increases of 25 percent in vegetable, 76 percent in fish, and 28 percent in milk production.[58]

World Bank figures show a similar trend. For example, vegetable production in the West Bank went from 182,300 tons just prior to the Intifada (in 1986–87) to 215,500 tons in 1989–90, an increase of nearly 20 percent.[59] The local production of eggs in Gaza doubled to 145 million from 1986–87 to 1991–92.[60] The increases in animal husbandry were similarly dramatic, as table 13 shows. All areas of animal husbandry expanded during the Intifada, including head of cattle (by 44 percent), sheep (30 percent), goats (33 percent), layer hens (twelvefold), and broiler chickens (threefold).

TABLE 13

Livestock Increases in the West Bank during the Intifada

	Cattle	Sheep	Goats	Layer Hens	Broiler Chickens
1986	8,000	263,200	157,400	93,000	7,500,000
1987	8,800	284,500	174,300	100,000	11,500,000
1988	10,700	314,000	186,200	251,000	6,900,000
1989	10,100	339,500	195,300	500,000	18,000,000
1990	11,200	345,300	210,800	603,000	35,000,000
1991	10,700	340,500	219,400	841,000	22,900,000
1992	11,500	336,700	210,000	1,170,000	22,800,000

Source: World Bank, *Developing the Occupied Territories, Volume 4: Agriculture* (Washington, D.C., 1993), p. 76.

The growth in food production and livestock holding was, in part, a result of the expansion of the agricultural labor force in the West Bank and Gaza and the concomitant decrease in the number of Palestinians who worked in Israel. During the first year of the Intifada, according to Israeli statistics, there was a 23 percent reduction in the number of days Palestinians labored in Israel (down 19 percent for workers from the West Bank and 29 percent for those from Gaza), indicating both the large number of Palestinians who quit working in Israel altogether and the larger number who worked in Israel less frequently out of choice or through curfews and border closures. In 1987, Palestinians who traveled to Israel worked, on average, twenty-two days per month. During 1988, the figure dropped to seventeen days per month.[61] In all, the agricultural work force employed in the West Bank and Gaza expanded by nearly one-third during the Intifada, as the World Bank figures compiled in table 14 demonstrate.

TABLE 14

Agricultural Work Force in Palestine during the Intifada

	West Bank	Gaza	Total
1987	29,800	8,600	38,400
1990	37,800	12,400	50,200

Source: World Bank, *Developing the Occupied Territories, Volume 4: Agriculture* (Washington, D.C., 1993), p. 83.

Finally, imports from Israel decreased during the Intifada. In the three-year period between the start of the Intifada and the beginning of the Gulf war there was a sharp drop in the level of imports of foodstuffs from Israel. The consumption of Israeli eggs, milk, vegetables, and fruit in the occupied territories as a proportion of total Palestinian consumption of these items declined by at least 50 percent in each case. The decline in Israeli imports reflected both an increase in Palestinian production and a decrease in overall consumption. Living modestly—without large weddings and parties for other social occasions, and without excessive consumption—was a major social by-product of the Intifada, both as a goal of the leadership and because of the continuing financial hardships of the population as a whole.

Besides the various Israeli punishments and strategies which sought to undermine the self-sufficiency movement, and the closure of the Jordanian market to West Bank produce, the movement itself engendered some unforeseen problems. For example, in the great rush to produce and market more milk—at one-half the cost of Israeli Tnuva—the pasteurization process was often bypassed, leading to a substantial increase in the number of cases of brucellosis among Palestinians. Moreover, as one Palestinian economist noted, "Farming is more complex these days than planting a few seeds. The new amateur farmers soon discovered the real costs of production are high."[62] As the difficulties of modern farming became apparent, a number of Palestinians dropped out of the movement. Also, the explosion in the production of vegetables drove some prices down, leading to a further loss of income among farmers. As one Salfiti explained,

We were very successful in growing vegetables, replacing the Nablus market. And we didn't import anything from Israel. But we may have been too successful because the supply drove down the prices, leading to a situation where farmers cannot rely on just their agriculture to make a living. Many farmers have combined efforts and are working a rotating system where one person watches several farms for one day while others work elsewhere. People can supplement their income this way. I could no longer make ends meet, so I am now teaching in this school [in al-Bira], but I keep my brother informed on what to do to keep the farm going. I still go back once a week to help out.[63]

These problems aside, the self-sufficiency movement was a compelling political event. Perhaps the most important—but least quantifiable—result of the movement was the enthusiasm and sense of communal self-empowerment it engendered. Euphoria is commonplace in revolutionary movements, and the Intifada was no different. A great many Palestinians believed, especially in the first year of the uprising, that total disengagement was possible. Yasir Arafat's repeated claims that an independent Palestinian state was "just a stone's throw away" added to the emotional rush. As a result of this enthusiasm, crops were planted with much passion but often without much expertise in terms of fertilizing, spraying, and marketing. Many Palestinians, however, were more open to seeking expertise. An American involved in providing such assistance commented that "the most significant change that the Intifada has brought in the field of agricultural assistance is that partners [i.e., Palestinian farmers] are easier to find now. Even those people who have not been active in the past are getting involved in agricultural programs."[64] The fervor to get involved actually forced PARC to cut back on its rearing and distribution of chicks and rabbits in 1989, as local cooperatives and individuals had greatly expanded their programs in these areas.

While dependence on Israel was far from broken, the Intifada's back-to-the-land movement provided a central political rallying point—something that everyone could participate in to one degree or another. Furthermore, significant increases in Palestinian agricultural production were made under what were, at best, very difficult circumstances. However, the most important change was psychological. As an aid worker told me, "Of course, a national agriculture economy cannot be based on gardens. The real importance is the change in attitude."[65]

The medical and agricultural relief committees which were built in the years leading up to the Intifada were part of a larger strategy to recruit Palestinians to organizations with new bases of social and political relations. In spite of both the political rivalry which often plagued the medical and agricultural committees and the sporadic resort to patronage politics by the Fatah-allied committees, these organizations laid the foundations for national health care and agricultural development systems. By providing badly needed services during the Intifada, they also enabled the Palestinians to better sustain and deepen the process of disengagement. In sum, the professional relief organizations were vehicles for a new Palestinian elite with an agenda quite different from the old notable class to help mobilize the community, overcome traditional social cleavages, and engage in collective national action.

The social base of the new Palestinian elite, of which the activists involved in the building of the professional relief organizations are part, is very similar to the social base of what was often described as the "new middle class" in Arab politics during the 1950s and 1960s. It was this class—the well-educated, nonlanded, salaried middle class—that made up the political arm of the movements which took power in Egypt in 1952, Syria in 1963, Iraq in 1968, and elsewhere in the Middle East in this period. Without assuming a teleological evolution, it was as if the Palestinians were going through a similar phase—but a generation later. The time lapse could easily be explained by the stultifying effects of life under military occupation. In particular, not only did this new middle class seek to supplant the traditional notable elite; it also had to confront the far more powerful military and human resources of Israel. Another important difference is that the army in the earlier cases was seen as the coercive arm of the new middle class, which enabled this class to come to power. Needless to say, the new Palestinian elite in the occupied territories had no military with which to take power.

In effect, the modern organizations which the new elite built in the 1980s and with which they helped to politically mobilize Palestinian society, were the "army" with which the new elite "took power"—i.e., became the dominant political elite within Palestinian society in the West Bank and Gaza. In the post-Oslo period, Arafat and the Palestinian Authority set about curbing the authority of this new elite through co-optation, coercion, and forced marginalization.

4

Abu Barbur

ELITE CONFLICT AND SOCIAL CHANGE
IN BAYT SAHUR

The most significant sociopolitical phenomenon to come out of the Intifada was the creation of alternative structures of authority at the local level—primarily neighborhood, popular, and relief committees. Interestingly, even though these new structures were generally based on the modern principles of individual association and democratic hierarchy, they often operated within the local clan, or *hamula*, configuration. In fact, the most successful attempts at modern social organization in the West Bank town of Bayt Sahur, near Bethlehem, were found in the neighborhoods where the hamula structure was intact and where refugee migration had changed the local demographic balance little. In the case of Bayt Sahur, significant changes in social relations within the hamulas occurred, brought on in part by the rise of a new elite with a more egalitarian ideology. A generation of military occupation did not destroy all the old forms of social organization—Israeli policy, after all, often sought to bolster the old notable elite and its bases of power—but it impacted the remaining structures. Thus, even though traditional forms of social interaction remained—in this case the hamulas—their meanings and their claims on members were altered. The base for political recruitment within the hamulas, however, persisted.

The experiment in mass mobilization through organization-building created new social relations and modes of social interaction based primarily on nonfamilial criteria. This process came to fruition during the Intifada when, for the first time in the history of Palestinian resistance, organization, not familial ties, was the primary vehicle through which social action was conducted.

This chapter is a case study of the rise of these informal associations during the uprising in the town of Bayt Sahur, a largely Christian town of 12,000 people located adjacent to Bethlehem in the southern half of the West Bank. Although many towns and villages engaged in popular organization-building, Bayt Sahur offers the best and most famous example of the role of popular committees (*lijan sha'biya*) in the Intifada. It was the best example because Bayt Sahur was by all accounts the most highly organized community in the occupied territories. This can be explained in part by the relative affluence and high levels of education of the residents; in the words of one, "We are the Japan of the West Bank—a community of highly educated, independent, and enterprising people."[1]

It was the most famous community immersed in building popular committees—and, by extension, engaged in civil disobedience—because of a highly publicized tax boycott and its subsequent suppression by the Israeli army. The civil disobedience campaign caught the eye of a number of foreign journalists, such as Anthony Lewis and Glenn Frankel, and other prominent figures, including Nobel Peace Prize laureate Desmond Tutu, who made a much-publicized visit to Bayt Sahur on Christmas Eve 1989. Such international ties helped to build a sort of political safety net for residents of Bayt Sahur, one in which other Palestinian communities did not necessarily share. In the words of one local leader, "the Israelis know that if they shoot one of us, it will be condemned at the United Nations the next day."[2] In fact, the high level of international publicity may have actually helped to increase local involvement in the informal organizations.[3]

This chapter will deal with the rise of local organization and autonomous political action in Bayt Sahur during the Intifada and the concomitant struggle between competing elites in the community. The development of independent and effective grassroots associations in Bayt Sahur (and elsewhere in the West Bank and Gaza) politically threatened both Israel and the PLO in Tunis, and both sought to reverse the gains for their own reasons. Israel's response was to brutally crush the tax boycott in Bayt Sahur; the PLO's was to quietly undermine the authority of the new elite by allying itself with the notable class. The end result of this struggle was the incomplete consolidation of local authority by the emerging elite in Bayt Sahur. This same pattern was seen throughout the West Bank and Gaza, where real authority had devolved to local political actors during the Intifada but where the resources of Fatah and Israel were used to try and reverse this trend.

The Formation of Neighborhood and Popular Committees

Like much of the Palestinian community, Bayt Sahurians were caught by surprise by the outbreak of the Intifada in Gaza.[4] For the first month or so very little happened in the town, but attention was kept on the nascent uprising, and debate centered on its sustainability. By the middle of January 1988, people in Bayt Sahur—and elsewhere in the occupied territories—began to realize that the Intifada was a momentous event which was not likely to abate anytime soon. With this in mind, a Bethlehem-area relief committee was formed out of existing organizations, charitable societies, women's committees, and the like. Originally, the relief committee was to include the towns of Bethlehem, Bayt Jala, and Bayt Sahur; however, there was reluctance on the part of the representatives of Bethlehem and Bayt Jala to proceed. They argued that such an overarching committee should be organized along factional lines— that is, that local PLO leaders should be in charge. Finally, an agreement was made to minimize the expressly political flavor of the committee.

This regional relief committee collected both money and merchandise to distribute to the areas hardest hit by curfews, raids, and other afflictions. Although the objective was to assist local inhabitants during times of need, assisting other communities was not precluded from the plans. Residents often improvised as to what to contribute. Employees and workers were asked to give a day's wages, professionals 5 to 10 percent of their salaries, and merchants variously, depending on their business. While this early attempt at local organization set the tone for later events, the regional relief committee quickly disintegrated, since the residents of Bayt Jala and Bethlehem were less committed to its success. As the regional mobilization failed, local organization strengthened.

In the aftermath of this early failure, Bayt Sahur organized itself into thirty-five distinct neighborhoods for the purpose of political and social action. Each of these neighborhoods comprised between forty and sixty homes. Beginning in the spring of 1988 each neighborhood held a series of "town meetings" to discuss what could be done both to participate in the Intifada and to protect the town during curfews and school closures. Typically, forty to fifty individuals attended early meetings in each neighborhood before the work was delegated to elected representatives.[5] Either during the first meeting or in another early meeting, between five and ten representatives from each neighborhood were elected in order to organize that neighborhood's activities.

Each neighborhood committee representative was in charge of one aspect of the response to the exigencies of the Intifada. The committee member would thus lead what came to be the defining aspect of Bayt Sahur's Intifada, a popular committee. Each neighborhood committee had popular committees that dealt with collective security, education, food storage and distribution, health, and agriculture.

Committee members organized guard duty for each neighborhood whereby residents were assigned one night a week to spend watching for army or settler raids in order to promptly alert the rest of the town. This was made necessary, in part, by the mass resignation of local policemen and other Palestinians employed by the military administration. The rooftop with the best view of surrounding roads was chosen as the neighborhood's lookout post. Guard duty was done primarily by adults, rather than the *shabab*, or activist youth.[6] Night watch often became a social event, where friends were invited to help pass the time. To expedite communication between those people participating in guard duty, a list of relevant phone numbers was distributed to those concerned. In the event of an emergency, such as an attack by Israeli settlers, a system was thus in place to mobilize large numbers of people quickly.

As schools were ordered closed by the Israeli military for most of the first two years of the Intifada, Palestinians developed a system of informal or popular education (*al-ta'lim al-sha'bi*). Since Bayt Sahur had a large number of well-educated people, finding relatively qualified individuals to teach neighborhood children was not difficult, although some neighborhoods were better endowed with teachers than others. In some cases, teachers were "exported" from one neighborhood to another to teach.[7] In general, since neighborhood committees broadly reflected hamula geography, teachers often taught their own relatives. As one teacher said, this provided "a greater incentive. Anyone would prefer to see his own family members educated."[8] Course work concentrated on Arabic and math.

The decision was made at many neighborhood committee meetings early on in the Intifada to have a neighborhood store so that, in case of an extended curfew, there would be enough supplies to last two to three months. In order to purchase such supplies in one neighborhood, each household was asked to contribute twenty to thirty shekels ($10 to $15). Goods with relatively long shelf lives, such as sugar, rice, and seeds, were purchased with this money. Food was usually stored in spare rooms or garages of local homes. Members of local women's committees, especially the PFLP-associated Union of Palestinian Women's Committees, were actively involved in food distribution.

Because of the large number of injuries and illnesses that resulted from the suppression of the Intifada (ranging from shootings and beatings to nutritional problems due to curfews) each neighborhood had a popular committee that dealt with health issues. The popular health committees included doctors, those with first-aid training and other volunteers. Initially, several makeshift underground clinics were formed by the popular committees, and later a licensed clinic was established to centralize and upgrade health care in Bayt Sahur (discussed below).

Much of the initial enthusiasm for the Intifada in Bayt Sahur was translated into backyard farming as a means to decrease dependency on Israel. Thus, a number of families began small vegetable plots in their backyards. The popular agricultural committees, like their health counterparts, tended to coordinate neighborhood efforts with a more centralized body—in this case, a newly formed agricultural information and supply center.

The work of the popular committees was facilitated by a questionnaire distributed in Bayt Sahur. It asked about numbers of children needing schooling, availability of water (i.e., cisterns, in case of a water shutoff), numbers of unoccupied rooms in the house (for use in popular education or food storage), available land for planting, numbers of cars (in case a need for emergency transport arose), and the like. In one area of Bayt Sahur, every household from seven contiguous neighborhoods filled out the questionnaire—a 100 percent return from about 350 homes.[9]

It is important to note that until August 1988, involvement in these types of nonviolent popular committees was legal under Israeli military rule. Mass involvement in popular committees in Bayt Sahur may well have occurred even if such participation had been illegal; after all, popular participation continued well after August 1988, when a ten-year jail term became the penalty for membership in popular committees. But it seems clear that the initial lack of penalty for membership in these private voluntary organizations encouraged relatively nonpoliticized and nonfactional elements to participate actively. For a number of Bayt Sahurians, this was a first attempt to confront the occupation. One resident credited the increase in political participation, at least in part, to the sudden "availability of more leisure time" due to school closures, strike days, and job layoffs.[10]

It was not the intent of the organizers of neighborhood committees to create structures which would continue indefinitely. Neither should one view the rapidity with which the popular committees came into being as evidence for some sort of master plan worked out in advance. Rather, innovation and communication played key roles. When one neighborhood committee came up with a good idea, such as a neighborhood store, others quickly adopted it.[11]

The success of neighborhood and popular committees in Bayt Sahur was due to an unusual mix of modern and traditional elements. Of foremost importance was the assertion of a new leadership: an educated, articulate, technocratic class, which was able to wrest control of the town away from the traditional notable leadership epitomized by the mayor, Hanna al-'Atrash. It was this new leadership that pushed for a higher degree of nonfamilial organization in town and for greater democratic decision-making within the neighborhood committees. This leadership stratum viewed with favor the fact that the large majority of neighborhood committee representatives were elected by popular vote and not simply appointed by a local patriarch. Thus, even though the neighborhood committees were never intended to be permanent, they did reflect the more egalitarian political values of the new elite which was responsible for their creation. In short, the neighborhood and popular committees of Bayt Sahur were the vehicle which the new elite used to mobilize the population against the Israeli occupation while simultaneously subverting the traditional Palestinian elite.

Yet, it is difficult to separate many of the neighborhood committees from the hamula structure in Bayt Sahur. The most successful neighborhood committees and popular committees came from areas where the hamula structure was strong, often where one or another clan was predominant. Those areas of Bayt Sahur that consisted primarily of nonclan nuclear families—often refugees from the 1948 war—tended to have less success in popular organization. The chairman of one such neighborhood committee, Majid Nassar, told this story:

> The neighborhood here is made up of nuclear families, as there is no great hamula or subhamula located in this area. My family, for example, is from [what is now Israel] and only came here in 1948 with the war. Our neighborhood committee was an example of how not to operate. First of all, the executive committee [of the neighborhood committee] was not elected, as happened elsewhere. Rather, names were nominated and just approved. Four of the five members were from the traditional elite and were aged fifty-five to sixty, while I am thirty-six. They just sat around and did nothing, as they were used to everything being brought to them. They were useless. One had an activist son who suggested that this strip of property here should be used for communal planting and that his father owned it. We thought this was a good idea and went to this man— remember, he was a member of our executive committee—and he refused to let it be used. You see it now, it lies unused collecting garbage. Every couple of weeks there would be a meeting of the representatives of the local ten or twelve neighborhood committees. These men never wanted to go, so I went to all of the meetings; usually I would bring a local young activist. The neighborhood as a whole met about once a month. This neighborhood committee was among the least effective in Bayt Sahur.[12]

The Hamula Structure

Despite the vagaries of war, displacement, and migration due to the conflict over Palestine, Bayt Sahur's demographic structure has remained remarkably stable this century, dominated by two hamulas (see table 15). About 2,000 of Bayt Sahur's 12,000 people have come to reside in the town without prior family ties, most as a result of the 1948 war. Of the remaining 10,000 people, about 80 percent belong to either the Qazaha or Murajda hamulas.

TABLE 15

Primary Hamulas and Extended Families in Bayt Sahur

Hamula	Qazaha	Murajda
Family	1. Qassis	1. Banura
	2. Qumsiya	2. Khayr
	3. Abu Farha	3. 'Awwad
	a. Muslih	4. 'Ayyad
	b. Abu Sa'da	
	4. Ishaq	
	5. Rishmawi	

The Christian Qazaha hamula initially consisted of three extended families which came to Bayt Sahur in the seventeenth century from the Wadi Musa area in present-day Jordan: the Qassis, Qumsiya, and Abu Farha branches.[13] The Hazbun branch of the Qazaha also came to Bayt Sahur at this time but shortly thereafter settled in nearby Bethlehem. In addition, the al-Rishmawi family, not originally from the Qazaha clan, migrated from southern Syria during the same period and was integrated into the Qazaha hamula. All of these families, as well as the Ishaq branch which came some years later, migrated to Bayt Sahur to escape religious persecution at the hands of the Ottoman Turks during the seventeenth century.[14]

The Murajdas were Coptic Christians who migrated from the village of Rushda in Upper Egypt in the first half of the eighteenth century. Four brothers—Banura, Khayr, 'Awwad, and 'Ayyad—came to Bayt Sahur and were the founders of the four main branches of the Murajda hamula.[15] The Mameluke policy in Egypt of compelled conversion to Islam precipitated the exodus.

Even with the migration of Christian families to Bayt Sahur, Muslims made up the majority of the population of the town in the early nineteenth century. The demographic turning point came in 1839 when Muslim soldiers from Palestine fought alongside Ibrahim Pasha of Egypt against the Ottoman armies of Mahmud II. A large number of the soldiers died during the campaign (most from heat and dehydration, not battle). As a result, three-quarters of the Muslim male population of Bayt Sahur was wiped out, leaving a Christian majority.

Since 1945 the population of Bayt Sahur has increased more than fourfold, as may be seen in the population tables shown in table 16.

Extended families in Bayt Sahur have continued to live in clusters, even if the location of the neighborhood has changed. For example, the

TABLE 16

Population of Bayt Sahur, 1945–90

Year	Population
1945	2,770
1961	5,316
1967	6,812
1975	8,028
1981	10,000
1990	12,000

Source: Tuma Banura, *The History of Bethlehem, Bayt Jala, and Bayt Sahur* (in Arabic) (Jerusalem: Matb'a al-Ma'arif, 1982), pp. 219–20.

extended Banura family initially settled in what became the center of town, but as the town grew, most relocated *en masse* to the "Latin" area adjacent to Shepherd's Field, about a mile away from their old quarters. The land to which they moved had been in the family for generations and had been used for livestock grazing. At least one branch of the Banura family remained in town. The point, however, is that when the time came to create neighborhood committees during the Intifada, 70 to 80 percent of the neighborhoods were peopled primarily by individuals from one or another extended family.[16]

Seemingly, there is a paradox between the modernist nature of the new elite's ideology and the fact that the most successful neighborhood committees were found in areas where the hamula structure was still intact. After all, one would expect that the best areas for social reconstruction would be found where the traditional structures were weakest. Conversely, in the areas where the hamula structure was strong, one would expect to find less of an emphasis on democratic process and more on patriarchal delegation. The paradox can be resolved by noting that there is a fundamental difference between social structure and social meaning—between form and substance. While the hamula structures and relations have persisted over time, what they actually mean to their individual members has changed. The claims of the hamula patriarchs to have the final say in the decision-making process are now widely seen by Bayt Sahurians as anachronistic, and those people with nationalist credentials earned in the confrontation with Israel are seen as having a greater mandate for communal authority.

More specifically, while hamulas have long since lost their primary economic and security functions and the hamula patriarchs have been discredited as political figures, the social content of the hamulas has persisted. In particular, the hamulas have acted as places of refuge—of emotional (and occasionally physical) safety. In emergency situations such as the Intifada, a premium is placed on instinctive trust. This is even more important in circumstances where secret collaboration by fellow nationals with one's enemy is common. Clearly, social relations within a hamula will be marked by a higher degree of instinctive trust than relations between atomized nuclear families.

In addition, through access to modern education, many Bayt Sahurians absorbed Western political values and integrated them into a number of social structures, including the hamulas. The changes in the claims that hamulas made on Bayt Sahurians were wrought primarily by this educated new elite, which had begun to displace the hamula patriarchs and other traditional leaders prior to the Intifada but was thrust into a leadership role during the uprising. As the elite changed, so too did the hamulas. After all, social structures tend to reflect the ideological preferences of those who dominate them. Social institutions can "learn" and change—either through experimentation from within or importation from without. In Bayt Sahur—and elsewhere in the occupied territories—the hamula form endured, but its meaning was altered significantly during the Intifada.

Members of the new elite could claim membership in the hamulas and gain the natural base for political recruitment that the hamulas provided while reconstructing the existing relations within the hamulas. The leaders of the "mixed" neighborhoods—where no single extended family was predominant—could match neither the intrinsic recruitment base of the hamulas nor the level of trust which such familial ties generated. Trust was an important element governing social relations in the occupied territories—especially after the penalty for involvement in popular committees of any kind became ten years in prison.

The maintenance of the hamula form as an arena for resistance points to the inherently ambiguous content of nationalist ideologies regarding substantive sociopolitical change. By its very nature, nationalism glorifies the traditions—real or invented—of the community, thereby inhibiting, although not eliminating, calls for social transformation. In other words, there are limits to the potential for significant social change if the vehicle for that change is tied to a preexisting social order. Even when revolutionary, nationalists are not Leninists.

The Shed, the Greenhouse, and Backyard Farming

Primarily because of the work of a handful of local residents, Bayt Sahur became a leader in the West Bank in backyard farming. The individuals who formed the Agricultural Committee of Bayt Sahur had advocated and partially implemented a policy of food self-sufficiency through small-scale farming as early as the 1970s.[17] However, until the uprising, their vision of greater self-sufficiency was largely ignored. The Intifada provided them with an audience and an opportunity to greatly expand their efforts.

The men, led by Jad Ishaq, Issa al-Tawil and Garasmus Kharrub and backed by fourteen local investors, created a central location for the distribution of gardening supplies known as the Shed. The Shed sold seeds and seedlings (bought from Israeli businesses and from nurseries in Palestinian towns), drip irrigation pipes (known locally as "black snakes"), and fertilizer, and even had a small tractor which was lent out on demand. While it was in operation, the Shed distributed tens of thousands of seedlings in Bayt Sahur and the surrounding areas.[18] The activities of the Shed were coordinated with the agricultural popular committee from each neighborhood. Those popular committees would first designate plots of land to farm and then approach the Shed for advice and supplies. The Shed, open every day from 6:00 a.m. to 10:00 p.m., was the only place in Bayt Sahur that was exempted from closing on strike days.

According to the leader of the Shed, Jad Ishaq, all supplies were sold at cost. However, one local merchant accused Shed members of selling for profit supplies they had received free of charge from various Palestinian concerns. The merchant had apparently been hurting financially because the low cost of Shed supplies had driven down the prices of his own products. Nothing ever came of the merchant's accusations, and Shed members vehemently denied any profiteering. Several local leaders, including at least one Shed founder, believed that the Palestinian Agricultural Relief Committee (PARC) was behind these rumors of wrongdoing, as the Shed represented its greatest rival. This is a plausible argument on two grounds. First, since PARC was associated with the Palestine Communist Party and the Shed was not factionally tied, ideological resentment may have been involved. Second, since the European Community offered to help fund the Shed, PARC may have perceived this as encroachment upon its economic turf. For its part, PARC denied any such unsavory motivation and pointed to its agricultural work in Bayt Sahur, including the distribution at half price of 3,600 liters of olive oil, three and one-half tons of cereals, and 3,500 seedlings, as well as its ongoing work with twelve agricultural popular committees in Bayt Sahur.[19]

The Shed spearheaded a virtual green revolution in Bayt Sahur. As a founder of the Shed noted, "You would go to the neighborhood committee meetings and all they would talk about was the farming. Everyone would watch how the crops were doing and compare, saying things like 'my seedlings are five inches high and yours are only two.'"[20]

After Israel closed the Shed and imprisoned its founder, Bayt Sahur was without an agricultural center for only a short period. In its place, local activists established a small cooperative nursery and greenhouse to continue the green revolution, although in somewhat altered form. Undertaken primarily by PFLP activists not associated with the earlier Shed, the cooperative included thirty farmers and a number of other backyard enthusiasts. They would purchase good quality tomato, eggplant, and other seeds—often from Israeli concerns—grow them in the greenhouse, and sell the seedlings to local farmers at prices substantially lower than market price. The cooperative still managed to turn a small profit.[21]

Animal husbandry was likewise encouraged in order to minimize dependency on Israeli products. With this in mind, Bayt Sahur's agricultural activists were in the forefront of a drive to purchase sheep, chickens, and goats, as well as build pens for the livestock, so that dairy and poultry needs could be met locally. A similar process occurred throughout the West Bank. The most famous example of this strategy arose when local residents formed a cooperative and purchased eighteen pregnant cows from an Israeli kibbutz in order to provide milk for Bayt Sahur.[22] When the Israeli military authorities were informed of the sale, soldiers went first to photograph and then to confiscate the cows.[23] By then, however, the cows were in hiding, and became the subject of spirited negotiations between the military administration and the would-be dairy farmers. The Israelis finally relented when residents convinced the officials that they possessed the proper permits for the cows, and that "these were not political cows."[24] The incident was not without cost, especially for the cows: thirteen died as they were shuttled around in hiding. In time, their numbers were replenished and they eventually provided a portion of the milk consumed in Bayt Sahur.

Health Committees and Clinical Subterfuge

Throughout the occupied territories during the Intifada, new medical clinics often replaced hospitals as health care providers. Many of these clinics were illegal back-of-the-house operations, providing rudimentary care to those injured during the Intifada. The impetus for such an increase in underground clinics, besides the obvious increase in need, was an Israeli military order which stipulated that hospitals which treated patients with Intifada-type wounds (e.g., gunshots) must hand those patients over to the Israeli army. Often, soldiers would not wait for patients to be treated but would arrest such individuals at the entrance to hospitals instead.

In Bayt Sahur each of the thirty-five neighborhoods had a popular committee dealing with issues of health. Lectures on hygiene, treatment of basic injuries, and liaisons with two makeshift underground clinics were provided by these popular committees. However, there was a real sense in Bayt Sahur that while guard duty, education, and food storage were best handled on a neighborhood basis, medical care should be undertaken on a community-wide basis.

Establishing licensed clinics involved obtaining permission from the Israeli authorities. Since that permission most likely would not be forthcoming during the uprising, another way was found. The Greek Catholic convent in Bayt Sahur had run a licensed clinic until 1974, when it was closed down for various reasons. However, the license remained valid. Several residents approached the convent with the idea of establishing a first-rate, low-cost medical clinic under the convent's auspices. The convent was receptive to the idea. Thus, "officially," the convent's clinic "re-opened" after a fourteen-year closure.

Bayt Sahur's medical clinic opened on September 19, 1988, nine months into the Intifada. In its first fifteen months of operation the clinic treated over 15,000 patients.[25] It quickly became a major health center for the whole Bethlehem area, including some of the eastern villages. The Israeli occupation forces, for their part, were less than amused by the success of what some were calling the "Hadassah of Bayt Sahur"—a reference to a well-known Israeli hospital in Jerusalem. As a result, the Israelis initiated a policy of harassment, whereby the doctors associated with the clinic (initially one full-time and five to six part-time) would regularly be placed under "day arrest." The doctors would be told to report to military headquarters at 8:00 a.m. and then be released at 8:00 p.m., never having been charged and often not having been spoken with. In addition, officials from the military government and Shin Bet (Israeli secret police) would frequently stand outside the clinic in order to see if "Intifada patients" were being treated. Providing medical care to Palestinians injured in confrontations with soldiers, without the prompt disclosure to Israeli authorities of the names of those treated, constituted grounds for closing any clinic. It was common knowledge that Bayt Sahur's clinic was treating Intifada patients, but the Israelis could not prove it. In any case, the clinic was often closed for days at a time in the early months of its operation, although such harassment diminished considerably by 1990.

Part of the reason for the clinic's success was the low cost of seeing a doctor. It cost the equivalent of $2.50 for most appointments and $4.00 for seeing the gynecologist. Any follow-up appointment within a week was gratis. All medicine came from the seven West Bank pharmaceutical companies and was distributed at cost. Twenty percent of the patients received free examinations and medicine. About half of the total costs of the clinic were covered through patient fees. The rest came from international and local donations, with a large part being contributed by the Union of Health Work Committees, the PFLP-associated medical committee. Dr. Majid Nassar, the clinic's head, estimated that the clinic saved local residents about $240,000 in its first fifteen months of operation.[26]

Bayt Sahur's medical response to the Intifada was not limited to the clinic. In addition, the local YMCA in May 1989 opened a rehabilitation program for people injured during the Intifada. Like the medical clinic, the rehabilitation program was sanctioned by a preexisting charitable institution, in this case the YMCA headquarters in Jerusalem. The need for such a program was pressing, as tens of thousands of Palestinians had been injured in the Intifada, many permanently. The center specialized in the psychological aspects of injuries, that is, helping people deal psychologically with often-permanent disabilities. Once again, it was members of the new elite in Bayt Sahur who were behind the program. For example, the director of the program, Rifa't al-Qassis, was a university-educated administrator. He had been active in the student movement at Bethlehem University, had been arrested on a number of occasions for his political work and imprisoned without charge (administrative detention), and had been issued a "green card" which prevented him from leaving the West Bank (even to go to East Jerusalem).[27]

The IDF responded to the YMCA's rehabilitation program in much the same way they had to the medical clinic: harassment, but not closure. Eight times in its first three years of operation the YMCA's clinic was raided for political incitement. In one raid, the Israelis confiscated the clinic's records, including many confidential doctor-patient files. In another raid, they arrested ten program counselors and sentenced one, Ghassan Jarrar, to deportation.[28]

The medical clinic and the rehabilitation program, like the Shed, institutionalized popular committee functions and were undertaken by individuals not associated with the traditional political actors in Bayt Sahur. All of these cases represented relatively successful attempts at functional disengagement from Israeli concerns. Not only were these institutions symbols of independence and self-reliance, but they were indicators of how much authority had devolved to the grassroots during the Intifada.

Creating a Parallel Municipal Authority

The mayor of Bayt Sahur, Hanna al-'Atrash, was one of a handful of traditional notable leaders who were voted into office in the 1976 municipal elections. Although scions of notable families won in most districts, they were generally of a nationalist, PLO-affiliated bent. 'Atrash, like Elias Freij in Bethlehem, was more conservative and had closer ties to Jordan than most of his counterparts. While the Israeli authorities dismissed the nationalist mayors in subsequent years, 'Atrash and Freij were kept on, as they were not viewed as political threats (i.e., through association with the PLO) to Israel.

'Atrash was widely ridiculed during the Intifada by Bayt Sahurians, being viewed more as an obstacle to be overcome than a participant in the struggle against Israeli occupation. As one local leader stated,

> Our mayor is part of the problem. Before the Intifada, he was the leading advocate of our paying taxes. Then comes the tax boycott here and all of a sudden 'Atrash goes to Washington, D.C., and says "we will never pay taxes until we have independence." He just jumped on the bandwagon when it was convenient.[29]

Another resident added, "the municipality is no more than a mediator to the military government. The municipality lost the chance of a lifetime in the Intifada by not supporting the town in the tax revolt. This was the best chance for 'Atrash to be something here—but he lost it."[30]

A local activist, Ghassan Andoni, told the story of the planning for the November 1989 Day of Prayer, a much-publicized event in which individuals from all over the world were invited to Bayt Sahur to pray for peace and the end of the occupation:

> The Day of Prayer was actually arranged before the tax raid. We had sent invitations to international leaders, including Presidents Carter, Gorbachev, and Mitterrand. We were told that Jimmy Carter was interested in actually coming but he wanted the mayor, Hanna al-'Atrash, to sign the invitation, instead of the more vague "People of Bayt Sahur." Who knows which people of Bayt Sahur? Anyway, I took the invitation to 'Atrash and asked if he would sign it personally. Not only did he refuse to sign the invitation, but I was arrested by the Israelis two days later.[31]

It was clear to Andoni that 'Atrash had informed the Israeli authorities of his activities in organizing the Day of Prayer. On another occasion, an invitation to Nelson Mandela to visit Bayt Sahur was penned, and "instead of asking the mayor to sign the invitation, a group of us went to him and told him to sign it. He was left with very little choice."[32]

Contempt for the mayor was so strong in some quarters that he was referred to as *Abu Barbur,* colloquial Palestinian Arabic for "father of phlegm."[33] In a letter distributed to Jerusalem-based media in July 1988 and signed by "The People of Bayt Sahur," 'Atrash was referred to as the "compromised mayor."[34] Perhaps the greatest public affront to 'Atrash's authority came with a much-publicized Christmas Eve 1989 visit to Bayt Sahur by Desmond Tutu. In what should have been 'Atrash's moment of glory, the mayor was pointedly shunned by the organizers, who made sure that he was not involved in the proceedings.[35]

In fact, 'Atrash either opposed or was uninvolved in every major event and new institution in Bayt Sahur during the Intifada. The mayor did not participate in the founding of Bayt Sahur's medical clinic and repeatedly refused to allow the municipality's resources to be used to assist the clinic. For example, twice the clinic sustained damage due to sewage accumulation combined with winter rains (the clinic sat at a low point in town) and clinic officials asked the municipality to help dredge it. Twice the mayor refused. After the clinic moved to a new building in 1990, its officials asked the mayor to extend the adjoining pavement two meters to reach the clinic's new front doors. Again the mayor declined.[36] The mayor was not involved in the Shed, the greenhouse, the rehabilitation center, or the dairy cooperative. Nor was he involved in the creation or running of Bayt Sahur's "rapprochement center," a locus for ongoing talks between Palestinians and Israelis. In the end, he even opposed Bayt Sahur's campaign of civil disobedience, from the mass return of identification cards to the tax boycott. In fact, at the behest of the IDF, he implored the merchants who began the tax boycott to pay their taxes.[37]

Although 'Atrash was a focus of criticism, it was the larger stratum of traditional leaders in Bayt Sahur that was pushed aside early in the Intifada. In neighborhood committees, popular committees, the Shed, and the medical clinic, the *mukhtar*s, the municipal authorities, the patriarchs, and other traditional leaders of Bayt Sahur were hesitant to get involved and were often not encouraged to do so. The shabab, so often credited with leading the Intifada, were important in terms of energy and involvement. But it was the "midgeneration" in Bayt Sahur that provided the leadership and functioned as the real builders of the Intifada. These were generally well-educated men in their twenties and thirties who bridged the gap between the oldest generation, who had flourished under Jordanian rule, and the shabab, the youths who had known only Israeli occupation.

It was this new leadership stratum that came to the fore when Bayt Sahur created a parallel municipal authority, known as the Sulha committee.[38] In early 1989, twenty-two organizations in Bayt Sahur—clubs, clinics, PLO factions, representatives from the municipality—met and established the Sulha committee in order to coordinate the activities of the entire town. Seven people were elected to this executive committee and charged with the duties of raising money to distribute to needy families, settling disputes, and coordinating Bayt Sahur's response to the Intifada. Like the medical clinic, the Sulha committee operated under a license that had been granted twenty years earlier but had not been used, so its existence was not kept secret. The participating institutions each agreed to contribute 100 Jordanian dinars (at the time about $250) to start and ten dinars a month thereafter. Thus, the Sulha committee had an initial budget of about 2,000 dinars, out of which it would give needy families (largely those families whose primary breadwinner was in jail or out of work) 20 to 30 dinars a month.[39] When funds ran low, more would be solicited, although occasionally the treasury was completely emptied.

Settling local disputes became a primary function of the Sulha committee. The traditional method of solving disputes, especially in the more conservative southern part of the West Bank, is based on Bedouin customary law (*al-'urf al-'asha'iri*). When there was a problem between families, there would be a three-day cooling-off period, during which time delegations from the affected families would meet. Next, the family at fault would admit its guilt and send a delegation to the wronged party in order to work out suitable compensation. In more extreme cases, especially if a killing had occurred, outside mediators would be chosen who would give binding arbitration. For disputes in Bayt Sahur, these mediators would come either from traditional notable families or from the nearby al-Ta'amra Bedouin tribe.

One indication of the decline of the traditional leadership in Bayt Sahur was that disputes during the Intifada were settled by the Sulha members, whose authority was based on nationalist credentials, not notables whose authority was based on familial status. In the words of one Sulha member, the committee "did not set out to be an alternative to this system of mediation, that is, to be the final arbiters. But that is exactly what happened. The moment the Sulha was created we were given full recognition by the community."[40] The nature of disputes changed during the Intifada. Before the uprising, problems would often involve entire hamulas, in classic feuds. During the Intifada, such disputes were limited and tended to involve only immediate families or even individuals.

When individuals were found guilty of various infractions, fines of up to 300 shekels (about $150) were assessed and redistributed by the Bayt Sahur relief committee to needy families. In one case in June 1989, following a period of bad blood between two families, an individual threw a stone through a window of the other family's home, slightly injuring a women inside. The Sulha committee intervened, demanding—and promptly receiving—an apology and a fine. According to a member of the Sulha committee, "the Israelis were furious that a family would pay fines to the Sulha committee but would not pay taxes to them. They saw us as a new government. This was a very frightening development for the Israelis."[41]

In another instance, community activists repeatedly approached a well-known collaborator, Mahmud Zahlan, and asked that he cease his collaboration.[42] Zahlan had been involved in the Village League policy in the early 1980s. Under this policy, the Israeli government (then under the leadership of Menachim Begin) empowered and sometimes armed usually marginal elements in the Palestinian population, who then would act on behalf of the Israelis in the occupied territories. It was common during the first year of the Intifada for collaborators to publicly renounce their relationship with Israeli authorities, and not be penalized by local activists. In fact, the head of the Village Leagues in the Bethlehem district (which included Bayt Sahur), Bishara Qumsiya, denounced his own collaboration to a gathering at the Bayt Sahur Orthodox Church in March 1988, declaring, "I will be your servant and I swear never to betray you again."[43] Those who refused to renounce their collaboration were often attacked, and many were killed after the first year of the uprising. Zahlan refused to renounce his activities and, as a result, had his home burned in September 1989.

One area where some traditional leaders were consulted by the Sulha committee concerned land disputes. As one Sulha member put it,

> These traditional leaders were the only residents who knew the borders of property. There are some strange rules for the sale of property here. For example, if a family wishes to sell a parcel of land, his neighbor has a right to buy it first. In addition, after ten years, if the land has not been developed, the old owner has the right to buy it back at the same price. In one case during the Intifada, the Sulha committee had to intervene between two families who bought the same parcel of land without the other knowing. The problem was solved equitably.[44]

According to all accounts, however, the traditional and municipal leaders were not pleased with the creation of the Sulha committee, but often they would cooperate because they had no alternative. In fact, the municipal officials were so irritated that their authority was being undermined that they withdrew their initial—and tentative—support from the Sulha committee shortly after it was formed. As one member of the Sulha committee explained,

> The municipality was very hesitant in supporting the restructuring of the community. They had to be dragged along in everything. The municipality was faced with the choice of joining the Sulha committee and trying to get power from the inside, or staying away and waiting for the Israelis to arrest us. The municipality was always on the edge—they would step in, step out, and step in again. When it became clear that the Sulha committee was running afoul of the security services, the municipality withdrew entirely.[45]

Again, it was not just the mayor and his municipality which opposed the Sulha. One of the more conservative members of the Sulha put it this way:

> A number of people opposed the Sulha early on, not just the mayor. Mukhtars and all elderly people opposed the Sulha on the grounds that its members were "not experienced," that the Sulha did not include those "who understand." Some felt the Sulha members, by their "inexperience," created more problems than they solved.[46]

For several months in 1989, the Sulha committee ran Bayt Sahur openly. In July 1989 five of the seven members of the committee were arrested by Israeli authorities and imprisoned without charge or trial.[47] Those arrested were confident that Bayt Sahur's traditional leadership stratum—up to and including the mayor—was at least partly responsible for their arrests. There was a sense that some of the old leaders, many with strong ties to the Israeli authorities, had informed the military administration about the activities of the Sulha committee with the intention of having its members removed from the scene.

It seems clear that the ensuing siege of Bayt Sahur by the Israeli army was due only in part to the refusal by residents to pay taxes. The siege and confiscations were about control—about which authority was greatest. But the showdown was not just between Israel and Bayt Sahur. A secondary struggle was also going on between two competing political elites within Bayt Sahur, with the traditional elites riding the coattails of the Israeli army in trying to suppress a new leadership in Bayt Sahur which was epitomized by the Sulha committee. Both the Israelis and the Palestinian traditional elite had an interest in crushing any genuinely popular and effective alternative structures of authority in Bayt Sahur.

Israeli Tax Policy in the Occupied Territories

Prior to the outbreak of the Intifada, the West Bank and Gaza did not represent a fiscal burden for Israel. Revenues collected in the occupied territories covered all Israeli expenditures there, so that, essentially, Palestinians paid the costs of their own occupation. In addition to underwriting the occupation, Palestinians also subsidized Israel itself. In fact, approximately $100 million annually was transferred to the Israeli treasury from various direct and indirect taxes collected from Palestinians in the occupied territories.[48]

The Intifada initially shifted the financial burden for the occupation more onto Israel itself as tax revenues from the West Bank and Gaza dropped sharply in 1988. In fact, in the first six months of the Intifada, tax revenues declined by nearly half.[49] The early revenue decrease was attributable both to the tax boycott and to a decrease in the tax base, as Palestinian earnings also dropped precipitously.[50] Israeli scholar Meron Benvinisti calculated that the gross domestic product of the West Bank and Gaza fell by 25 percent in the first eight months of the Intifada.[51]

Calculations of taxes owed and the collection of those taxes became part of a larger Israeli strategy for dealing with the uprising. After the mass resignation of Palestinian employees of the civil administration in March 1988, in conjunction with a general unwillingness on the part of

Israeli tax collectors to enter the occupied territories during the Intifada, the military government had no real means to gauge tax indebtedness in a systematic way. As a result, taxes were often calculated and collected in an arbitrary fashion. Incidents of this nature were legion. For example, a nineteen-year-old Bureij refugee-camp resident was told to pay $23,500 in taxes in spite of the fact that he was unemployed and had never held a job; the same day, a few miles away in Gaza, another Palestinian was told to pay $8,000 in back taxes on his store, even though he did not own one.[52] Store owners were often compelled to pay both current taxes and the following year's expected taxes.[53]

Military Order 1262, enacted in December 1988, allowed the military administration to link the issuance of licenses and permits to the payment of taxes. Thus, for a Palestinian man to receive a driver's license, travel permit, identification card, birth certificate, permission to visit relatives in Ketziot/Ansar III prison, construction permit, import/export license, or similar documentation, he would have to receive a "good conduct" certificate from Israel's secret police, the Shin Bet.[54] The good conduct certificate was issued only to those Palestinians who had paid all assessed taxes. The Israeli human rights organization, B'tselem, characterized the order as illegal and noted that even this order had been violated in a number of cases: Palestinians were denied permits because of taxes owed not by themselves but by relatives; identity cards of Palestinians were often confiscated to compel them or a third party to pay taxes (it was illegal to be without an identity card); car registration documents were confiscated until taxes were paid, at times with no evidence that any taxes were owed. As B'tselem noted, "exorbitant assessments" could not usually be paid, resulting in extensive attachment of property, often worth more than twice the sum originally assessed.[55]

A new tax was introduced during the Intifada for vehicles from the occupied territories owned by Palestinians (Israeli settlers in the occupied territories were not similarly assessed). Widely believed to be retaliation for the stoning of Israeli cars in the West Bank and Gaza, the new tax was dubbed *daribat al-hijara*—the stone tax—and averaged $450 per car.[56]

As the Intifada wore on, and tax revenues continued to fall in spite of the measures just noted, the occupation authorities relied increasingly on large tax raids in conjunction with a military show of force in order to assert control. This tactic met with success in terms of total revenues collected. By the end of 1989 tax receipts had returned to about 95 percent of their pre-Intifada levels, although they were being collected from only 50 percent of potential taxpayers.[57] In short, half as many Palestinians were paying twice as much in taxes. It was only a matter of time before there would be a showdown between the Israeli military and the town most famous for tax resistance: Bayt Sahur.

The Siege of Bayt Sahur

In bayan 6, dated February 5, 1988, the UNLU implored Palestinians to build popular committees and other appropriate organizations in order that "complete civil disobedience" ('*isyan muduni shamil*) could be undertaken, including the nonpayment of taxes to Israel. The people of Bayt Sahur widely heeded the call to abstain from paying taxes while under occupation. In the words of one resident, "the Israelis use us as simple laborers. We don't have any services in town, no national insurance, no unemployment benefits. They don't allow us to develop a real modern industry. Why, after all, should we pay taxes?"[58] The town even circulated a leaflet stating:

> We, the people of Bayt Sahur, being an integral part of the Palestinian people and its Intifada, refuse to pay taxes to the occupiers of our land, considering such payment to be a symbol of slavery and oppression. We consider the occupation of one people by another to be a clear violation of all international laws and religions, and it is in violation of the most basic human rights and democratic principles. We strongly believe that every citizen has to pay taxes to his national government in order to enable it to perform its duties and obligations. No taxation without representation![59]

The first crackdown began in an unusual way. A resident of Bayt Sahur, Kamal Abu Sa'da, was briefly interviewed by Israeli Television in a "man-on-the-street" episode, and was asked if he was paying taxes. He responded that he was not, because the UNLU said not to. For the next seventy-five days Abu Sa'da was kept under "day arrest," forced to sit at the Israeli military headquarters from 8:00 in the morning to 8:00 at night.[60]

Bayt Sahur was placed under military curfew on July 7, 1988, and a number of people were arrested and goods confiscated. In response, hundreds of residents turned in their ID cards to the municipality and held a peaceful sit-down strike, demanding that those arrested be released. Israeli authorities responded with force, arresting hundreds and sending a number of those arrested to Ketziot/Ansar III prison in the Negev desert. On July 17, the Latin patriarch of Jerusalem, Michelle Sabah, threatened to go on a hunger strike if the curfew was not lifted. Not wanting a public relations fiasco, the army lifted the curfew that day. The next day, a seventeen-year-old Bayt Sahurian, Edmond Ghannem, was killed by a stone dropped from an Israeli lookout post situated on the rooftop of a local building. Demonstrations and marches protesting the killing rocked Bayt Sahur for three days before curfew was reimposed.

In November 1988 the town again received a general notice to pay all taxes within thirty days. Several days later, troops entered four local pharmacies and arrested their owners. The four men spent nine days at the prison in Bayt Shamash before being released on bail. The military authorities had decided to confiscate the contents of the pharmacies but were prevented from doing so by the High Court of Justice. On June 22, 1989, the court issued a judgment that such confiscation could occur only after the owner had been given written notification to pay and ten days in which to do so. In violation of the court order, the army raided the Rishmawi pharmacy in Bayt Sahur on June 26, 1989. Elias al-Rishmawi, the owner of the pharmacy, recalled, "I can never forget the Israeli officer's response when I showed him the High Court's order. He looked at it, tossed it down on the desk and just laughed. I couldn't believe he could have such an open disregard for the Israeli High Court of Justice."[61]

By refusing to pay taxes to Israel's military administration, Bayt Sahur was becoming an example of the effectiveness of nonviolent civil disobedience for all Palestinians. Israeli authorities were clearly worried that such behavior might spread to the rest of the West Bank. Thus, on September 20, 1989, Israeli troops ringed Bayt Sahur with military checkpoints, closed all side streets, cut telephone lines, and declared the town a closed military area that nonresidents could not enter. Tax officials accompanied by armed troops began systematically raiding businesses and houses in order to collect money and valuables. Videotape smuggled out of Bayt Sahur showed soldiers removing couches, television sets, chairs and tables, and an array of other merchandise from homes and businesses. Many pharmaceuticals were confiscated and rendered unusable. By September 25, 1989, after five days of intensive seizures and nightly curfew, over forty businesses and four homes had had goods confiscated; the estimated worth of these goods was in the hundreds of thousands of dollars, far in excess of even the rather vague claims of what was owed in back taxes.[62] Without intended irony, Shalti'el Levy, the administrative commander for the Bethlehem area (which includes Bayt Sahur), reported on Israeli Television that "confiscations are being carried out in accordance with the law."[63] Al-Haq deemed these raids "blatantly illegal."[64]

On October 4, 1989, Israeli authorities lifted the curfew in Bayt Sahur in order to allow residents the opportunity to pay taxes voluntarily. No payments were made.[65] Infuriated, Israeli Defense Minister Yitzhaq Rabin vowed to "teach a lesson" to the residents of Bayt Sahur, saying that the civil disobedience campaign of Bayt Sahur must not be allowed to succeed.[66]

The siege to crush the tax revolt intensified two days later, in part because of passage of a United Nations General Assembly condemnation of Israeli practices in Bayt Sahur.[67] This time, Israeli military authorities borrowed a tactic from the UNLU, distributing leaflets throughout the town urging residents to pay their taxes and blaming an "irresponsible minority" for the troubles. The leaflet stated that other Palestinians were paying their taxes and warned that the world would soon forget Bayt Sahur as it had already forgotten the Intifada, leaving the residents to face the army alone. The leaflet concluded ominously, "You are standing alone. You are facing the Security Forces by yourselves, and we will not relent until we have fulfilled our duties."[68]

On October 31, after forty-two days of continuous tax raids, the siege was eased. By this time, approximately $1.5 million[69] worth of goods had been confiscated from 398 homes and businesses.[70] The head of the civil administration, Brigadier General Shaike Erez, commented, "We accomplished what we wanted, and more. We enforced the law and asserted our authority in Bayt Sahur. Where it is necessary, we will collect taxes by force."[71]

The withdrawal of the army from Bayt Sahur was widely viewed among Palestinians as a victory, albeit a costly one. As one local merchant said, "We have lost so much. But we did not yield, and we resisted all efforts to force us to pay taxes to the occupation."[72] One resident commented hyperbolically that "Today, Palestine has become a reality."[73] Such euphoria and defiance were premature, as the next day and on several subsequent days the town was again declared a closed military zone, although the confiscations had ceased. In addition, over time there was a growing realization that many residents had in fact quietly settled their tax bills with the Civil Administration, further muting the town's elation.

On November 5, Bayt Sahur hosted a Day of Prayer celebration. Even though Bayt Sahur had been declared a closed military area, a number of nonresidents were able to defy the order by staying in town for several days ahead of time or by surreptitiously making their way on foot. Included among the outside participants were a few Israeli Jews, Europeans, and Americans, including a special representative of former President Carter. The most prominent visitor to this largely Christian town was the mufti of Jerusalem, Shaykh Sa'd al-Din al-'Alami, who received thunderous applause upon his arrival in the churches of Bayt Sahur. During his visit, 'Alami issued a religious decree, or *fatwa*, forbidding the purchase of goods confiscated by the Israeli military during their tax raids on Bayt Sahur, on the grounds that such goods were "stolen property." 'Alami declared: "It is forbidden for a Muslim, Arab, or any man with a conscience to buy any of these unjustly plundered goods. Purchasing any such item is like participating in the theft of the plundered goods, and whoever does so deserves punishment for stealing his brothers' property."[74]

The plundered property was put up for sale by the government at the auction hall at Ben-Gurion airport shortly after the raids concluded. The goods confiscated from Bayt Sahur did not sell well, in part, perhaps, because of the tainted nature of their acquisition, but more likely because of the different tastes of Palestinians and Israelis. Additionally, most of the confiscated drugs from local pharmacies were either unusable because of the manner in which they had been handled (e.g., left sitting in the sun) or went unsold because Israelis generally will not buy pharmaceuticals manufactured by Arab companies. In any case, the total costs of the campaign against Bayt Sahur certainly exceeded the revenues earned by selling the confiscated goods. But no matter: the clash was always about control, not money.

In the end, Israel's dire warning to Bayt Sahur that it "stood alone" in its tax revolt proved accurate. While there were scattered attempts to replicate Bayt Sahur's model—in Kufr Malik and Ramallah, for example—no systematic campaign of tax resistance ensued. Given that civil disobedience has proved to be an effective "weapon of the weak" in other struggles and that Bayt Sahur's campaign was efficacious on several levels, the lack of a larger tax boycott implementation was curious. Three salient points make sense of this seeming irony. First, and most obvious, Israel's willingness to respond to such civil disobedience with overwhelming force had the intended consequence of scaring off potential followers of this strategy. Israel consistently and generally effectively implemented a policy of bringing disproportionate force to bear on the Intifada, limiting its mass appeal after its first few months. Second, the relative wealth of Bayt Sahur contrasted sharply with the poverty found in much of the West Bank and Gaza, so that Bayt Sahurians literally could better afford to withstand the ensuing fiscal onslaught. Residents of neighboring Dheisheh refugee camp, for example, simply could not risk losing what little they possessed.

The third reason for the failure of the tax boycott to spread is also the most relevant to the larger argument found in this book: the PLO in Tunis failed to support Bayt Sahur's campaign, as it feared the political consequences of such grassroots initiatives. The devolution of authority during the Intifada to grassroots activists—including PLO cadres—challenged Tunis's ability to control or even significantly influence Palestinian politics in the West Bank and Gaza. That kind of political autonomy was unacceptable to Tunis, and in this regard, it found common cause with Israel. Evidence for this lack of support can be seen most clearly in the PLO's failure to promote this type of campaign elsewhere. In various pronouncements coming out of Tunis, lip service was paid to Bayt Sahur's efforts, but little more. No overall strategy to guide other communities to follow Bayt Sahur was devised. No attempt to financially subsidize those people who had lost much in the tax boycott—as was common for the families of those killed or imprisoned during the Intifada—was forthcoming from Tunis. The whole issue of civil disobedience was virtually ignored after the last autonomous UNLU committee was arrested in March 1990. Leaflets issued after that time—written with the specific approval of Tunis—concentrated on discussing diplomatic developments and strike days, not grassroots strategies for disengaging from Israel.

Tunis's—and particularly Yasir Arafat's—disregard for Bayt Sahur's campaign of civil disobedience was strongly felt by members of the new elite in Bayt Sahur. In numerous interviews, founders of the civil disobedience campaign in Bayt Sahur—Sulha members, institution builders, and leaders of the tax boycott—were nearly unanimous in their view that Tunis not only did not support Bayt Sahur's efforts but actually tried to thwart them by privately urging others to pay their taxes and by more closely aligning itself with members of the old elite. It was in this period, for example, that relations between Arafat and Elias Freij, the longtime mayor of neighboring Bethlehem and quiet opponent of Bayt Sahur's campaign, began to warm considerably. It needs to be reiterated that this conflict was not between supporters and opponents of the PLO, as Bayt Sahur's Intifada leadership consisted largely of PLO supporters, primarily from the PFLP. Rather, it was among the first signs that the PLO in Tunis feared its declining role in the West Bank and Gaza, recognizing that its power was increasingly wielded by autonomous local activists—often PLO activists—whom it could not control. Therefore, Tunis sought to reconstitute its political base by relying heavily on the more pliant notable elite instead of its own cadres. This pattern was seen clearly in the post-Oslo period, especially following the return of Arafat to Gaza in 1994.

While Israel succeeded in breaking the tax boycott in Bayt Sahur, it did not rid itself entirely of the tax issue. In February 1992, merchants from Bayt Sahur filed suit in the Israeli High Court of Justice against the IDF and Civil Administration, charging them with the illegal collection of taxes. Led by Elias al-Rishmawi, the merchants charged the occupation forces with violating the High Court's own ruling on the extension of the value-added tax (VAT) to the occupied territories. The VAT, which significantly increased taxes paid by Palestinians to Israel, was imposed in 1976 and was ruled legal by the High Court in 1983 as long as it was applied equitably and for the benefit of the local population.[75] The Rishmawi petition argued that the IDF and Civil Administration violated both provisions of the court's ruling. First, on the principle of equality of taxation, the petition showed convincingly that actual tax rates between Israelis (even settlers living in the occupied territories) and Palestinians were greatly unequal. Palestinians had a lower income threshold for triggering taxation and had higher overall rates of taxation at similar income levels. Second, by pointing out that no detailed budget for the expenditures of tax money was ever published by the Civil Administration, there was no evidence that the revenue was being reinvested locally. The strength of the case forced the IDF and Civil

Administration to ask the High Court for a series of long delays in responding to the petition, until finally the Israel-PLO agreements made the case moot.

Incomplete Consolidation and the Retreat from Politics

The major social aspect of the Intifada—what gave it shades of being a social revolution—was the challenge to and partial displacement of a whole class of elites by a competing class with a very different social and political agenda. But this revolution was incomplete; for a variety of reasons, the old elite was never fully removed from the political scene. In places, in fact, the old elite was able to regain some of its lost power and standing. Moreover, after the Oslo Accords, Arafat further resurrected the notables as a pillar in his new political order. Thus, while the notables had been largely marginalized politically in the first two years of the Intifada, they were able—with the help of Israel and Tunis—to recapture some of their lost power over time. The new elite still held the balance of local power, but since it was not fully consolidated, its authority was not decisive.

The incomplete nature of the Intifada's social revolution was seen in microcosm in Bayt Sahur. Of the new elite's projects, some were successfully institutionalized, prospering even in the post-Intifada period, while others failed. Community leadership was retained largely by the new elite, but not decisively so. After all, the Sulha was disbanded and the mayor, *"Abu Barbur"*—tying his fortunes to Arafat and Fatah—survived the Intifada, both physically and politically. This was made possible by the relative depoliticization that marked Bayt Sahur during the last years of the Intifada and the post-Oslo period. The retreat from politics in Bayt Sahur was a by-product of both Israeli punishment and PLO encouragement.

The new elite of Bayt Sahur was able to institutionalize several of its political projects founded during the Intifada. Of greatest significance, the medical clinic expanded to become perhaps the best clinic of its type in the whole of the West Bank and Gaza. The excellence of the clinic led a number of foreign donors to assist in purchases of medical equipment and provide further political protection to the activists who ran the clinic. Likewise, the YMCA's rehabilitation program outlasted the uprising and continued to treat patients who sustained permanent injuries during the Intifada. The rapprochement center also continued to function, even branching out into "alternative tourism."[76] Finally, while Bayt Sahur sold the last of its famous cows to the Israeli Tnuva milk company in April 1994, it did so only after plans for a dairy plant in Bayt Sahur had been approved. The new dairy began operations in 1995.

Not all of the Intifada projects survived. All of the neighborhood and popular committees ultimately gave way to local political factions as the mass base of the Intifada subsided. While the Shed was closed by Israeli authorities before the 1989 siege, the greenhouse failed on its own. It closed its doors in 1993. Perhaps most important, the Sulha committee finally disbanded. After Israel released the five arrested members of the Sulha from prison, the Sulha changed its activities to be more in line with prevailing legality. As one member put it, "there was increasing concern with individual security—the members did not want to court arrest."[77] The Sulha began to concern itself with more traditional practices, "to work within the system more," leading its most active member, Ghassan Andoni, to quit in protest.[78] Another Sulha member defended the change:

> The Sulha did go mainstream, but you have to remember these are people who had jobs and families. It's hard to maintain stamina under the circumstances. People got scared about the ten-year prison sentence, especially after some were jailed. The military governor gave a not-so-veiled threat when he mentioned [the name of] one Sulha member and shrugged, "What does he know about *sulha* mediation?"[79]

The Sulha disbanded after it could no longer perform its primary function of maintaining community solidarity through solving local problems. There was a direct correlation between the decline in community unity and the weakening of the Sulha's authority. Three cases in particular demonstrated the Sulha's declining authority. In the first instance, there was a dispute between two neighboring families about the building of a veranda by one family. To make matters worse, the families were identified with two different political factions, Fatah and the PFLP. The argument got heated, factional allies were brought in, and the two sides skirmished with heated words and stones. The Sulha was called in to solve the problem but could not. One family finally left Bayt Sahur.

In the second case, in March 1992, a seven-year-old Bayt Sahur girl was killed by a driver from the nearby Ta'amra Bedouin community. The driver, a well-known local collaborator, was briefly arrested by the police but was quickly released. The Sulha was unable to reach a settlement between the girl's family and the Ta'amra. The family then requested that the mayor intervene with the military authorities, giving new life to the mayor's role. While even the mayor was unable to solve the problem, the shift away from the Sulha was important.

In the most damaging case for Sulha authority, a Bayt Sahur commercial landlord raised his rental rates after four years of keeping them low (in line with UNLU instructions). It was common to return to pre-Intifada rates during this period, and this landlord was among the last to do so. Two merchants refused to pay the increase, and the case went to the Sulha committee. The Sulha ruled in the landlord's favor and demanded that the merchants pay the higher rent. Although the merchants had accepted Sulha mediation, they refused to honor the Sulha's ruling. Since the Sulha had no legal standing, it could not compel the merchants to pay. The Sulha was shown to be powerless when its authority—always based on voluntary compliance—was ignored.

As Arafat increasingly relied on the old notable elite as a base of his political power in the occupied territories, the mayor remade himself into a Fatah ally. 'Atrash began attending Fatah functions in Bayt Sahur well before Oslo was announced, then came out in favor of the agreement later on. He routinely praised the work of Arafat and the Palestinian Authority. Symbolically, his political return was signaled when he forced a local teacher to issue a public apology to him for using his nickname, *Abu Barbur*, in public. Even with his more visible posture in the aftermath of the Intifada and his new backers in Fatah, 'Atrash opposed holding local elections. While the mayor and his traditional elite allies had been politically resuscitated from above, Bayt Sahur had changed too much since 1974 for the mayor to win a local election. 'Atrash and the old elite of Bayt Sahur—like elites elsewhere in the West Bank—had been too discredited to hope for grassroots support.

The decline of the Sulha and partial political comeback of the mayor all took place within the context of a general depoliticization in Bayt Sahur. While the retreat from politics was most clearly seen after 1991, it can be traced to two earlier specific circumstances. The first was Israel's assault on Bayt Sahur for its civil disobedience campaign. Not only had numerous families and businesses lost so many of their possessions, but they had done it alone, without the rest of Palestinian society following their lead.

The second reason for the decline of political involvement was the campaign of the PLO in Tunis to discourage autonomous grassroots activism in the West Bank and Gaza. The lack of support for Bayt Sahur's Intifada has already been noted, but the process went further than this one case. There was a general discouragement by the PLO in Tunis of all autonomously organized political actions. As one member of the Sulha neatly summed up the PLO's position, "The popular committees were viewed by the PLO as a separate power base which threatened their position."[80] Tunis's tactic was epitomized by Arafat's repeated claim following the 1988 Algiers PNC declaration that an independent Palestinian state was just "a stone's throw away." If that were the case, then no rational individual would risk imprisonment or worse by engaging in political activism when the outcome was already assured.

Bayt Sahur's Intifada was among the most compelling local examples of the devolution of authority during the uprising. From the civil disobedience campaign to the autonomous organization of political action to the partial institutionalization of grassroots politics, Bayt Sahur was in many ways an extraordinary case. At the same time, it epitomized many of the larger themes that characterized the Intifada and post-Oslo periods. Such issues included the partial democratization of familial structures, autonomous popular organization building, and the related conflict between two distinct sets of elites. Most of all, the incomplete consolidation of power by the new elite epitomized the real but indecisive sociopolitical transformation the Intifada spawned.

In general, new elites come to power in traditional societies during periods of crisis, when routine—the basis of any traditional authority—is no longer tenable. The Intifada was just such an emergency situation, in which a new elite with new skills was needed. The new elite brought with it a modernist ideology stressing individual association and democratic hierarchy, and this ideology undermined the bases of authority for the patriarchal leadership of the clans, as well as for other traditional leaders. In Bayt Sahur, this elite conflict was seen clearly in the struggles between the Sulha committee and the mayor and between the neighborhood committees and the hamula elders. The conflict was not just between competing elites but between different types of elites, one emphasizing modern values of social relations and authority, the other more traditional ones. At the same time, the new elite utilized some of the traditional forms of social organization—particularly the hamula structures—but infused them with very different patterns of social relations.

5

Popular Committees in the Intifada

The types of social and political relationships created during the decade of grassroots mobilization which preceded the Intifada became tangible early in the uprising in the form of popular committees (*lijan sha'biya*). Local popular committees, the dominant form of sociopolitical organization throughout the Intifada, were largely responsible for the Palestinians' ability to sustain and deepen the uprising. In many ways, popular committees were an extension of the politically tinged social programs undertaken in the years before the uprising by the newly formed grassroots organizations. The popular committees were, at base, the organizational expression of the new Palestinian elite's ideology.

Three overarching points inform this chapter. First, the extent of everyday activities undertaken by popular committees shows how far authority had devolved in Palestinian society during the Intifada. Decisions formerly taken on the municipal or national levels were often made during the Intifada by self-appointed neighborhood groups or individuals. Both the old notable elite and the Palestine Liberation Organization in Tunis were often incapable of controlling or even significantly influencing decision-making at this level. Second, many of the social relations forged by the new elite prior to the Intifada were indispensable to the creation of these alternative forms of authority. Finally, the devolution of authority during the Intifada led directly to many of the problems experienced by the Palestinian Authority in the post-Oslo period. Essentially, an outside power—the PLO in Tunis—tried to impose its centralized power hierarchy on a population in which day-to-day authority was located at the grass roots. In other words, the disjunction between the grassroots organization of authority in place in the West Bank and Gaza and the logic of power consolidation by the PA often led to stalemate. The PA responded to this situation by trying to divert resources from nongovernmental organizations and other representatives of grassroots authority. This issue will be taken up again in chapter 7.

The Role of Popular Committees

The popular committees were formed as a response to concrete problems that the Palestinian community faced in the early weeks of the Intifada. In particular, Israel's decision to impose long curfews on wide areas of the occupied territories—as a form of collective punishment—made it difficult for the community to purchase food. The threat of widespread hunger during such curfews forced Palestinian leaders to choose between ensuring the supply of basic foodstuffs or ending the nascent uprising. Thus, the first popular committees were formed in order to organize the clandestine storage and distribution of food within besieged communities. Other popular committees formed early for community protection, particularly those committees which organized guard duty to alert residents to approaching army patrols.

The success of the first popular committees in supplying emergency services to communities under siege helped to consolidate the early gains of the uprising. More important, after the mass demonstrations of the first few months gave way to a more drawn-out process of national disengagement from Israel, popular committees were a crucial cornerstone for the institutionalization of the Intifada. The range of functions performed by popular committees was wide, and the division of labor within and between the various committees was never delineated with any precision. However, all the committees reflected the central self-help and self-sufficiency tenets of the Intifada's ideology. Moreover, the activities of the functionally diffuse popular committees were essential in strengthening the cohesion of Palestinian society in the face of Israeli attempts to suppress the uprising.

As the Intifada wore on, however, most popular committees became dominated by factional activists, losing the broad social base that had initially made them so powerful. In some cases, committees were disbanded altogether after the first two years of the uprising. The political "professionalization" of the committees and their absorption by political factions was perhaps inevitable, given the severity of Israeli reprisals against individuals involved in any kind of popular committee. Only the most politically committed individuals would risk ten years in prison for undertaking such activities.

Formation and Work

The sociopolitical structures from which popular committees came varied widely. In the town of Bayt Sahur, as discussed in chapter 4, the popular committees were functional subgroupings for larger neighborhood committees, which themselves were tied to the social geography of local extended families. In the neighboring village of Tuqua, popular committees were organized by the Fatah-allied Shabiba youth organization, which greatly expanded its membership (including many adults) in the early months of the uprising.[1] In the Rafadiya district of Nablus, the major PLO factions, together with several "clean, well-known, and well-educated persons," formed a governing popular committee during a neighborhood meeting on February 15, 1988.[2]

The primary work of popular committees dealt with food storage and distribution, guard duty, alternative education, backyard farming/self-sufficiency, and health care. Virtually every community in the occupied territories organized committees to deal with these issues. In addition, popular committees collected funds—a form of self-taxation—to support their work and compensate families that had suffered in the Intifada, arranged visits to injured people in hospitals and to the families of those killed during the uprising, organized teams to clean the streets when garbage was accumulating and to assist local farmers at harvest time, and generally helped implement directives of the Unified National Leadership of the Uprising (UNLU). Regular meetings of these types of popular committees were held openly in the first months of the Intifada when popular committees were legal.

More militant forms of popular committees were also organized, in particular the strike forces (*quwat al-dariba*), which were embedded in the existing factional structures. The strike forces were responsible for a number of attacks on Israeli soldiers, but were primarily implementers of UNLU decisions. Strike forces, for example, enforced both the commercial strike hours set by the UNLU and the UNLU's announced policy of boycotting Israeli goods where possible. In a number of cases in the first two years of the Intifada, stores were cleared of their Israeli merchandise, which was placed on the street and burned. Strike forces were also responsible for organizing demonstrations in the occupied territories. Finally, many of the collaborator killings discussed in this chapter were undertaken by strike forces.

Most popular committees were nonviolent. Nonetheless, Israel outlawed the committees in August 1988. The military government correctly saw that the popular committees were "undermining the Israeli government apparatus in the territories [by] establishing an alternative apparatus in its place," and thus viewed the popular committees as a "primary threat."[3] While this action did not stop the popular committees from continuing their activities, it was central in the growing factional quality of the committees. In other words, the widespread communal voluntarism which marked the early months of the Intifada gradually gave way to a more specialized spectrum of activists.

The UNLU

In many ways the UNLU was the single most important popular committee of the Intifada. While it would be incorrect to suggest that any single group controlled the Intifada, the UNLU certainly had a significant impact, both in coordinating Intifada activities and in communicating local initiatives to the wider national audience through its periodic dissemination of leaflets, or *bayanat*. More important, the UNLU acted as a national symbol—an anonymous, local leadership which Israel seemed incapable of silencing. In actual fact, the grassroots UNLU was ultimately stopped through waves of arrests, although a tamer, higher-profile membership assumed its mantle. As with all autonomous organizations which arose in the Intifada, neither Israel nor the PLO in Tunis wanted to see the UNLU prosper.[4]

The UNLU was formed in the early weeks of the Intifada by activists from Fatah, the DFLP, and the PFLP. The Palestine Communist Party did not join the UNLU at first, believing that the Intifada would not last. Having built a significant institutional base in the occupied territories, the Communists had the most to lose by joining the Intifada in such a significant way. Several months into the Intifada, the PCP began to participate fully in the UNLU. From early 1988 to March 1990, the UNLU consisted of one representative from each of the four factions. Ultimately, four UNLU groups were created, each new group necessitated by the arrest of the preceding UNLU. In all, from the beginning of the Intifada to March 1990 and the demise of the UNLU as a distinctive organization, the UNLU had seventeen members.[5]

The UNLU consisted of the best and the brightest of local PLO grassroots cadres, not the recognized top political leaders. The factions inside the occupied territories decided that the UNLU representatives should come from among the young, smart, rising stars in each faction. While such people were highly thought of in their respective factions, they would still be relative unknowns to the Shin Bet, therefore unlikely candidates for early arrest. The membership of the UNLU neatly encapsulates the profile of the new elite: none came from notable families; all but one had a university education, nearly half (eight) had attended Bir Zeit University; most were either journalists, engineers, unionists, or current university students; and they came primarily from refugee camps and villages, many in the Ramallah and al-Bira area.

The UNLU was known publicly only through its periodic leaflets. The leaflets were issued approximately twice a month during the first two years of the Intifada, and more sporadically after that. The bayanat would contain commentary and instructions on a number of issues, from backyard farming to collaborators to diplomatic initiatives. They would also contain a schedule of upcoming events, including planned strike days and other symbolic forms of resistance.

Perhaps the greatest role the UNLU played through the leaflets was as mediator of the local conflicts that naturally arose during the extended uprising. Much of the UNLU's mediation activity dealt with undramatic, even mundane, issues. For example, the collapse of the Jordanian dinar—a widely used currency in the West Bank—exacerbated the problem of rising prices for rental units, particularly in East Jerusalem. In order to stem the growing discontent among renters, the UNLU called for landlords to limit rent hikes, and for consultation as to what an appropriate rent would be. The UNLU regularly urged merchants not to raise prices for their products, considering the economic plight of many Palestinians during the Intifada. In bayan 42 (July 1, 1989), the UNLU called upon Palestinians to "boycott all Zionist products" while encouraging the consumption of indigenous substitutes instead. Realizing that such actions would put upward pressure on the prices of a number of Palestinian goods, the UNLU went on to say: "Merchants, institutions, and factory owners are asked to comply with the [previously] set prices, refrain from raising them, and protect the market from speculation." Muhammad Khalid, a member of the last UNLU group, commented on one such mediation:

> On one occasion, the issue of closing time for sewing factories in Tulkarim couldn't be resolved locally so it came to us. These factories employed around 5,000 people. Recall that stores had 8:00–11:00 a.m. hours, but factories stayed open regular hours.[6] But the local shabab [youth activists] couldn't understand why these factories stayed open past 11:00 a.m., and they were giving the factory employees and owners a hard time. So we put it in a leaflet—over the PFLP's objection—that it was proper for these factories to remain open. This seemed a trivial thing for many Palestinians—I was reminded of it and given a hard time over it in prison—but so many people just didn't understand the market, the need to employ, to produce. We were not out to kill ourselves economically. But many just didn't understand that these sorts of issues were really important. This was true even for the UNLU members often.[7]

The last group of UNLU members was arrested in March 1990. Because of the circumstances of the arrests and the method of interrogation—those caught were immediately asked about UNLU activities, with the interrogators having inside knowledge of many details—there most likely was a mole, or collaborator, inside the network. In any case, by this time, the leaflets had lost their central role in the uprising, in large measure because they no longer were meaningful to the everyday lives of most Palestinians. As Khalid continued,

> Most of the UNLU members had lost sight of the real world of markets and

stores and earning a living. If you get paid a salary [even during strikes] then it is easy to talk about fifteen-day strikes, as the PFLP routinely did. It was this gap between the lives of UNLU members and the experience of most Palestinians that was primarily responsible for people becoming less committed to the bayanat.[8]

After March 1990, the functions of the UNLU were taken over by well-known political personalities from each faction. These public figures continued to write (or, more precisely, controlled the writing of) the leaflets, which acquired a different tone in the years that followed. It should also be noted, however, that these figures wrote some of the bayanat during the interregnums between the arrest of one UNLU group and the construction of the next. These figures included Faysal al-Husayni (Fatah), Zuhara Kamal (DFLP), Ghassan Khatib (PCP/PPP), and Hani Bayadun (PFLP). Because of their connections to their respective PLO factions in Tunis, these figures represented a transition from grassroots to traditional factional leadership. In other words, March 1990 marks the date when Tunis was finally able to control decision-making at the top level of the Intifada and to ensure that such decisions more accurately reflected its own thinking.

There is reason to believe that this change in the UNLU's constitution suited the interests of both the PLO and Israel. That established leaders in the PLO would not want an alternative leadership to arise in the West Bank and Gaza—even by those who came from PLO ranks and expressed fealty to PLO goals—seems self-evident. As I argue throughout this book, the PLO in Tunis sought to bolster the Intifada in areas that it controlled, while it sought to undermine those phenomena that it did not control. The whole structure of alternative grassroots authority, in particular the popular committee framework, was a development beyond Tunis's reach, and therefore it was viewed as a potential political threat. One circumstantial piece of evidence supporting the view that the PLO was pleased with the change of leadership of the UNLU is the fact that despite much evidence of a mole's existence, the PLO never investigated who was responsible for the arrests of four groups of UNLU members.

The change in the UNLU was also apparently supported by Israel. A known and more established leadership was preferable to a diffuse and grassroots one. Unlike the earlier versions, the new UNLU leadership had recognizable names and a political "address." In fact, it was this group of people with whom Israel began negotiations in Madrid and Washington a year later. Circumstantial evidence for this proposition is found in the fact that while all early members of the UNLU were captured and most imprisoned, no public personality was ever arrested for his or her UNLU activities, even though their names and activities were well known.

Other Domains

While the UNLU was the best known of all the popular committees, it was also the smallest. Other sectors had many more people involved in the work of popular committees, and also impacted the day-to-day lives of many Palestinians. Two very different domains stand out in the number and variety of popular committees playing key roles in the implementation of communal requirements: creating an alternative education system in the face of extended school and university closures, and solving internal civil and criminal disputes in the wake of the collapse of the judicial system during the Intifada (see later sections of this chapter). Such divergent examples demonstrate the range of activities in which popular committees engaged.

A number of the problems faced by these voluntary organizations in providing education and an alternative system of justice were not solved adequately. The mode of implementation and the types of results varied widely from region to region, from village to village, and often from neighborhood to neighborhood. Neighborhood schools were not widely successful if uniform quality and sustainability were the measures employed. Standards of justice, as in other revolutionary movements, were often crude, harsh, and without central control. This was particularly true of the pattern of collaborator killings in Nablus.

In spite of such severe drawbacks, the networks of popular committees essentially succeeded in their mission. These alternative organizations were able to compensate, at least in part, for the withdrawal or collapse of normal social services and were crucial for sustaining the Intifada over the long term. In short, popular committees, which provided basic and needed services, created the necessary space for the Intifada to continue.

Popular Education

The UNLU repeatedly called on popular committees in general and those concerned with education in particular to organize daily life in the Palestinian community. For example, in bayan 16 the UNLU called on Palestinians to

> accelerate the work to form popular committees in all locations. Popular committees and other specialized committees are entrusted with organizing the requirements of daily life and guaranteeing essential services and supplies, such as food, health, education, and security. The popular committees represent the people's authority and function as alternatives to the crumbling apparatus of the occupier, as well as an essential instrument for the success of civil disobedience. We call upon all teachers to

participate fully in the process of popular education and to escalate their struggle to protest the continuing closure of educational institutions and the refusal of the occupation authorities to pay teacher salaries.[9]

These types of exhortations to strengthen popular education—even when schools were open—were a constant feature of the UNLU leaflets. Again, in bayan 19, the UNLU stated:

> We urge students, teachers, and academic institutions to continue education and to compensate for lost school time on official holidays, while affirming total adherence to the strike on full strike days. Popular instruction should be used as a means of raising educational standards and assisting students in compensating for curriculum not covered at school.[10]

In this section, I examine the creation of an informal educational system by the Palestinians during the first two and one-half years of the Intifada in order to show the level of community mobilization that the Intifada engendered. As a rule, the older the students, the better organized the informal education. Hence, university education during formal closure of all Palestinian universities fared significantly better than primary school classrooms.

None of this is to suggest that popular education proved to be a reliable substitute for formal schooling in terms of educational achievements. Quite the contrary: in virtually every regard the closure of schools proved disastrous for Palestinian society in ways which popular education could not rectify. The problems were legion: many students would not attend classes for fear of arrest; there was no quality control of teachers or curricula; the hours spent in "class" were a fraction of normal; no lab or computer classes were possible; the backlog of students waiting to enter a grade level once schools reopened was enormous and extremely disruptive; once schools did reopen, student discipline was low, with widespread and coercive cheating on the *tawjihi* examination[11] plaguing classes for several years; a number of students expected to be "graded" on their Intifada activities, not their classroom achievements. Thus, I am not arguing that popular education proved to be a scholastic success, although given the closure of schools it was certainly better than nothing. Rather, I am suggesting that the community mobilization that marked popular education was indicative of the larger devolution of authority and activism which occurred during the Intifada.

The K–12 Levels

On February 3, 1988, Israel ordered closed until further notice all schools in the West Bank because they had become "centers for organizing and stimulating violence."[12] The closure affected all 611 kindergarten and elementary schools, 321 middle schools, and 262 secondary schools.[13] Within a week all East Jerusalem schools were also closed; thus, over 1,200 schools and more than 300,000 students were affected. Excepting occasional brief openings, the schools remained closed throughout 1988. On January 21, 1989, all West Bank schools were ordered closed until further notice. They were allowed to reopen again eight months later. From late 1989 until the August 1990 Iraqi invasion of Kuwait, when curfews were reimposed on the occupied territories, there were a number of spot closures but no comprehensive closure orders. The particularly harsh extended curfews of 1990–91 resulted in a total cessation of school activity in the occupied territories. Schools in towns under curfew were, of course, closed *de facto*, as residents were not allowed out of their homes. In all, pupils had a total of 35 actual days of school (out of 210 scheduled school days) during the 1987–88 academic year and 40 actual school days the following year.[14] While open school days increased substantially in the 1989–90 academic year, the 1990–91 year was virtually completely lost because of curfews.

Thus, West Bank schools were largely closed for four years. Gaza did not experience the kind of formal mass closures of schools that prevailed in the West Bank. However, spot closures were frequent. For example, in the semester September 1988 to January 1989 there were at least thirty-six closures affecting a minimum of thirty-one schools. These closure periods varied widely; in the case of at least five schools, closure was indefinite, i.e., "until further notice."[15] Gaza had a series of *de facto* mass closures during its frequent curfews. School closure was clearly used by Israel as a form of collective punishment.

In response, Palestinians, through popular committees, implemented a system of informal classes that would help to educate their youth in the absence of formal schooling. For most educators, the aim was not to completely revolutionize Palestinian education but rather to fill in for the schools during their closures. There was no question for these teachers that when schools reopened, the informal education sector would close down. This attitude, although practical, served to undermine any chance of institutionalizing alternative education, for each time the Israelis reopened the schools, the informal sector was dismantled. Restarting it during the next closure was always a difficult task.

By April 1988 popular education had caught the imagination of a number of educational reformers. The initial euphoria as to what could be accomplished by informal education belied the actual results. For a minority of educators, the possibilities included a total disengagement from Israeli control and the chance of "fundamental changes in the ways Palestinians think about education."[16] Munir Fasheh, an early proponent of popular education, argued that the process could be a first step in dramatically upgrading the quality of Palestinian education:

The Palestinian education system has inherited the worst of everything from its various rulers. The British system was basically geared toward creating officials for the Mandate government. The Jordanian system stressed our Arab heritage more but, since it was based on the British system and encouraged rote learning, it too was flawed. The Israelis maintained much of the Jordanian system but took away the meaningful aspects of the history of Palestine, the Arabs and Islam. In 1980, sixth- and seventh-grade textbooks still talked about man's continuing quest to reach the moon and about the "kingdom" of Libya and its pastoral economy [the Libyan monarchy was overthrown the same year that man reached the moon, 1969; oil has dominated the Libyan economy since the 1960s]. There was no education before, so the closures haven't meant much. [Popular education] has caused people to be more receptive to ideas and changes that will make Palestinian education more meaningful. The closures have been a blessing in disguise.[17]

The popular education committees were organized by neighborhoods and usually involved both teachers and parents in a joint attempt to maintain a semblance of educational normality. The classes generally took place in local homes, since the school facilities were physically closed, although in some towns mosques and other facilities were used. The lessons usually concentrated on math and Arabic.

Classes occasionally took on political overtones. In the West Bank town of Salfit, for example, parallel classes were held in the local mosque and the union building. Families with links to Hamas sent their children to the mosque, while families with more secular political ties, especially with the Palestine Communist Party and the Democratic Front for the Liberation of Palestine, had their children attend classes at the local union building. According to one teacher, the mosque classes had significantly higher enrollment. In some ways, the mosque classrooms were more socially progressive than the regular gender-segregated schools, as integration of the sexes in the classroom was practiced due to necessity. The teachers in the informal sector of Salfit were all volunteers without previous teaching experience, ranging in age from seventeen to twenty-two. They taught in the facilities which more closely paralleled their own political views.[18]

Clearly, the Israelis were concerned about the growing autonomy of the Palestinian community as it began to disengage itself from its long-standing dependence on Israel. The initial success (or, at least, excitement over the possibility of success) of popular education and other areas of informal Palestinian organization led to the outlawing of all popular committees by Israel's defense minister Yitzhaq Rabin in August 1988. In justifying this action Rabin initially responded that these committees encouraged "violent activity." However, he went on to state what was undoubtedly the underlying motive for outlawing them: the popular committees were "undermining the Israeli government apparatus and establishing an alternative apparatus in its place."[19]

The military government was serious about ending informal education and took measures—some of which would seem farcical were it not for their impact—to carry out the decision. On September 6, 1988, for example, a high school class which was being conducted at the facilities of the Society of Friends of al-Najah University in Nablus was raided (and the society ordered closed indefinitely) and two students and two teachers were arrested. The director of the society was told he would be charged and prosecuted for "permitting make-up classes to take place on the premises."[20] These actions were, as one Hebrew University professor said, "a deliberate attempt to suppress all manifestations of Palestinian self-organization and to increase their ties of dependency on Israel."[21]

Informal classes at the K–12 levels ceased as a widespread phenomenon after the first year of the uprising. In retrospect, popular education as it was actually implemented had a series of critical flaws. Most obviously, the quality of education varied widely, depending largely on the creativity of individual teachers. Middle-class neighborhoods which could afford to supply the necessary materials had a significant advantage over poorer areas. This situation, of course, exists in many areas. However, in the midst of a national uprising when all classes and social forces are expected to share the resulting burdens, such class cleavages could only enhance division. Further, no accreditation could come from these classes, so formal advancement was impossible. The absence of degree-granting powers clearly showed that popular education was only a stop-gap measure to slow the educational decline. Moreover, the relatively low maturity level of students who participated in these classes—they were, after all, children—cast doubts as to whether the lessons could continue indefinitely. The students were, according to the prevailing laws, participating in a criminal activity and could not be counted upon to resist Israeli pressures to reveal the locations of their classrooms and the names of their teachers. For all of these reasons, the attempts by popular committees to initiate widespread and sustained informal education met with only limited success.

The level of enthusiasm for popular education was always significantly higher than the degree of accomplishment. In some quarters, the enthusiasm did not wane. For example, during August and September 1989 the self-described Popular Education Committee (*lajnat al-ta'lim al-sha'bi*) distributed a forty-four-page pamphlet entitled "Issues of Pedagogy" (*qadaya tarbawiya*) in which, among other things, it instructed people in how to set up their own informal education classes.[22] A more promising form of informal education was begun in 1991–92 by the Friends School in Ramallah with the composition of a series of home-schooling books. The user-friendly series was designed to give students a more systematic education during extended closures in the future.[23]

These efforts notwithstanding, the constant opening and closing of schools, in addition to the possibility of arrest for those participating in the popular committees, made popular education at the K–12 level problematic. However, the degree of grassroots activism that went into establishing a system of popular education—even with all of its insurmountable problems—was indicative of the distribution of authority during the Intifada. That is, the initiative for political action clearly came from below.

The Palestinian Universities

Palestinian universities in the West Bank and Gaza are centers not only of education but of politics as well. The political importance of universities in Palestinian society far exceeds the political impact of universities in the West. In the mid-1980s, Palestinian universities took on added political importance. In the words of two Palestinian observers, "Following Israel's invasion of Lebanon and the departure of the PLO from Beirut, the struggle for survival between the Palestinian people and Israel shifted to the occupied Arab territories, with the universities becoming the forefronts [*sic*] for this struggle."[24]

The universities have always been a bellwether for prevailing Palestinian political attitudes, at least at the elite level. Thus, in the mid-1970s, when Palestinian universities were first being established, the student councils and various university-based groups were dominated by secular nationalists—usually PLO affiliated—and Communists. Between 1979 and 1987, Islamic groups began to control many student councils and organizations and constituted a sizable minority in those that they did not lead. Whatever their political coloration, students were among the best organized and most influential sectors of the Palestinian community on the eve of the Intifada.

Beginning in late 1986—a year prior to the Intifada—Israeli authorities increasingly relied on a policy of university closure as collective punishment for political activities. For example, Bethlehem University was closed by military order five times for a total of thirty-five days between February 18 and October 18, 1987. On October 29, 1987, it was ordered closed; the onset of the Intifada meant that it stayed closed for four years. Bir Zeit University was closed down five times for forty-eight days between December 8, 1986, and August 13, 1987. Al-Najah University in Nablus was repeatedly closed by the Israeli military: eleven times for seventy-nine days between December 31, 1986, and July 4, 1987. Likewise, the Islamic College was closed often: six times for forty-four days between February 16 and October 14, 1987. By comparison, Hebron University was closed twice for a total of forty-one days.[25] All Palestinian universities were ordered closed by Israel from the beginning of the

Intifada to 1991. By the fall of 1991, all Palestinian universities, with the exception of Bir Zeit, were allowed to reopen, but their activities were greatly curtailed.

The closure by military order of all Palestinian universities during the Intifada had the intended consequence of preventing students *qua* students from participating in the uprising. In other words, student organizations were not crucial to Palestinian activities during the uprising, as university closings left them without a forum for gathering and formulating strategy. Yet, university students were involved in the Intifada as individuals, often acting locally as part of neighborhood popular committees or strike forces.[26]

In the wake of prolonged closures, the Palestinian universities attempted to provide continuing education for their students on an informal basis. Unlike their K–12 counterparts, university classes cannot be said to have been organized by popular committees in a strict sense, and Palestinians themselves would not refer to the underground university classes as examples of popular committees. I am applying the term here because such activities were illegal, functionally specific, and organizationally informal. In other words, underground classes, even at the university level, exhibited characteristics similar to popular committees.

Bir Zeit and Bethlehem universities were the most successful at providing such informal education. The most obvious reason for this success is their location close to East Jerusalem, where classes could be held with somewhat less difficulty than elsewhere in the territories. Even though the existence of informal classes was well known—Bir Zeit even published in its newsletters the numbers of students attending these classes—they remained illegal.

The Israeli authorities generally seemed to turn a blind eye to these prohibited courses, cracking down only when they wanted to send a political message. On April 19, 1989, for example, the *Jerusalem Post* carried on its front page a story about a police raid in East Jerusalem which "uncovered a network of illegal classes" from Bir Zeit and Bethlehem universities. The existence of such informal classes may actually have served Israeli purposes by eliminating the political aspects of campus life while allowing the authorities to point out to their international and domestic critics that classes continued and a number of students graduated with degrees.

BIR ZEIT

Although the roots of Bir Zeit date from 1924, the school became a full four-year university only in 1972. Since that time it has generally been considered the premier Palestinian university and, under normal circumstances, has an enrollment of approximately 2,600 students.

The Israeli military authorities ordered the university shut on January

9, 1988, and it remained closed for four years. In fact, in the fall of 1991, when all the other Palestinian universities were allowed to reopen, Bir Zeit's closure remained in effect. Realizing early on in the Intifada that the closure might be for an extended period, university officials began to organize informal classes for advanced students. The first session ran from July 1 to September 30, 1988, and served 240 students, 80 of whom graduated after the completion of the three-month period. According to Dr. Nabil Kassis, then vice-president for academic affairs at Bir Zeit, the instruction

> focused on mature students who had already finished most of their course work at the university and who [were] able to make do with a minimum of contact with the instructor. No courses with laboratory work were offered. Only theoretical courses and courses which rely on student reading were offered. Most classes were restricted to a maximum of five students, and followed a tutorial mode of teaching.[27]

Informal courses continued and expanded in the following months. During the spring of 1989, 500 students participated in the "university without walls" program. Even though military harassment continued—university administrative offices in the nearby town of Ramallah were raided on May 25, 1989—and the campus facilities remained closed, informal education became widespread and somewhat institutionalized. In the eight-week summer session in 1989, for example, the university offered students 146 different courses (the last pre-Intifada university catalogue listed a total of 612 course offerings). Classes in the physical sciences and engineering commanded the greatest number of listings in the 1989 summer session, with 67, while 43 courses were offered in the humanities, 13 in the social sciences, and 23 in other subjects, including business and physical education. Even a physics lab was offered at a nonuniversity location.[28]

BETHLEHEM

Located just south of Jerusalem, Bethlehem University was founded in 1974 by the Christian Brothers and is affiliated with the Vatican. While the university maintains a clear relationship with the Vatican and its faculty and staff are overwhelmingly Christian, the student body of 1,500 is about two-thirds Muslim. This figure should not be surprising, given the virtual disappearance of the Palestinian Christian community, which now comprises less than 3 percent of the Palestinian population.

Because it was closed on October 29, 1987—more than two months before other universities met the same fate and more than one month before the Intifada began on December 9—the university had time to prepare for informal sessions.[29] In fact, by the summer of 1988 tutorials had already begun "quietly" at the university.[30] In October 1988 the

Israeli military raided the campus and stopped the informal classes. However, in January 1989 informal courses began in earnest with a six-week session, followed by an eight-week session in March and April and a six-week session in May and June. On August 7, 1989, a new eight-week quarter—"or nine if there are too many strike days"[31]—began. Some 550 students enrolled in the August–September session, although the actual number of students who attended would be smaller since withdrawals were not recorded. As with Bir Zeit, classes were generally designed for juniors and seniors, but some lower-division students were accommodated. For example, in the Faculty of Nursing, all 17 fourth-year students returned to take off-campus courses, while 17 of 19 third-year,[32] 17 of 23 second-year, and 15 of 30 first-year students also participated in the informal classes.[33]

As the campus facilities were closed to students, classes were held at unusual locales. For example, in the summer 1989 session, courses were offered at a converted storeroom at a resthouse, a hospital (for classes and labs), three hotels, a child care center, a local club, a secondary school, a hostel, and Jerusalem-based Catholic facilities, among other places.[34] Private homes had been used frequently in previous sessions. Perhaps the most unusual location for a classroom was "on the stairs under the railings outside the Brothers' residence."[35] The British Cultural Center even offered its library for use by the students of Bethlehem University, volunteering to stock textbooks that the university requested. During this same session, the university offered 103 courses, compared with 366 scheduled offerings in the fall semester of 1987. In contrast to Bir Zeit, Bethlehem's courses were primarily in the humanities and education (71), while the hard sciences accounted for 13 classes and 2 labs. Social sciences comprised 11 courses, while the remaining 7 classes were primarily in business.[36]

The little laboratory work that was undertaken was, out of necessity, done creatively. For example, paper chromatography replaced column chromatography,[37] utilizing simpler equipment at much-reduced costs. Labs at three local hospitals as well as outpatient clinics were used for microbiology and other science courses. Students were often asked to bring their own materials or, when experiments could be done at home, were given both the instructions and the supplies to complete these tests on their own. Intifada students in general had a great deal of motivation—viewing such activity as part of the overall struggle—which made such changes easier.[38]

The quality of education during the informal sessions was a subject of intense debate at Bethlehem University. One professor, Walid Dajani, argued in a key faculty meeting on December 2, 1988, that the informal sessions were "playing into the Israelis' hands" because the military authorities, while preventing any kind of demonstration at the campus against the ongoing occupation, could point to the continuation of classes in order to silence critics. Such a situation could continue indefinitely, he argued, as it pleased the military authorities, leaving the university to offer inferior education. Another professor, Manuel Hassassian, argued that figures showing the number of students who graduated under the informal regimen in the various universities were "mere bragging" and that the quality of teaching was obviously inadequate. The clear implication of these arguments was that the university should press for full academic freedom and if the military authorities continued to close the campus then the informal sector should likewise cease.[39]

The belief that informal education at Bethlehem University was inadequate was not shared by all. One professor argued that their "grades showed that Intifada students had bettered their predecessors in stability and academic achievement."[40]

In a telling letter, one of the brothers noted that although rote learning often plagued Arab education, it was made quite difficult by the type of classes offered in the informal courses, which stressed independent thought and creativity out of necessity. Owing to shortened schedules in Intifada classes, instructors were unable to present all of the material which would have been examined during the pre-Intifada format. This left students responsible for the necessary further reading and ruminating. The brother continued by noting that under normal circumstances, the teacher often

> says that the students cannot manage without his covering everything in his lectures. [This] belittles the intelligence of our students, and makes them dependent on the teacher for learning and for judgment. This is hardly a preparation for life, where personal judgments have constantly to be made.[41]

The brother argued that informal education during the Intifada had a dramatic impact for the better on the quality of education in terms of fostering independent judgment and intellectual maturity. He concluded by noting, a bit sarcastically, that "even if we revert to fifteen-week semesters, off-campus methodology must be adopted, if ever we want to liberate our students from servile dependence on our brilliance."[42]

The Intifada allowed the Palestinian community in the occupied West Bank and Gaza to build, in part, the basic infrastructure of an autonomous civil society. At the very least, creating an informal institutional framework for providing needed services during the uprising was necessary to sustain anti-occupation activities. Education, one such informal institution, had mixed results. The informal classes at the K–12 level at least slowed the march toward educational disaster promised by the prolonged school closures. Had schools remained closed constantly, instead of experiencing the roller-coaster ride of openings and closings, and had participation in informal schools not been illegal, then popular education may have been more successful. The Palestinian universities, or "terrorist colleges" as they were called by Prime Minister Yitzhaq Shamir,[43] were quite a bit more successful with the experiment in informal education, having sustained educational activities in spite of the obstacles that the Israeli authorities placed in their path.

Revolutionary Justice

One of the most intriguing facets of the Intifada was the way in which the Palestinian community tried to solve internal disputes in the face of the complete breakdown of institutional means of social problem solving. In particular, without a legitimate court system to sort out various kinds of legal disputes, how did Palestinians attempt to address internal problems during the course of the uprising? The question goes to the very heart of the process of state-building: In the nascent phase of creating national means for the solving of communal problems—often done in the midst of revolutionary transformations—what types of relationships and standards can emerge? Do elites—and others—conceive novel ways of dealing with such problems, or does society fall back on traditional forms of problem solving, or are hybrids constructed? The Palestinians' experience with such questions is examined by focusing first on the creation of mediation committees (a reconstituted "tradition") and multifunctional judicial popular committees. Later, the chapter focuses on the question of how Palestinians dealt with the issue of collaborators.

The Israeli Court System

Military occupation is not generally conducive to a functioning and proper legal system. The situation in the West Bank and Gaza prior to the Intifada was no different; a mishmash of courts and jurisdictions cohabited but never cooperated. The multitiered court system in the West Bank and Gaza included civil and criminal courts, which handled most cases involving taxes, land, or petty crimes, and Islamic *shari'a* courts, which handled personal status matters but were limited in their jurisdiction by the requirement of mutual consent. Various other courts were also established, including municipal courts, administrative tribunals, and settler courts. The most important bodies, even before the Intifada, were the military courts, which handled all security cases, many financial cases, and any other case which the military governor thought appropriate. The High Court of Justice in Israel would also hear special Palestinian cases as its jurisdiction evolved.

The Intifada significantly changed this court system in at least three ways. First, virtually all cases during the Intifada were handled by the military courts. Such cases ranged from tax resistance to rock throwing to traffic citations, as well as the usual security offenses.[44] Essentially, every facet of Palestinian life during the Intifada was deemed security-related, and thus was handled by the military courts. This shift severely overloaded the system.

Second, partly through overwork and partly by design, the process of military court justice became a form of collective punishment. Through a pattern of delay tactics, cases, often involving minor matters, were not heard for months; as bail was rarely granted, this process resulted in long prison stays. According to the Israeli human rights organization B'tselem, "imprisonment for the duration of legal proceedings has become an accepted form of punishment."[45] B'tselem claimed that 90 percent of all military court cases were delayed, either because the Israeli army failed to bring the defendant from jail to the courthouse, "misplaced" the case file, or failed to bring in prosecution witnesses. When this happened, the suspect would remain in jail until another court date was set. B'tselem also observed that 20 percent of the prosecution witnesses (usually soldiers or policemen) failed to appear, and that there was usually no correspondence between the list of hearings on any given day and the defendants brought to court. The report concluded that "punishment precedes conviction. The detainee is punished by imprisonment, and only when he is ready to confess does he obtain a release or notification of when he will be freed."[46] Amnesty International also criticized the military court system, arguing that the conviction-to-acquittal ratio of twenty-five to one in the first two years of the Intifada, in addition to the problems B'tselem mentioned, compelled most detainees to plead guilty regardless of their actual guilt.[47]

The third and perhaps most significant change was the virtual abandonment of the civil and religious courts during the Intifada. In the first two years of the uprising, these courts operated at about one-third of their normal caseload.[48] This reduction was due to a number of phenomena, including the transfer of cases to the military courts, the economic hardships faced by Palestinians who thus could not afford to bring cases,[49] and the lack of enforcement of judgments, owing to the mass resignations of Palestinian police. In addition, because of the perceived need to enhance unity in the midst of the uprising, local grievances were often not pursued by the aggrieved parties.

The most important reason for the lack of Palestinian civil cases was the construction of an alternate framework of justice during the Intifada. Instead of settling disputes in "Israeli" courts, Palestinians created their own bodies to mete out justice. Such bodies were often based on customary law and traditional mediation institutions but were sometimes self-appointed "revolutionary" committees.

Mediation Committees

Community-based mediation or reconciliation committees are a traditional feature of Palestinian—and Arab—society. Disputes between individuals or clans in the Arab world are often resolved by the active mediation of village elders, by a committee appointed by those elders, or by one approved by the parties to the dispute. While such practices were of diminishing importance in Palestinian society in the decade prior to the Intifada, they never entirely disappeared.

Mediation committees made a dramatic comeback during the Intifada for all types of disputes, as they were viewed as an indigenous alternative to the corrupt court system. However, such committees underwent a fundamental restructuring in their substance, if not their form, as they no longer consisted of traditional village elders. Instead, most mediation committees during the Intifada comprised nationalist leaders with a history of confronting the occupation. Those individuals who had often interacted with, and accommodated, Israel's military government lost stature in the community and were generally shut out of the mediation process.[50]

Nationalist leaders associated with various grassroots organizations were often asked to mediate disputes during the Intifada. In one typical case, a worker who belonged to the Palestine Communist Party's General Federation of Trade Unions (GFTU) was injured in an automobile accident in Abu Dis, near Jerusalem. Since no independent settlement was reached between the parties, the worker asked officials from the GFTU to represent him in the mediation process. He preferred union representatives to local notables because of their nationalist credentials.[51]

Judicial Popular Committees

A second institution for solving disputes and enforcing decisions which was utilized during the Intifada was the judicial popular committee. While the UNLU was in many ways the ultimate judicial committee in the Intifada, its decision-making was not based on face-to-face encounters with participants. Rather, like any higher political or judicial body, it tended to issue judgments removed from the actual participants in a dispute. The kinds of judicial committees discussed here, then, are somewhat different from the UNLU, in that they operated in direct contact with the people they judged and upon whom they made demands. Specifically, these judicial popular committees organized guard duty after Palestinian policemen resigned; gathered financial contributions to enable popular committees to buy food, fertilizer, and the like; ran "popular courts"; enforced punishments, including house arrest; and regulated the flow of workers into Israel through the confiscation of identification cards. Unlike the mediation committees, judicial popular committees had no traditional antecedent in Palestinian culture. As such committees had more to do with enforcing decisions than making them, their members tended to be younger than those on the mediation committees. In addition, there was a clear overlap between members of judicial committees and the more violent strike forces (*quwat al-dariba*).

Guard committees were formed initially in January and February 1988, during the height of a confrontation over merchant hours.[52] During this period, Palestinian merchants were required by the UNLU to close their shops at 11:00 A.M. as part of the larger civil disobedience campaign. The ongoing partial strike was deemed illegal by the military government, and it ordered merchants to keep their shops open during normal business hours. Palestinian merchants refused to comply with this order and continued to close their shops, prompting Israeli soldiers to break the locks off the doors, forcing the shops to "reopen." In an escalating battle of wills, the UNLU suddenly reversed the times of the strike and ordered merchants to close in the mornings and open from 2:00 P.M. to 7:00 P.M. The merchants complied, leading the soldiers to forcibly open the shops in the morning and close them in the afternoon. Conceding defeat in this test—in hindsight, the defense minister Yitzhaq Rabin called the forced openings and closings of the stores "a mistake"[53]— Israel finally relented, and by the spring of 1988, the UNLU had a free hand in determining strike hours. Commercial hours were gradually lengthened by the UNLU, and in late 1991, leading Palestinians issued calls to end the commercial strike entirely, arguing that it hurt primarily Palestinians. The commercial strike died with a whimper a year later, already widely violated and by then uniformly resented by the commercial class.

Local activists took it upon themselves to provide protection for shops forced open by Israeli soldiers. Thus, popular committees designed to prevent robberies of unattended Palestinian stores were born. They enjoyed considerable success, especially in the early months of the Intifada. The job of such committees was made notably more difficult in March 1988, when, at the directive of the UNLU, Palestinian policemen working for the occupation authorities resigned. Two-thirds of all policemen employed in Gaza resigned, leading to predictions of an imminent crime wave. However, crime in Gaza actually declined by 25 percent during this period.[54]

In order to help support the activities of popular committees, especially in providing financial support for the families of those killed, injured, deported, or imprisoned during the uprising, funds were collected on a door-to-door basis in much of the occupied territories during the first year of the uprising. In fact, the UNLU had urged such a system as early as March 1988:

> We call on our people in villages, cities, and camps to establish donation funds for financial and in-kind donations, to be supervised by national and popular local committees. These funds will be used for those in need in that particular locality. We warn, however, that no donations should be given to people outside those committees which you have established yourselves.[55]

By 1989, suspicions were increasingly raised about the misuse of funds, leading the UNLU to urge the collection of only voluntary contributions and to cease collection of a fixed amount on a door-to-door basis. Prior to this time, the UNLU had openly criticized those who accused Palestinian activists of embezzlement, suggesting that such accusations were initiated by "the Zionist enemy and its collaborators."[56] The change to a completely voluntary system of contribution effectively halved the amounts collected, at least in the Nablus area, although the difference was often made up by contributions from East Jerusalem organizations.[57] Accusations of misuse of funds persisted, leading the Nablus committees to announce via loudspeakers in September 1989 that no contributions should be given unless the popular committee in question presented a stamped certification from the UNLU attesting to its validity.[58] Similar problems plagued the Tulkarim refugee camp, where judicial committee activists publicly announced in February 1990 that all those who collected funds must not cover their faces with a kafiya, the traditional Palestinian headdress (and often a symbol of resistance during the Intifada).[59] Those who were caught collecting money fraudulently—claiming it was for the Intifada but using it for personal gain—were dealt with harshly. In one instance in late 1989, a thirty-six-year-old Palestinian man apprehended while collecting money fraudulently near Ramallah was severely beaten.[60]

The strong communal solidarity which marked the first two years of the Intifada began to show cracks in early 1990 as intra-Palestinian robberies increased significantly. In the absence of a legitimate court system, such cases were "tried" in "popular courts," often after an interrogation by a usually self-appointed judicial committee. While this practice was applied to alleged collaborators, prostitutes, and drug dealers, it was also undertaken for other offenses, such as burglary, destruction of property, and kidnapping. In Nablus, such interrogation committees formalized their position by printing their own letterheads and "security dossiers," which were labeled "General Security System,

Palestine National Liberation Movement—Fatah, Unified National Leadership, Nablus, State of Palestine." The dossiers included their own logo and contained lines indicating the name, age, and profession of the accused, as well as the charge.[61]

Communal splits were evidenced by events in Nablus in late 1989 and early 1990. A number of residents had been abducted, questioned, beaten, and then released with the announcement that they had been found "innocent." Such actions led Fatah, in two different leaflets, to condemn the perpetrators and demand an end to such practices. In addition, Fatah activists marched through the old city of Nablus publicly denouncing the abductions and a related crime wave.[62] The rate of kidnappings slowed considerably, but the robberies did not. On March 12, a jewelry store in Nablus belonging to Wajdi Qamhawi was burgled and four kilograms of gold was stolen. A local militant group claimed responsibility, saying that the gold was taken "for a good cause."[63] A few minutes after Qamhawi's shop was robbed, the "Military Police of Fatah" marched through Nablus's casbah with loudspeakers condemning the theft and vowing to apprehend those responsible.[64] The next day, the "General Security Services" of Fatah issued a leaflet that condemned the robbery of Qamhawi's store.

Those judicial committees that were widely backed had the power to impose various types of sanctions on individuals, from organized social ostracism to death. Perhaps the most intriguing form of routine punishment meted out during the Intifada by these committees came in the form of house arrest (*iqama jabriya*). The fate of the 'Asha family in Nablus is a case in point.[65] Eight members of the family had been "convicted" of collaboration with Israeli authorities and were put under house arrest for six months. Two members of the family were exempted from the punishment: the father, so that he could work and buy food, and one son, who was being held without charge by Israel in Ketziot/Ansar III prison. Another son was confined to the home for a further six months. No visitors were allowed. When the initial six months expired in November 1989, activists from the "Security of the Revolution" publicly announced that the family members (with the one exception) were free to come and go and that visitors were now permitted. Neighbors then stopped by to congratulate the family on the lifting of the ban.

What was remarkable about this house arrest was that the family willingly abided by the popular committee's decision. As the father was allowed to go to work, contacting Israeli authorities about his family's predicament would have been easy. To do so, however, would have led to permanent ostracism from the community or worse; this possibility led the family to accept the ruling of the local popular judicial committee. In addition, the family's neighbors apparently also abided by the decision and refused to visit the 'Ashas during the period of the ban. The decision of the judicial committee in this case relied more on moral imperative for enforcement than on actual coercion. In other cases of house arrest, coercion was more blatant.[66]

In addition to execution and house arrest, judicial committees or strike forces would implement a range of punishments, including different types of ostracism and beatings. Often these decisions were carried out in public. In a fairly typical episode in September 1993, a strike force in Gaza rounded up three residents suspected of stealing $30,000 from a Palestinian moneychanger. The three were publicly interrogated and confessed to the crime. The interrogators then turned to the large crowd and asked what the appropriate penalty should be. The crowd demanded the death penalty. The interrogators overruled the onlookers, instead shooting the suspects in the legs before releasing them.[67]

On issues where there was little factional agreement, competing judicial committees often found themselves working at cross-purposes. For example, throughout the Intifada the issue of Palestinian workers in Israel was a source of profound disagreement. In contrast to the other members of the Big Four of the PLO, the PFLP routinely urged all Palestinians who worked in Israel to quit their jobs immediately and permanently. The other factions agreed that an end to the employment of Palestinians in Israel was a primary goal but argued that it must be done only insofar as there was a parallel increase in the Palestinian economic infrastructure that could absorb the labor. Otherwise, unemployment and poverty would only increase and lead to a decrease in communal unity, since the decree would almost certainly be violated by those facing starvation. This internal PLO debate was reflected on the street after Israel issued magnetic identification cards to all Gaza Palestinians in 1989 in order to better control the flow of labor. Possession of such a card became mandatory for all Palestinians wishing to enter Israel from Gaza. In response, popular judicial committees associated with the PFLP confiscated these cards from Palestinians to prevent them from working in Israel. After a heated debate within the Palestinian community, the more pragmatic forces won out, and the cards were returned to their owners. Although the PFLP never did drop this demand, it did not press the issue after the long curfews and associated hardship resulting from the Gulf war.

Collaborators

Armies of occupation routinely seek a collaborationist "native pillar" in order to make the task of social control over a hostile population easier. Israeli policies in the West Bank and Gaza after 1967 emphasized the need to build and enhance an indigenous network that would cooperate with Israeli authority on different levels. During the first decade of military occupation, when the Labor Party was in power, the main thrust of Israeli policy was to bolster segments of the population that had some potential for popular legitimacy and yet were removed from the growing ideological dominance of Palestinian nationalism. By so doing, it was thought, the Israel Defense Forces (IDF) could play a less visible role, thereby decreasing the potential for open conflict. Thus, while thousands of undercover Palestinian collaborators were recruited, the major Israeli effort of social control during this period went into politically bolstering the waning notable social class.[68] Such practices, it was hoped, would eclipse the growing power of the PLO in the occupied territories.

This hands-off approach was rejected by the Likud Party when it came to power in Israel in 1977. During Likud's rule from 1977 to 1992, it consistently and openly pursued permanent Israeli control of the occupied territories and sought to eradicate all manifestations of Palestinian nationalism. Such a policy had two principal consequences. First, the army acquired a more prominent role in the policing of the occupied territories, even as power was formally assumed by a "civil administration."[69] Second, the effort to support a native pillar with a degree of standing within the Palestinian community was dropped, and in its place Likud bolstered what can best be described as a Palestinian mafia: the Village Leagues. As a result, the nationalists who won the 1976 municipal elections—including a number of notables affiliated with the conservative wing of Fatah—were dismissed, and some were deported. The 1980s saw intensified efforts to recruit and strengthen a network of Palestinian collaborators.

Recruitment

The recruitment of collaborators focused on three types of individuals: criminal collaborators, utilitarian collaborators, and notables. The criminal collaborators were Palestinians from the margins of society, often drug dealers and prostitutes, who were recruited by the Shin Bet (the General Security Services, or secret police). In general, these social marginals were given protection by Israel and allowed to practice their trades in exchange for information and, often, cooperation in recruiting fellow Palestinians into collaboration.

A common form of recruitment by criminal collaborators was through *isqat*, a "bringing down" of a person. Isqat is usually associated with the sexual compromise, through entrapment, of a female. In the Jerusalem-area town of Bayt Hanina, for example, a house of prostitution was founded in the 1980s by advertising itself as the "Association of the Orphans and Widows of the Massacre of Sabra and Shatila."[70] The two Palestinian organizers appealed to the wives of imprisoned Palestinians and the widows of those killed by Israel to come to the association and receive aid. The women who were persuaded to come were raped and then blackmailed into becoming prostitutes and collaborators. If they refused to cooperate, their families would be notified of the rape. There is no greater shame a woman can bring upon her family in the Arab world than such illicit intercourse, whether through consent or rape.[71] To prevent such humiliation, the women often agreed to collaborate. In a similar case, the owner of a house of prostitution in Bayt Jala, Nina Mattar, photographed a local mukhtar completely naked and gave the photograph to the Israeli police, who used it, presumably, to blackmail the mukhtar into collaboration.[72]

An even more common means for recruitment of criminal collaborators was through the drug trade. Israeli forces were widely viewed as encouraging, protecting, and often arming Palestinians involved in the sale of drugs. In exchange for information and fellow recruitment, the drug dealers were allowed to prosper in their trade, protected by the security services. Occasionally this policy backfired, as it did in the case of Muhammad Halabi, convicted of the 1989 murder of seven people in the Tel Aviv–Jaffa area. Halabi was a collaborator from Gaza who was armed by Israel and had permission to sleep overnight in Israel, and whose known criminal activities—Halabi was one of the leading drug dealers in the area—were ignored by the police. Halabi's activities had led Hamas to call for his execution; Halabi may have committed the murders to "disprove" the allegations. In a 1993 case, a collaborator killed his Shin Bet handler, again in attempt to clear his name of suspicion of collaboration in the Bethlehem area.[73]

The predominant view of the relationship between crime, armed Palestinians, and collaboration was expressed by Palestinian editor Ziad Abu Zayyad:

> One of the reasons for the success of the Israeli occupation is that since 1967 the Israelis have succeeded in building a very wide network of collaborators and spies inside the Palestinian community. Most of these [collaborators] come from the underworld . . . and receive arms from the occupation authorities. They are people involved in drugs, crime, and prostitution, and they become collaborators in order to get the protection of the occupation. They are being blackmailed. Drug dealers need to be collaborators to protect themselves. For Palestinians in the occupied territories, if someone carries a gun supplied by the Shin Bet he is [automatically] considered a collaborator.[74]

The most formalized Israeli attempt to arm and empower Palestinian social marginals was found during the early 1980s in the Village Leagues policies. The espoused aim of the Village Leagues was to undermine Palestinian nationalism—in particular the influence of the PLO—and to negotiate limited, fixed autonomy for Palestinians in the Israeli-occupied territories. In exchange, Israel would maintain permanent sovereignty over the areas. Failing to find Palestinians with standing who would participate in such a venture, Likud was compelled, according to Salim Tamari, to rely on "the socially marginal and politically ostracized elements among the peasantry as the backbone of Village League membership." Tamari continues: "Itinerant laborers, drifters, former members of the British police force and Jordanian *mukhabarat* [secret police], land brokers [for Himnuta—a land purchasing company for the Jewish Agency], and village transport workers constitute main sources for league recruits."[75] Several of the Village League heads were known to be illiterate, and a large number came from the criminal underworld.[76]

The second major source of collaborators was the judicial and administrative systems. Most undercover collaborators—intelligence agents (sing., *'amil al-mukhabarat*)—in the occupied territories were recruited through deals to reduce prison sentences or to acquire administrative favors. Palestinians arrested for various offenses frequently were offered greatly reduced sentences in exchange for information. For those Palestinians facing multiple years in prison, and especially for those not convicted of political crimes, an offer of freedom and, in some cases, cash was hard to resist. In addition, a number of Palestinians were recruited in exchange for specific administrative services. The range of common permits used to recruit collaborators was extensive, including permits for family reunification, travel abroad, family visits from abroad, any kind of travel documents, permission to work in Israel, driving licenses, and building permits.[77] People seeking family reunification permits in order to allow their wives and children to live in the West Bank or Gaza tended to be the most vulnerable to collaboration, given the high emotional stakes. Permission for family reunification was granted often as *quid pro quo* for agreeing to provide information to the intelligence services.

A former Shin Bet recruiter emphasized the need to look for people who were in need of special favors:

> You don't just take people off the street. The first thing is that you look for people who are involved in [political] activity. From them we look for the people who have a good motive for enlisting. For example, a bad economic situation, family reunification, need for help, for assistance, cutting a prison term; the need for medical treatment is a good motive.[78]

As B'tselem correctly points out, this system worsened considerably after the Intifada began:

> With the outbreak of the Intifada, the phenomena indicating a policy of arbitrary denial of services worsened. During the first three years, the receipt of most permits was made dependent on seven different authorities, including the police and the GSS [Shin Bet]. Granting of services was

often made conditional upon agreement to collaborate with the authorities, and along with special benefits and extortion, was a common recruitment practice.[79]

If Palestinians protecting their often illicit activities were criminal collaborators, then this second type can be labeled utilitarian collaborators. In this case, the Palestinians were not socially marginal, but rather came from the mainstream of society. Rarely suspected of collaboration, these informants had greater access to political life within Palestinian society than their criminal counterparts. Utilitarian collaborators generally did not undertake collaboration with enthusiasm, but rather viewed it as the lesser of two evils.

The third group of collaborators—or, at least, so they were often perceived by Palestinian militants—consisted of some members of the traditional elite who had cooperated with the military government in the administration of the occupied territories. Generally, these notables agreed to play their traditional role as intermediaries between the state (in this case, Israel) and the local population in order to preserve their social, political, or economic status. It should be emphasized that not all or even most mayors, mukhtars, and other members of the traditional elite were viewed by most Palestinians as collaborators per se. Rather, they were viewed generally as political obstacles and a drag on the Intifada. The Intifada, it must be noted, was not just an uprising against Israeli occupation; its secondary target was the traditional Palestinian elite. The UNLU would occasionally criticize these notables by name, as they did in February 1988: "We have to marginalize the agents of Jordan, like [Bethlehem mayor Elias] Freij and [former Gaza mayor, now deceased, Rashad] Shawwa and others who are poles of Amman and Arab reaction."[80]

As official intermediaries to the military government, notable "collaborators" were public in their activities, in contrast to the overwhelming majority of collaborators. Only a small handful of nonnotable collaborators were open in their work, usually because they helped secure permits and other favors from the occupation authorities in exchange for cash. While fewer and fewer resources flowed through notable intermediaries to the community, mayors and mukhtars would still be able to secure an occasional permit or the like for a constituent. In return for continued status, these men were expected to report back to the military government on developments in their towns or villages.

Most political notables were sufficiently marginalized by the inattention paid them. The Israeli-appointed mayor of Nablus, Hafiz Tuqan, from one of the most important notable families in the West Bank, resigned early in the Intifada because he lacked funding—he had 10 to 15 percent of his normal budget—and because popular committees were providing many of the municipal services usually performed by the city.[81] At the behest of the military governor, the mayor of Bayt Sahur, Hanna al-'Atrash, urged local businessmen to pay their taxes instead of persisting with the nascent tax boycott. He was ignored. In the words of one West Bank Palestinian, "It's a matter of getting rid of all people appointed by Israel and Jordan. They are tools. We are cleaning out the cities. This is the real Intifada."[82]

Occasionally, notables would be assaulted. The mayor of Qalqilya, al-Rahman Abu Snina, and a number of his assistants were repeatedly attacked by Palestinians denouncing their collaboration. The secretary of Qalqilya, Yusuf Milhem, was seriously wounded in a December 1988 attack, then was shot to death the following September.[83] In another instance, Ibrahim Brahma, the mukhtar of the village of Talluza, near Nablus, was killed by assailants accusing him of collaboration. Interestingly, Brahma had been given a sixteen-year jail term by Jordan in 1963 on charges of spying for Israel but was released by Israel immediately following the 1967 war.[84] At least ten mukhtars were killed by Palestinian militants during the Intifada.[85]

This network of different kinds of collaborators engaging in diverse levels of collaboration was not merely an inconvenience for Palestinians or a hindrance to mobilization efforts but often represented, indirectly or directly, threats to their physical safety. Information passed to Israeli authorities by collaborators would often result in arrests, beatings, imprisonment, or the denial of various kinds of permits. The deportation of Palestinians or the capture of "wanted" Palestinians was invariably based on information provided by collaborators. Israeli military courts rarely allowed a defendant or his lawyer to see the evidence used to convict him, in order not to potentially compromise the collaborator who provided it.

Reliance on collaborators as a "native pillar" of Israeli power increased dramatically after the first year of the Intifada because, in the words of one military source, "the days when the *mukhtar* would have done it are gone."[86]

The Killing of Collaborators

One important early accomplishment of the Intifada was the temporary collapse of the network of collaborators in the occupied territories. The weakening of the collaborator network actually began just prior to the Intifada in some areas, especially Nablus and Gaza.[87] The process of rooting out collaborators accelerated and expanded rapidly after December 1987. During the first several months of the Intifada, thousands of collaborators—generally the utilitarian ones—publicly renounced their collaboration and, following UNLU orders, were usually accepted back into their communities without retribution. In the early spring of

1988, for example, Nablus collaborators were publicly encouraged to go to the local mosque on a particular day and renounce their behavior. According to one eyewitness, hundreds of Palestinians came, many of whom had not been suspected of being collaborators.[88]

As a rule, Palestinians respected the UNLU orders not to harm those collaborators who renounced their collaboration early in the Intifada. During the first year of the uprising, about a dozen collaborators were killed; the number went up tenfold in subsequent years. Most of those killed early on were among the most visible collaborators, often precipitating their own deaths by employing violence. For example, in February 1988 in the village of Qabatya, near Jenin, a well-known collaborator, Muhammad Ayad Zakarna, was murdered only after he opened fire on fellow villagers who were urging him to cease his collaboration. His shooting spree left a four-year-old child dead and thirteen persons wounded. Zakarna's house was raided, and he was lynched and left hanging on a utility pole for all to see.

The collapse of the collaboration network early in the Intifada prompted Israel to intensify its recruitment efforts. In addition, those collaborators it did recruit, or those that had been exposed, were often used in much more explicitly coercive ways. The military government encouraged collaborators to attack Palestinians directly, even going so far as providing paramilitary training to thousands of collaborators in the occupied territories to help suppress the Intifada.[89] As a result of this policy, armed gangs of collaborators were given wide latitude by the army to terrorize Palestinian civilians. Often these collaborators were housed close to permanent army roadblocks to be better protected against retaliation. Such collaborators were responsible for a number of killings, robberies, beatings, and destruction of property, as well as for helping the army to make arrests of wanted Palestinians. Even the "extrajudicial killings" by Israeli undercover units disguised as Arabs (Hebrew: *mista'arvim*) often relied on collaborators to point out the intended target moments prior to his execution. Such death squads were used in the execution of scores of Palestinian activists.[90]

Israel's success in rebuilding its collaboration network by late 1988 had two significant and closely related results. First, as more and more collaborators were being used in more obvious ways and their connections to Shin Bet made clearer (through the increased distribution of guns, more visible protection, etc.), their vulnerability was likewise increased. The subsequent dramatic increase in the killing of collaborators should not be a surprise. While only a few collaborators were killed in the first year,[91] over a hundred alleged collaborators were killed every year thereafter until the Oslo Accords were signed in September 1993. The collaborators' increased visibility, attributable to their need for protection, left unrepentant collaborators even more exposed. Ironically, Israel may have inadvertently spurred the killings by being more open in its protection of collaborators. By more aggressively embracing collaborators, Israeli officials thought, other collaborators who might be wavering in their commitment would maintain their relationship; Israel was sending a signal that it would not desert its native pillar. The message was heard not only by collaborators but by their enemies as well.

Second, the reestablishment of the collaborator network forced the UNLU to rethink its announced policy. During the first year, the UNLU generally urged tolerance for collaborators who renounced their activities, and persuasion, pressure, and ostracism—not death—for those who did not. Beginning in late 1988, when it was clear that the collaborator network had been effectively rebuilt, the UNLU took a more hardline stance, urging more active attacks on collaborators. From late 1988 to early 1990, when the UNLU as a distinctive and authoritative body ceased to exist, most leaflets demanded retribution against collaborators, including urging their "judgment day." The UNLU justified its open call for the execution of collaborators:

> We must continue to pursue the traitors used by the occupation authorities, so that they may be made examples for all those who deviate from their people and their cause. The UNLU will punish them not because they are political opponents with differing points of view, but because they are tools of the occupation who are provided weapons with which to kill and terrorize our people.[92]

The UNLU had clearly changed course on the collaborator issue by the close of 1988, with the thrust of its new policy to take a more militant and vengeful approach. Still, a number of leaflets contained conflicting sentiments regarding appropriate behavior toward collaborators. One paragraph might urge ostracism or perhaps sanction the murder of collaborators provided permission was granted by higher political authorities. A later paragraph in the same leaflet would take a much more militant stance. Such was the case in bayan 44, which at one point urged that "no collaborator should be liquidated without a central decision by the supreme leadership, and national consensus, or before advance warning to repent." Further down the page, no caveats were inserted when dealing with collaborators:

> Escalate the confrontation against prominent traitors. Persecute the collaborators whom the enemy is organizing into armed militias in order to attack honorable nationalists. Let the land burn under the feet of the occupation troops, border guards, settler gangs, and collaborators, because the only language the enemy understands is that of force, suffering, and continuous losses.[93]

By all accounts, a number of "collaborator killings" were in fact murders unrelated to the Intifada or to collaboration. Some were associated with personal feuds or criminal activity but were reported as, or assumed to be, collaborator killings. A number of "honor killings" of noncollaborating individuals engaged in "immoral" behavior also occurred. In a small number of cases, honor killings of women by their own kin took place and were labeled as collaborator killings. One such murder that occurred in the Nablus casbah in December 1989 was reported as a collaborator killing. Two months later it was revealed that the victim's brother-in-law had confessed to the slaying, saying that the victim had violated his family's honor. The killing was unconnected with the uprising.[94]

Other killings were the result of mistaken identity. For example, in December 1989, Ma'mun al-Masri of Bayt Iba, near Nablus, was killed when local militants mistook him for a known collaborator. When the mistake was discovered, activists speaking on behalf of the local Fatah leadership and the UNLU proclaimed Masri to be a martyr (*shahid*) of the uprising.[95] In a small number of cases, there was genuine disagreement between competing factional strike forces as to whether an individual was a collaborator. Thus, one group would kill a "collaborator" who was immediately proclaimed a martyr by another faction. Such was the case for Nabil 'Abd al-Hamid Jawadat, whose October 1993 killing was condemned by Fatah, the PFLP, and the PPP but condoned and justified in a Hamas leaflet. Fatah then publicly honored his family.[96] In a number of cases, militants sent letters directly to the victim's family, explaining the reasons for a particular killing.[97]

In order to protect undercover collaborators who had been exposed or open collaborators who could no longer be protected, Israel established two "collaborator villages" in the occupied territories, one in the West Bank and one in Gaza. At their peak, these villages housed hundreds of former collaborators and their families. The largest, Fahma, in the northern part of the West Bank, had been a Jordanian army camp prior to 1967. It is surrounded by an Israeli military camp, guaranteeing the security of its inhabitants. The second, Dahaniya, is south of Rafah, adjacent to the Egyptian border. It can be entered only through an IDF checkpoint. Other collaborators were allowed to move to Israel, an option which expanded considerably after the Oslo Accords. All collaborators were allowed to carry Israeli identification cards.[98]

The Crusade for Revolutionary Purity

The best-known groups involved in the killing of collaborators during the Intifada were founded in Nablus as violent splinter factions ambiguously associated with Fatah and the PFLP. The gangs, known as the Black Panther (*al-fahd al-'aswad*) and Red Eagle (*al-nasr al-'ahmar*) organizations, claimed to belong to Fatah and the PFLP, respectively, while those PLO factions often criticized their actions. People involved with the Black Panther and Red Eagle organizations tended to be semiliterate young men in their late teens and early twenties. Jabar Hawash, for example, was just sixteen years old when he left the Black Panthers and formed the Red Eagles.[99] The two groups were responsible for the killing of dozens of Palestinian collaborators, mostly in 1989. Many of the killings were done openly in the streets of the Nablus casbah, some after purported "trials" of the accused. One killing was dramatically re-counted by an eyewitness:

> There were seven of them, standing in single file [in the casbah], wearing olive drab uniforms and red kafiyas. Three carried pistols sticking out of their pants, and four carried hatchets. Speaking through a megaphone, their leader [made an announcement]. The leader stopped talking, and one of the gang members stepped out of the line. At that moment, a woman passed by, and he called to her: "Umm Rami, come here." He asked her two questions: "How many women did you employ as prosti-tutes? How many youths have you betrayed to the authorities?" Before she could say a word, he pulled a gun and shot her six times in the head. She fell on her face, without a sound. Another person in the line dragged her to a corner, and propped her up on her knees. The leader announced: "We have killed a collaborator, come out and see." Thousands of casbah resi-dents streamed to the area, and, for half an hour, women spat at her and some kicked her in the head. No one dared to remove the body. People said: "Let her stay there, until the army arrives."[100]

The gangs were finally routed by the Israeli army in late 1989. Army and Shin Bet personnel were involved in an assault on a Red Eagle safe house in November 1989, killing the organization's leader and arresting a number of other members. A few weeks later, elite Israeli troops assassinated three leaders of the Black Panthers,[101] then the Israeli army conducted its largest sweep through the Nablus casbah since the 1967 war, conducting house-to-house searches and mapping out uncharted quarters. Scores of Palestinians were arrested, a number of whom be-longed to the Black Panther gang. A number of collaborator killings by reconstituted Black Panther and Red Eagle gangs occurred in the months following the crackdown, but the groups were not able to fully recover from the assault.

The assault on the Black Panther gang came just days after the group had effectively imposed a curfew on the Nablus casbah in order to interrogate several Palestinians about their involvement in the arrest of a number of activists. For the Israeli authorities, the ability to effectively impose a curfew on a large area in central Nablus challenged Israel's control of Nablus and was therefore intolerable. An editorial in the *Jerusalem Post* captured this sentiment well:

> Some might argue that as long as it was a matter of Palestinians killing Palestinians, Israeli intervention was not needed, or even counterproduc-tive. To allow the Nablus casbah to be taken over by the Black Panthers would, however, have been politically unwise. It might be tantamount to

conceding the Arab capital of Samaria [northern West Bank] to the paper-state of Palestine. At the very least, it could be interpreted as an admission of Israel's inability to keep control of the occupied territories.[102]

What the Black Panther–Red Eagle episode clearly showed was the revolutionary zeal of the uprising. In the Intifada, as in many other revolutionary movements, there was a drive to purify society, to rid the Palestinian community of "unclean" elements. The appeal of such a puritanical view of society during the Intifada was demonstrated when Israel Television, seeking to publicize the bloody events in Nablus, interviewed Jabar Hawash after his capture. By his own admission, Hawash had questioned 140 collaborators and had participated in a number of killings. Hawash dispassionately described several killings in which he had participated, including the murder of his own cousin, a woman known as Umm Barakat. When asked why he had done these things and how they had helped the Intifada, Hawash responded:

> Our people have slowly become purified. When someone linked to [Is-raeli] intelligence sees someone else like him has been killed, he stops what he is doing. One thing is important to us: that our people be pure, and that they all follow the straight and narrow. That's what we want.[103]

Instead of being repulsed by Hawash's actions, many Palestinians were enthralled by them.[104] In fact, the Hawash interview, conducted in Arabic, was at the center of discussion in the West Bank for days afterward, and most of the sentiment was favorable to Hawash. As one Palestinian explained, "People were proud and pleased at what Hawash said, particularly his explanation that he wanted to purify our society. People were impressed that he was even prepared to kill his own cousin. When he spoke, he wasn't afraid."[105]

The crusade to purify society could be seen in three separate aspects of the collaborator killings. First, the killings usually were characterized by dramatic overkill. Often, collaborators' bodies were mutilated be-yond recognition in the process. The force employed in the execution of collaborators usually greatly exceeded that which was necessary to kill the person. It was as though the villagers or townspeople were not just out to kill a quisling of the enemy but to exact a brutal vengeance for past deeds and, more important, to cleanse themselves through the total destruction of their own enemies. In a manner reminiscent of Frantz Fanon's Algeria, brutal violence was employed as both a purifying and an empowering vehicle in the revolution.[106] One prominent Palestinian described the overkill involved:

> The brutality involved in their killings is a reflection of anger, frustration, rage—not self-control. It goes beyond capital punishment, as that is viewed as a necessary evil. With collaborator killings there is an obvious pleasure involved.[107]

Second, a number of Palestinians were killed not for their collaboration but for "immoral behavior." As noted, the criminal element in Palestinian society was often linked to collaboration. That said, a number of killings during the Intifada were of Palestinians accused of promiscuity or drug dealing where no claim was made that the individual had been a collaborator. The Intifada, it was felt by many, was a time to cleanse one's own society of Palestinians who had strayed from the correct path. Attacks on hangouts of "spies and '*araq* drinkers" were easily accepted.[108]

Third, the drive for purity could be seen in the common refusal of Palestinians to bury the bodies of murdered collaborators in their local cemeteries. Part of the reason for this, of course, was to shame the collaborator one final time. Another reason, it seems, was the sense that collaborators physically carried social pollution with them: even in death, the filth of collaborators could contaminate the sacred soil. Such was the case for Muhammad Hatatba, a murdered collaborator from Bayt Furik, where the villagers refused to have his body buried in the local cemetery.[109] In another case, Sara al-Ribashi of Hebron was murdered for collaboration and promiscuity in March 1990 (her husband had been killed earlier for collaboration and drug dealing). After an autopsy was performed at the Israeli Institute for Forensic Medicine at Abu Kabir, her body was returned to Hebron where local activists as well as cemetery officials refused to bury her corpse. The military government intervened and had her body sent for burial in East Jerusalem. Cemetery officials there also refused to bury her. Finally, after more shuttle grave-digging, her body was buried back in Hebron under armed guard.[110]

Ignoring the PLO

It is not clear that the PLO ever controlled the strike forces and judicial committees which dealt with collaborators. It is evident, however, that when the PLO in Tunis, its allied high-profile personalities (*shakhsiyat*) in East Jerusalem, and even the UNLU tried to end or substantially reduce the killing of collaborators they were unsuccessful. This issue, like many others in the Intifada, was driven from the bottom up and was carried out by widely diffused and largely autonomous groups. The level of killings declined substantially only when the Intifada itself ended, or, at least, when the Oslo Accords produced a different political reality on the ground.

The PLO in Tunis was little concerned with the issue of collaborator killings until it became clear in late 1989 both that the murders were detracting from the politically beneficial image the Intifada had generated in the West and, more important, that the groups could not be controlled from above. At that point efforts were made to curtail the killings. Yasir Arafat made the first of numerous personal appeals to end the killings of collaborators in October 1989 in a radio broadcast.[111] In coordination with Tunis, the Fatah leadership in Nablus, the site of many of the killings, issued several leaflets condemning the killings and ordered their followers "to stop the killings of those who have gone astray and [instead] use all methods to restore them to the national line."[112] A few weeks later, Fatah called upon "national forces and all our organizational units to stop immediately and finally the killings of collaborators. Only the President of the State of Palestine [Yasir Arafat] has the authority to issue a decree to execute collaborators."[113] In addition, marches were held in the Nablus casbah by members of Fatah to demand that the killings end.[114] Such direct appeals from the Fatah hierarchy had little impact on the numbers of collaborators killed.

Recognizing that there was little they could do to stop a number of the groups engaged in killing collaborators, Tunis opted to establish parallel strike forces staffed by more reliable cadres. The founding of the Fatah Hawks was largely a response to the inability to control other groups. Originally formed in Rafah in Gaza, the Hawks proved—initially—to be more amenable to the demands of Tunis, to the point of keeping files on every person they interrogated, including justifications for punishments. However, even the more disciplined Hawks would sometimes disobey explicit orders from the ranking Fatah leadership not to kill a suspected collaborator.[115] Moreover, the Fatah Hawks in Rafah were led in 1992 and early 1993 by Yasir Abu Samhadana, a man responsible for more collaborator killings than any other single individual. Famous for refusing to mask his identity, Abu Samhadana was responsible for the killing of thirty-seven alleged collaborators, personally executing at least twenty-five himself. Even the Fatah Hawks proved too independent for Arafat and the Palestinian Authority: a section of the group, led by Ahmad Tabuk, had to be crushed by the Palestinian police in December 1995.

Many well-known public officials identified with Fatah in the occupied territories also spoke out against collaborator killings from 1989 to 1993, but to little avail. At various times Faysal al-Husayni, Haydar 'Abd al-Shafi, Ziyad Abu Zayyad, Sari Nusayba, and other prominent personalities urged restraint in the killings. All of these individuals recognized the difficulty of the problem—how should a society under occupation deal with such dangerous elements in the absence of courts and jails? Or, as human rights lawyer Jonathan Kuttab argued,

> The population involved in the Intifada is physically endangered by many collaborators, most of whom carry guns issued by the Israeli authorities and use them on fellow Palestinians and others. They provide the authorities with information that jeopardizes the lives, liberty and property of the

general population. Hence, in addition to the need to provide sanctions that would punish or deter such individuals, there is also the need to protect the community from the danger. While I have no problem opposing the death penalty in an organized state, I am not sure that I can posit as a universal rule that collaborators cannot be subjected to this punishment anywhere and anytime unless I can think of effective alternatives.[116]

None of these individuals believed, however, that the uncontrolled killing of collaborators helped the Intifada or the Palestinian cause. Sari Nusayba, a respected philosopher and political activist and current president of Jerusalem University, was critical of the killings, and unlike most Palestinians, he downplayed the importance of collaborators to Israeli policies of control:

> The dynamic of the Intifada only gets defused by violence, such as the collaborator killings. This is an escapist action. The main thrust of the Intifada is not violence—violence is a marginal phenomenon which only results in a scattering of the main thrust. I don't agree that collaborators were a primary means of control for the Israelis. If Palestinians think this, then they are only negating the revolutionary consciousness. The real base of control was Palestinian acquiescence. Collaborators were the parasites on the situation, not the foundation of control. Collaborators are only useful to the extent that they are allowed to be useful by the Palestinians. Violence against them should only be used as a last resort. Don't forget that a lot of collaborators have been forced into this position by the Israelis. Of course, there are the Mafia types who are armed and dangerous. If they are attacking a Palestinian home, then of course killing in self-defense is justified. But on the whole it only detracts from the effectiveness of the Intifada.[117]

Perhaps most symbolic of the failure of PLO elites to effectively stop collaborator killings was the controversial *mithaq al-sharaf*, or honor pact, of 1992. Involving many of the most prominent public political personalities in the occupied territories and with the explicit support of Arafat, the honor pact called for the cessation of all intra-Palestinian killings. The pact had no significant impact on the rate of collaborator killings.

The rejection of the nationalist elite's calls to cease the killings had a class sentiment as well. Members of this elite—such as Faysal al-Husayni, Sari Nusayba, and Sa'id Kan'an—often came from the same class of nationalist notables that had been a target of some activists during the Intifada, and they were resented by many grassroots militants and others for trying to capture what they did not produce. Palestinian journalist Jamal Hamad captured this sentiment well:

> The members of these groups [who killed collaborators] felt that their leaders, who belonged to wealthy and aristocratic Jerusalem and Nablus families, had "stolen" the Intifada from them and captured the media and

publicity limelight, while they were the ones actually paying the price of suffering and sacrifice. From their perspective, the situation gave them a perfect opportunity to impose their control, rejecting the elitists' authority of the local leadership and even that of the PLO leadership.[118]

Even the UNLU, which had taken a hardline approach to collaborators in late 1988 and 1989, began to change its view in late 1989. The UNLU then began to appeal for restraint:

First, concerning collaborators: We repeat that all strike force cadres and popular committee members should maintain strict discipline, to prevent any disorder that the enemy might exploit on the ground or in the media. Patient scrutiny and sober examination are required before issuing hasty accusations. The highest authorities should be notified in full before judgments are passed or warnings given. Give time for repentance. Try to reform [the suspected collaborator] before applying any punishment.[119]

With the arrest in March 1990 of the last group of grassroots UNLU members and the appropriation of the UNLU by more prominent and "connected" politicos, published leaflets stressed further the need to control collaborator killings. For example, in leaflet 84 (July 4, 1992) the UNLU attacked all intra-Palestinian violence, and stressed

the need for and the importance of maintaining the gains and achievements of the Intifada, especially the ethical values and concepts it produced. These include solidarity, cohesiveness, and the spirit of love, tolerance, and unity among all parties, forces, groups, and sects. We must work to entrench civilized democratic dealings, away from fanaticism and extremism. We must respect institutions, their laws, regulations, and bodies. We must also fight the practices of extortion, hegemony, and monopoly, which are alien to our people's values and traditions, and which inflict serious damage on the march of our people and our valiant Intifada.

The inability of the PLO, the leading public figures in the West Bank and Gaza, and the UNLU (comprised of members of the new elite) to stem the flow of killings was due primarily to the diffuse and autonomous nature of many Intifada activities. Certainly an additional part of the explanation for the continued killings was that Islamist groups, such as Hamas, never made a concerted attempt to end the killings. However, there is no evidence that even the secular strike forces were much impacted by the calls to end the killings.

The devolution of authority in the Intifada to the lower strata in Palestinian society could clearly be seen in the widespread phenomenon of popular committees. Fluid, multifunctional popular committees are common in revolutionary movements. When the normal functions of the state break down, are withdrawn, or are rejected, alternative structures of authority are often created to fill the vacuum. This process leads to what scholars have termed a situation of dual or multiple sovereignties. It is, in essence, the nascent phase of state-building: the transference of authority from one set of formalized institutions to other emerging, functionally diffuse, nondelineated bodies. Such committees commonly focus on widely divergent issues—from alternative educational systems to revolutionary justice—but share the concern of denying the existing state authority and decision-making powers. In these cases, authority is closely linked to the provision of social goods. As revolutionary popular committees provide such social goods, not only can the movement be more easily sustained and the cohesion of the rebelling population strengthened, but the contours of authority in the emerging polity can be more readily ascertained.

In most cases, members of the new elite were central in the formation of popular committees for popular education, agricultural and medical self-help groups, or even the UNLU. In some cases, such as those involving "revolutionary justice," authority devolved beyond the ability of the new elite to control or even greatly influence. Here, authority was practiced on the street and reflected the unrestrained rage engendered by a brutal military occupation and its native pillar.

The PLO in Tunis was not enamored of popular forms of authority which it could not control. As a result, the factionalization of many popular committees after the first year of the Intifada could be seen, in part, as the PLO's attempt to capture and contain the spread of popular forms of authority. Even the PLO's failed attempt to stop the killing of collaborators should be seen in the context of a larger struggle for control between the PLO leadership and its own nominal cadres on the ground. That authoritative decisions, often involving life and death, were being made by Palestinians pronouncing fealty to the Palestinian cause but outside of effective PLO control, was intolerable for the ranking leadership. This was seen directly after the Tunis leadership moved to Gaza in 1994, when it fired many popular Fatah cadres with Intifada experience because, it seems, they were considered too independent.

Many popular committees disappeared as the Intifada waned; others were captured by the PLO or suppressed by Israel. What remained were the patterns and relations of authority engendered by the Intifada. The diffuse, grassroots nature of decision-making during the uprising—the distribution of authority—has made post-Oslo centralization attempts under the Palestinian Authority difficult.

6

Hamas and the Islamist Mobilization

The political mobilization of Palestinian society in the 1980s was not limited to grassroots organizations established by elites and factions affiliated with the Palestine Liberation Organization. A parallel mobilization was undertaken by activists from various Islamist groups, primarily the Muslim Brethren, in the occupied territories. Like that of the PLO, Islamist organization-building created new social relations and political ties between various strata of Palestinian society. In addition, it politically incorporated previously excluded groups who were now more open to recruitment because of the larger social changes—principally depeasantization and expanded education—which were transforming Palestinian society.

Islamism: An Overview

A great deal has been written in the West in the last two decades explaining Islamist movements—from the revolution in Iran to the rebellion of the Shi'a in Lebanon to the Jama'at groups in Egypt—as movements bent on turning back the historical clock hundreds of years, of returning to traditional ways. Alternatively, Islamism (or "Islamic Fundamentalism," as it is often inappropriately called) has been viewed as a movement of rage, of marginal groups that have been excluded from the social and global orders lashing out at persons who are seen to oppress them—Westerners, Christians, Israelis, national (Westernized) elites, and the like. Both schools of thought share a common theme: Islamism is fundamentally and irrevocably antimodern.

Such views are both misleading and miss what is important about Islamism. First of all, it would be wrong to speak of a single Islamist movement. The great majority of Islamist movements are fueled by local problems and local politics, although clearly there is an international demonstration effect which helps local groups to frame their grievances in certain ways and not in others. That said, it is important to note that the leaders of these movements (except the occasional spiritual leader who gives greater legitimacy to the movement) are more often than not firmly entrenched in modern society. That is, they have modern, secular educations, often having studied in Europe or North America, live in urban areas, usually capital cities, and are young (generally in their twenties and thirties). Often, their studies are in technical fields, such as engineering and medicine. They are almost never students of religious jurisprudence; nor have they studied in religious schools. In other words, leaders of the Islamist movements in the Middle East have virtually the same social profiles as those who, a generation earlier, agitated in favor of Ba'thism, Nasirism, and Arab socialism.

There should be nothing surprising in the fact that Islamist leaders have their roots in modern society. The intellectual vanguards—those who mold the ideology and provide the leadership—of most revolutionary movements, as Michael Walzer has argued, share similar, nontraditional backgrounds:

> By and large, while classes differ fundamentally from one revolution to another, vanguards are sociologically similar. They are recruited from middling and professional groups. The parents of the recruits are gentlemen farmers, merchants, clerics, lawyers, petty officials. Recruitment begins at school, not in the streets, or in shops and factories, or in peasant villages.[1]

The Islamist leadership of the revolution in Iran is instructive on this point. Clerics such as Ayatullahs Khomeini and Taleqani who were vital to the success of the revolution had bases of support outside the traditional religious institutions and cities of learning in Iran. Khomeini, of course, had been in exile from 1964 to 1979. Taleqani and other politically active clergy (who constituted a small minority of the 'ulama before 1978) had built their network of hard-core supporters largely from fellow prisoners in the shah's jails and from alienated university students. The most important revolutionary clerics were based in Tehran, not Qom or Mashhad or other religious cities in Iran. Nor did they come from provincial capitals.

However, the core cadres of the revolution in Iran were not the 'ulama but the radical lay Islamists. The social profile of these cadres was often young (twenties and thirties), urban (mostly Tehran), and well-educated (studied at secular universities in Iran or the West). Often, they were followers of Ali Shariati, an intellectual who blended Marxist concerns for social justice with Islamic themes of authenticity. Thus, while the traditional religious stratum gained much of the credit for the revolution in Iran, the lay Islamists—of the same profile that Walzer describes and very much a product of modern society—were the activists, the organization builders, and the bridge to strata of society not enamored of clerical politics. The fact that this sociological group splintered after the revolution does not alter the fact of their centrality in the affair.

Other examples of the essentially modernist roots of Islamism abound. The Tanzim al-Jihad group in Egypt, responsible for, among other things, the assassination of Egyptian president Anwar al-Sadat in 1981, also fits this description.[2] Nearly 70 percent of Jihad's members were either students or professionals. Over 77 percent were between the ages of twenty and thirty. A disproportionate number had studied engineering at secular universities.[3] Nearly every leader of the Islamic Salvation Front in Algeria came from the capital city of Algiers and had a higher degree in a technical subject, such as chemical engineering, and many had studied in top universities in France. The same is true for the (government-backed) Islamist movement in Sudan.

Manfred Halpern was right to suggest over thirty years ago that political power in the Middle East was increasingly being seized by a salaried "new middle class" of "managers, administrators, teachers, engineers, journalists, scientists, lawyers, or army officers." It is a "class of men inspired by nontraditional knowledge, clustered around a core of salaried civilian and military politicians, organizers, administrators, and experts."[4] Clearly, while this class did seize power through the army in a number of Arab countries, the relatively liberal scenarios Halpern forecast have not materialized.

What I am suggesting here is that the Islamist leadership in the Middle East is, generally, very much a component of the modernist, new middle class that Halpern described. However, its ideological framework runs counter to that predicted by Halpern and others in the modernization school. Modern, Western educations were supposed to breed greater secularization in the new middle class. But, for a number of reasons, significant segments of the new middle class have used Islamist ideologies, not secular-based ones, to address concerns of social justice, political power, and the distribution of resources. Such are the ideologies of authenticity.[5]

Even with the exigencies of life under Israeli occupation, the same cleavage was produced in the Palestinian middle class in the West Bank and Gaza: a dominant secular ideology of nationalism and an influential Islamist rival. The leaders of both camps came from more or less the same social backgrounds that Walzer described. There were class cleavages *within* the nationalist and Islamist camps, but not *between* the leadership stratum of each. The main fissure in the Palestinian new middle class was along ideological, not class, lines. Ideology, in this case, should not be construed as epiphenomenal, or as a mask to advance material class interests. However, how that ideology was put into practice—or, more precisely, who put the ideology into practice—within each of the large ideological groupings did often parallel class lines.

The prominence of Islamism in the Middle East in recent years is primarily attributable to the failures of secular regimes in their economic and political projects. The failures of the nationalist governments which came to power in the major Arab states in the 1950s and 1960s included the devastating military defeat at the hands of Israel in 1967 and the regimes' continuing inability to redress the loss of Palestine, the unequal distribution of resources, high levels of corruption and nepotism by "revolutionary" regimes, and retarded economic development. As a result of these failures, political discourse in the Middle East increasingly shifted to include penetrating Islamist critiques of secular Arab governments, most notably by the Egyptian writer Sayyid Qutb. While Palestinians living under occupation had a different set of political problems than other Arab Muslims, the impact of the larger Islamist discourse was likewise felt in the West Bank and Gaza.

Moreover, the successes of Islamism outside Palestine, particularly the revolution in Iran, bolstered the Islamist paradigm. The Iranian revolution demonstrated that a principally (although far from exclusively) Islamist movement could overthrow an oppressive, corrupt, American-supported, un-Islamic, heavily armed regime. This message was not lost on Islamists in Palestine, in spite of the Shi'i, Persian character of the revolution. Other dramatic acts carried out in the name of Islam intensified the Islamist demonstration effect in Palestinian lands. The assassination of Sadat in 1981 was one such act, as was the Shi'i movement against Israeli troops in Lebanon following the 1982 invasion and occupation. Palestinian Islamists have pointed out that the Shi'a of Lebanon, by making the human and material costs of continued occupation too high, were the only military forces ever to have driven Israel off land it had occupied.

Local events also empowered the Palestinian Islamist movement. The ascent to power in Israel in 1977 by the Likud Party, with its strong Jewish messianic ideological component, helped to shift the political discourse in Israel over the occupied territories from one of competing nationalisms to one of religious conflict. In response to Israel's heightened stridency along religious lines, Islamists claimed that the real struggle was, at base, a religious one, so that the proper response was not more nationalist ideology but a strengthening of Islam among Palestinians. It is one of the great ironies of the conflict that the political hardliners among both Israelis and Palestinians essentially agree on the terms of the struggle, if on little else.

Finally, as Emile Sahliyeh points out, Fatah tried to recruit the Islamist bloc in the occupied territories in its move to displace the Palestine Communist Party from its preeminent position as the major force behind grassroots organizations.[6] The PCP was the first to establish mass organizations in the occupied territories, and its hegemonic position in this regard was not challenged until 1979. The Islamists' brief alliance with Fatah increased both the Islamists' visibility and their legitimacy in the eyes of fellow Palestinians. It was only after this time that the PLO began to view the Islamist movement as a potentially serious political challenger.

The remainder of this chapter deals specifically with the Islamist movement in the West Bank and Gaza in the 1980s and 1990s: its origins, its development and competition with the PLO during the Intifada, and its reaction to the changing diplomatic environment.[7]

The Deepening Islamization of Palestinian Society in the 1980s

The growing influence of Islam—both behavioral and institutional—in Palestinian society during the 1980s could be seen at a number of levels, including social practices, institution-building, student body elections at universities, and public opinion surveys. In terms of social practices, during this period a number of women, especially younger ones, began wearing modest Islamic, or *shari'*, dress, a practice which had virtually disappeared from the Palestinian scene a generation earlier. The observance of other Islamic practices—daily prayer, Qur'anic recitation, fasting—was also on the increase, as a 1984 survey demonstrated.[8] These changes were especially strong among refugee-camp inhabitants. In addition, a 1986 survey revealed that over half of all literature carried in West Bank bookstores was of a religious orientation.[9]

Concurrent with the increased social expression of Islamic practices during this period was the more important establishment of institutions geared toward an Islamic reorganization of social life. It was this institutional network, built in large measure by the conservative, upper merchant class leadership of the Muslim Brethren, that was, in effect, taken over by a well-educated, younger, poorer, and more activist middle stratum within the Islamist movement prior to and during the Intifada. The most obvious institutional expression of the growing Islamist movement was the increasing number of mosques found in the occupied territories. The number of mosques in Gaza more than doubled between 1967 and 1987, with the greatest increase occurring in the decade prior to the Intifada.[10] The West Bank also experienced a mosque boom, with forty new mosques built annually.[11]

In addition to the significant increase in the number of mosques in the occupied territories, a number of schools of Islamic learning were established in the years preceding the Intifada. The most important of these seminaries was the Islamic University in Gaza, established in 1978 as a branch of Cairo's al-Azhar University, one of the oldest and most prestigious Islamic schools in the world. Colleges of Islamic law (*shari'a*) were established that same year in Jerusalem and Hebron.[12] Together, these schools produced many well-educated Muslim clerics who gradually replaced more traditional 'ulama as prayer leaders throughout the West Bank and Gaza.[13] Other manifestations of Muslim institution-building included the birth of a number of charity, or *zakat*, committees in the late 1970s which collected money to distribute to needy Palestinians,[14] the establishment of Islamic nursery, elementary and secondary schools, and the founding of Muslim associations for young men and women in Jerusalem and Gaza.[15]

The two most important Muslim institutions established prior to the Intifada were the Islamic collective (*al-mujamma' al-Islami*) and the Islamist student blocs at Palestinian universities. The Mujamma', established in 1973 by, among others, Shaykh Ahmad Yasin, a leading figure in the Muslim Brethren and later a cofounder of the Hamas movement, quickly became the primary organization of the Islamist movement in Gaza. All other Brethren institutions, including the Islamic University in Gaza City and 40 percent of all mosques in Gaza, came under the Mujamma''s authority.[16] The particular genius of the Mujamma' was to combine religious and social activities, so that the mosque was not only a place of worship but a provider of social services as well. In fact, the Mujamma' (and its offshoots) had a medical clinic, sports club, nursing school, activity rooms for women and girls, and a social gathering hall, in addition to its mosque.[17]

The flourishing of such Islamic institutions was, in part, a response to a similar—and more widespread—process undertaken by PLO factions in the occupied territories, a theme which runs throughout this work. The leadership of the Muslim Brethren saw that the PLO was formulating a policy of grassroots organizing as a means to widen and deepen the resistance to the occupation, and felt that there should be a parallel undertaking to expand the Islamist base.[18] The goal was to establish a viable Islamic alternative to the secular nationalism of the PLO through a process of religiopolitical socialization at all levels of society.

The strength of student Islamic blocs at Palestinian universities reflected the growing power of the Islamist movement in the occupied territories. Paralleling a similar divide in the larger Palestinian community, the student Islamist blocs encompassed two politically different types of Muslims. One genre consisted of socially conservative, quietist Muslims, often from rural areas, with little taste for activist politics. A disproportionate number of female students fell into this category.[19] The second type of student involved with the Islamist movement was more openly activist, was more likely to be from a refugee camp and male, and, in sociological terms, had the same "social profile" as activist colleagues in the local PLO factions. The leadership of the Islamist bloc at Palestinian universities fell into this second category.

Throughout the 1980s, Islamist blocs at Palestinian universities garnered significant support. In fact, in the aftermath of the Iranian revolution, Islamist blocs in the West Bank and Gaza gained control of a number of student councils. For the most part, however, alliances of various nationalist and leftist factions enabled the PLO to maintain its hegemony in West Bank universities while relinquishing authority to the Islamist bloc in Gaza. In effect, while the PLO—in particular, Fatah—remained the dominant political power at most Palestinian universities in the 1980s, the Islamists represented a powerful counterforce or opposition. In each of the three elections at Bir Zeit University which immediately preceded the Intifada, the Islamist bloc received approximately one-third of the total vote, second only to Fatah. In the 1985–86 and 1986–87 academic-year elections at al-Najah University in Nablus, the Islamist bloc won 38 percent and 41 percent of the vote, respectively. In both elections the Islamist bloc finished second to Fatah (which won 49 percent and 48 percent, respectively) but far ahead of the leftist PLO factions. Similar results were seen at Hebron University. At the Islamic University in Gaza, the Muslim Brethren swept every election in the 1980s. In the 1987 election, the Islamists won three-quarters of the total vote, with Fatah gaining most of the remainder. Only at Bethlehem University, with its official ties to the Vatican and large Christian minority, was the Islamist bloc of marginal importance.

In many ways, universities were more important than mosques in the Islamist movement in the occupied territories, principally because the universities had greater autonomy under the occupation.[20] Many mosques were linked to Islamic endowments, or waqfs, the administration of which tied the Muslim establishment more closely to Israeli and Jordanian authorities. The university Islamists, on the other hand, had no material interests fettering them to Israeli or Jordanian concerns, and thus were better able to construct ideologies independent of state interests. Israeli infringement upon Islamist autonomy at Palestinian universities was generally limited to military coercion during the occasional confrontation.

Various public opinion surveys during the 1980s also demonstrated the appeal of the Islamic idea. In a 1986 poll taken by Mohammad Shadid of al-Najah University and Rick Seltzer of Howard University,[21] nearly 30 percent of the Palestinians questioned responded that a future Palestinian state should be based exclusively on Islamic law (shari'a). A similar number of respondents felt that the hypothetical Palestinian state should be based on principles drawn both from the shari'a and Arab nationalism. Thus, nearly 60 percent of the Palestinians surveyed preferred some form of Islamic governance if and when an independent Palestinian state was formed. A secular democratic state, the long-standing formal position of the PLO, received a scant 10 percent, while a democratic (but not necessarily secular) Palestinian state garnered 21 percent.

The survey was not without its ambiguities. Even with such a demonstrably strong Islamist content to the answers, the officially secular and nationalist PLO remained the overwhelming choice as the preferred political leadership for over 72 percent of those surveyed. The authors surmised that a large portion of the 20 percent who refused to answer this question or had no opinion were supporters of Islamic groups. Moreover, in terms of individual leaders, Arafat garnered support from nearly 79 percent of all respondents, far outdistancing all other Palestinian and Arab leaders. Part of the explanation for why the survey showed seemingly contradictory themes—strong support for Islamist political solutions and for the secular PLO—is likely due to the conditions under which the poll was conducted. As the authors admit, recording opinions of people under military occupation is a difficult task at best. Often, those Palestinians asking the questions were viewed as representatives of either Israel or the PLO; thus, there may have been a tendency to give "correct" answers.

This seeming paradox of support for both Islamism and the PLO could be partially resolved by looking at the structure of Fatah, the largest faction within the PLO. A significant number of Islamist activists were affiliated with that organization for many years. As will be discussed, cadres from the Islamic Jihad and Fatah worked together both before and during the Intifada. Moreover, a number of Muslim Brethren members in Gaza who were involved in anti-Israel attacks in the 1950s later became high-ranking officers in Fatah.[22] Thus, unlike other factions in the PLO, Fatah—or, at least, certain members of Fatah, particularly the late Abu Jihad—was not viewed as irrevocably hostile to Islamism.

None of this is to suggest that relations between the PLO and various Islamist organizations were easy in the 1980s. In fact, relations between the two groups were often hostile. In January 1982, all secular groups, including Fatah, signed a statement of national unity which condemned the Muslim Brethren.[23] The single most important basis for coalition-making at Palestinian universities in the early 1980s was to prevent Islamists from taking control of student councils. Those efforts were generally, but not always, successful. Furthermore, there were a number of clashes between PLO activists and Islamists in Gaza in the months immediately preceding the Intifada and again after the first year of the uprising.

The activist variant of the Islamist movement made inroads into the Palestinian community during the 1980s largely because it gained a strong foothold among the intelligentsia: university students and faculty members, artists,[24] and others; that represented a sharp break with earlier generations, when Islamism was generally derided by this stratum as little more than mystification of an essentially political struggle. It was only in the context of the post-1967 Arab world and, in particular, the perceived failures of regimes based on secular ideologies that a "return" to Islam was viewed more in terms of a search for political authenticity than a denial of political consciousness. As noted, modern Islamism is not really a return to anything, but represents a politically new phenomenon.

Significant evidence bolsters the notion that there was a partial Islamization of the intelligentsia, beyond the strong showing of Islamist blocs at Palestinian universities. In the 1984 survey already cited, Shadid found that

> the survey data revealed that the revivalist [i.e., Islamist] trend was more evident among the youth and the college-educated. Of those that said they pray more than they did five years ago 14.7 per cent of the age-group twenty-five to thirty said they did, as compared to 1.6 per cent of those over fifty years of age, 11 per cent of those with college education and 5.1 per cent of the illiterate. This helps to explain why the Muslim Brethren concentrates its recruitment activities on the young and educated.[25]

In addition, the same survey found that while 11 percent of all West Bank and Gaza Palestinian women wore the Islamic shari' dress, 29 percent of female university students did.[26] Thus, university women were nearly three times more likely than other Palestinian women to dress in a way that would be openly identified by others as being sympathetic with the Islamist movement.

Another study, conducted immediately prior to the beginning of the Intifada, confirmed the strength of the Islamist trend among the intelligentsia. In a survey by Iyad Barghouti, 10 percent of the students at al-Najah University in Nablus were polled on their religious and political views.[27] In general, the results of the survey correspond well to what theories of development tell us to expect. That is, the most religious students had less education (i.e., were underclassmen), came from poorer classes and from families with few political activists, and had mothers who never worked outside the home. However, a number of findings do not "fit" well with such theories. For example, after a century of secularization, 71 percent of the male students and 84 percent of the female students usually observed religious occasions.[28] Moreover, students at the College of Science—the same students who scored highest on the tawjihi, a sort of SAT in much of the Arab world—were significantly more religious in their orientation than students in any other college. Perhaps there was a relationship between the certitudes provided by both religion and science.

The various surveys taken by Barghouti, Shadid, Sahliyeh,[29] and others, in addition to student elections at Palestinian universities, showed clearly that a large segment of the student population was strongly Islamist in its orientation. For the most part, these polls registered the existence of a large stratum of traditional, socially conservative Muslims, often from rural areas, whose political values were generally quietist and nonconfrontational in their implementation.

More important, these phenomena, taken together, also point to the emergence of a smaller stratum of activists within the Islamist movement who were increasingly ready to postpone the social Islamization of society until after liberation and immediately confront the occupation. This trend was epitomized by both the emergence of the Islamic Jihad movement and the spring 1988 palace coup within the Society of Muslim Brethren, which resulted in the creation of Hamas. The typical social profile of these Muslim activists paralleled that of the PLO organizers discussed throughout this work, and was centered on the educational experience.

While exceptions were plentiful, the usual social profile of a Palestinian Muslim activist was as follows: a male from middle- or lower-class origins whose father was a laborer (often a construction worker) or peasant (i.e., not from the traditional merchant class), who was part of the first generation in his family to get a university education, and who studied science, engineering, or medicine, not Islamic jurisprudence. The distinction between Palestinians who studied Islamic jurisprudence and those who received an education in more technical, scientific areas is crucial. The former were typically quietist, concentrating on the traditional Muslim Brethren concern of social transformation, while the latter were more likely to be involved in confrontational politics against the occupation.

The only significant difference in the social profiles of Palestinian Islamists and their counterparts elsewhere in the Middle East is that the Palestinian Islamists tended to be from refugee camps, not cities. This distinction is less important than it might seem, as many refugee camps in the West Bank have been absorbed by neighboring cities. The Gaza Strip—little more than contiguous refugee camps—is, in many ways, a large urban sprawl devoid of a real center.

Islamist Groups in the West Bank and Gaza before the Intifada

Of the various Islamist factions present in the occupied territories prior to the Intifada, two stand out in importance: the Muslim Brethren and the Islamic Jihad. The Muslim Brethren has traditionally been the oldest, biggest, and most influential of all Islamist groups in the Middle East, as it clearly was among Palestinians. The Islamic Jihad, which rejected the quietism of the Muslim Brethren, represented the small but growing confrontational nature of Islamist politics in the 1980s and was largely responsible for the onset of the Intifada.

Founded in Egypt in 1928 by Hasan al-Banna, the Society of Muslim

Brethren was, for most of its first half-century, an active opponent of many of the secular state policies adopted in the Arab world, in addition to opposing Western colonialism and Zionism.[30] During this period, the Muslim Brethren was illegal in most countries, especially Egypt, and was often harshly suppressed because of its politics and various assassination attempts. In Egypt, the movement was gradually co-opted by the upper stratum of the merchant class, which, with its amiable ties to the regime, supported the concept of passive social Islamization, not confrontation with the regime. In part as a response to this trend in the Muslim Brethren—strongly encouraged under the leadership of 'Umar al-Tilmisani in the 1970s—more radical Islamist groups formed in Egypt which sought the overthrow of the state and the killing of the state's "apostate" leadership.[31]

Unlike Egypt, Jordan generally tolerated the Muslim Brethren's political activities. In fact, the Muslim Brethren was the only continuously legal political organization in the West Bank when Jordan controlled the area from 1948 to 1967.[32] While under Jordanian authority, the Muslim Brethren generally limited its political activities to its social agenda. That is, it advocated the gradual Islamization of society through education and adherence to Islamic principles, especially those encoded in the shari'a.

The differences between Egyptian and Jordanian policies toward the Muslim Brethren between 1948 and 1967 go a long way toward explaining the disparate state of affairs for the Islamist movement in Gaza and the West Bank under Israeli rule following 1967. The fact that Nasir outlawed the Muslim Brethren gave its activists in Gaza experience in decentralized and clandestine organization-building. In spite of a number of crackdowns by Egyptian authorities, members of the Muslim Brethren successfully carried out a number of armed attacks against Israel in the 1950s. The combination of continued repression by Cairo and the co-optation of Islamic activists by Palestinian nationalist groups sucked the strength out of the Muslim Brethren movement in Gaza by the mid-1960s. A number of the Islamists involved in the planning and implementation of attacks on Israel in the 1950s later became leaders in Fatah when that organization gained hegemony within the Palestinian nationalist movement following the 1967 war.[33]

In contrast to the secretive and militant forms of Islamism in Gaza under Egyptian rule, the lawful status of the Muslim Brethren in the Jordan-annexed West Bank put no premium on clandestine organizational talents. In addition, since Jordan permitted no cross-border violence against Israeli targets, there developed no tradition of armed militancy against Israel in the West Bank, as there did in Gaza.[34] Whereas Gazan Muslim Brethren migrated to Fatah in the late 1960s, West Bank Brethren politically stayed put, as that organization was technically illegal but widely indulged by Israeli authorities. Thus, ties between

Islamist and nationalist organizations in Gaza have historically been very strong, while those ideologically differentiated organizations in the West Bank remained isolated from each other.

In part because of these very different histories and orientations, the Muslim Brethren in Gaza and the West Bank never formed a common organizational link. Even after the two remaining parts of Palestine were reunited under a common military occupation in 1967, the West Bank Brethren members continued to be associated with their colleagues in Jordan, not Gaza, while those in Gaza were generally independent of outside ties. Israel formally banned the Muslim Brethren but generally tolerated—and even supported—its activities.

In spite of both the harshness of military occupation and the persistent rhetorical attacks by nationalists on the seeming ideological acquiescence to the occupation by the Muslim Brethren, the leadership of the Brethren remained committed to the primacy of social Islamization, not confrontation with Israel. For the ideologues of the Muslim Brethren, it was impossible to separate Israel from a larger campaign by the West to discredit and undermine Islam; it was equally impossible to politically differentiate Palestinian Muslims from the greater Islamic world. At base, then, the question of Palestine for the Muslim Brethren was essentially an Islamic problem and had to be addressed in Islamic terms.

The Muslim Brethren believed that Palestine was part of a larger God-given Islamic endowment, or waqf; thus, no human had the right to cede control of any part of such lands to non-Muslims. For these reasons, the Muslim Brethren never distinguished between the parts of Palestine occupied in 1948—Israel proper—and the lands occupied in 1967—the Gaza Strip, the West Bank, and East Jerusalem. In contrast, the PLO after 1973 increasingly differentiated between the 1948 and 1967 lands, a process which was made explicit first in the November 1988 proclamation of a two-state policy and more formally in the 1993 Oslo Accords. The Muslim Brethren rejected what it viewed as an artificial divide between the West Bank and Gaza, on the one hand, and the rest of Palestine.

For the Muslim Brethren, Palestine had been lost in large measure as God's punishment for turning away from Islam. The logical first step in its recovery was for Palestinians to return to Islam, and only after that could Israel be confronted effectively. In fact, any jihad against Israel—which ultimately would be necessary—could not succeed until the people had embraced true Islam. It was for this reason that the Muslim Brethren concentrated its efforts on social and individual transformation and left the political struggle for later. A 1986 content analysis of Islamic literature carried in West Bank bookstores demonstrated that most articles dealt with problems of individual behavior and piety, not political or economic issues.[35]

According to the Muslim Brethren, the longer the nationalists rejected the overriding need to Islamize Palestinian society before any confrontation with Israel, the longer Palestinians would wait for true liberation and the reclamation of the land. The tendency of the PLO to mimic the ideologies and structures of the West, they argued, only undermined the larger struggle between *dar al-Islam*, the abode of Islam, and *dar al-harb*, the house of war—in context, the West. A return to "true Islam" (*al-Islam al-haqiqi*) constituted the only possible solution for the problem of Palestine. The ideology of nationalism was viewed by Islamists as no more than a tactical weapon:

> Nationalism can be used as an instrument to relieve the occupation. However, nationalism has no Islamic justification. Remember, it was ideas of nationalism that led both to the establishment of Israel in 1948 and to the betrayal of Palestine by nationalist Arab regimes.[36]

The ideological struggle between nationalists and the Brethren, as viewed by the latter, was neatly summarized by Shadid:

> The Muslim Brethren strategy is divided into two phases. The first phase would be to transform the society in the West Bank and Gaza into an Islamic society. The second would be to call for jihad (holy struggle) against Israel. During the first phase the primary contradiction is not with the forces of occupation, but with the forces of modernization and secularization that would delay or hinder the process of returning society to Islam. In essence, secularization and the nationalist struggle are posited as the primary contradictions rather than the occupation. The Brethren's strategy has therefore evolved to eliminate these threats; the use of literature, sermons from mosque pulpits and even physical violence is justified as a tool in the conflict with the nationalists.[37]

The relatively passive policies adopted by the Muslim Brethren leadership vis-à-vis Israel's military occupation of the West Bank and Gaza—the Islamization process could go on indefinitely—caused the Brethren to come under intense pressure from the nationalist camp. The Brethren was often ridiculed for its inaction in the face of occupation. Such arguments and pressure were especially intense on university campuses, where classes often split over the issue and student elections frequently centered on the subject. Despite its generally strong showing in university elections, the Islamist bloc was clearly on the ideological defensive throughout the occupied territories in the decade leading up to the Intifada. The sharp attacks by the nationalists on the political implications of Brethren policies increasingly had an impact on student activists within the Islamist movement.

The Islamist movement began to divide along class and ideological lines in the 1980s, a fissure that pitted the old elite of the Muslim Brethren against an activist middle stratum. In terms of social class, the leadership of the Muslim Brethren tended to be urban, upper-middle-class merchants.[38] In addition to being generally more well-to-do than their followers, the leaders of the Muslim Brethren had very close ties—including financial ones—with a number of conservative Arab states, principally Saudi Arabia, Kuwait, and Jordan.

Because of its economic stake in the status quo, the leadership of the Muslim Brethren in the occupied territories could in no way be construed as revolutionary. The Islamist ideology it propagated, unlike, for example, the ideologies of Ayatullah Khomeini, Sayyid Qutb, and Muhammad 'Abd al-Salam Faraj, reflected the Brethren elite's concern with not unduly disrupting the social and political order. Not surprisingly, the leadership of the Brethren constructed various alliances with non-Brethren notables and other wealthy businessmen and came to their defense when the notables were criticized by nationalists for their political inactivity.[39]

Unlike the leadership, many of the members of the Muslim Brethren had poorer, more rural, and conservative backgrounds. These members tended to support Brethren policies.

However, because of the Brethren's recruiting strategies in the 1980s, a middle stratum of activists developed which came to oppose the policies of their leaders. Recruitment focused on high school and college students, schoolteachers, and youths from camps and villages, and tended to stay away from the working classes.[40] The middle activist stratum which developed consisted primarily of university-educated men from lower-middle-class nonmerchant origins. In addition, this stratum was primarily based in refugee camps, domains which were formerly bastions of Arab nationalism.

The ideological fissures within the Islamist movement centered not on ultimate goals, as both sides wanted the establishment of an Islamic state in all of Palestine with strong ties to the larger Islamic world. Rather, the question was one of tactics: whether it was better to free the soul or the nation first. Should the occupation be confronted and rolled back first and society purified later, or was successful confrontation with Israel impossible without a genuine Islamic society being created first? Increasingly in the 1980s, the middle stratum of the Islamist movement chose the former course while the leadership of the Muslim Brethren maintained its long-standing position, which emphasized prior social Islamization. Thus, the fissure separating the two Islamist camps had overlapping class and ideological implications. The fact that the Muslim Brethren was decentralized under Israeli rule, owing to its official banning, allowed both tendencies to prosper and delayed a confrontation, at least until the Intifada began.

The first and most important activist-oriented offshoot of the Muslim Brethren to form was the Islamic Jihad, or *al-Jihad al-Islami*, founded in Gaza in the early 1980s by Shaykh 'Abd al-Aziz 'Awda and Fathi al-

Shaqaqi.[41] The Islamic Jihad differed from the leadership of the Muslim Brethren by advocating immediate confrontation with the Israeli occupation, although the formulation of this line of thought did not fully and clearly emerge until about 1986. Both of the founders had studied at Zaqaziq University in Egypt and were close to the Sayyid Qutb–influenced factions of the Egyptian Muslim Brethren, and both were ultimately deported by Israel from the occupied territories in 1988.

Jihad leaders believed in a dialectical relationship between political power and social piety. Because of the intimate relationship between the struggles to obtain political power and to purify society, they argued, one challenge should not be undertaken in the absence of the other. Therefore, confronting the occupation and Islamizing Palestinian society should be done simultaneously.[42] The fact that Islamic Jihad implemented its ideology through strikes against Israeli targets helped it gain adherents within the Islamist movement and support from Palestinian nationalists and leftists.

Jihad remained politically marginal for several years. The 1985 prisoner exchange between Israel and a Syria-based hardline, non-PLO Palestinian faction led by Ahmad Jibril proved a turning point for Jihad. Israel released approximately 1,000 Palestinian prisoners—650 of whom remained in the occupied territories[43]—in exchange for six Israeli soldiers captured in Lebanon. A number of those released were Jihad activists or persons recruited to Jihad during their prison stays who had the critically important political schooling that comes with any stay in Israeli prisons. The prisoners greatly expanded ties to other groups and activists, shared strategies and experiences with each other, and, generally, grew more hardened in their commitment to overthrow the occupation. It was following the prisoner exchange that Jihad began to call clearly for confrontation with Israel prior to the complete Islamization of Palestinian society.[44]   .

Largely as a result of their learning experiences in prison, Jihad activists began to establish a series of tightly knit and secretive cells throughout the occupied territories, but principally in Gaza.[45] Because of both the conspiratorial nature of Jihad's organizational structures and their members' abilities to evade detection by the Israeli authorities in the sprawling refugee camps which line the Gaza Strip, Jihad was able to carry out a number of attacks on Israeli targets and largely withstand the inevitable crackdowns that followed.

Islamic Jihad was politically closer to the PLO than it was to the Muslim Brethren in the occupied territories. In fact, prior to the Intifada, Jihad was outspoken in its criticism of the Brethren both for its inaction against Israeli occupation and for its rhetorical and physical attacks against Palestinian nationalists.[46] For its part, the Muslim Brethren resented Jihad's bid to undermine its hegemony in the Palestinian

Islamist movement, realizing that both groups were fighting for the sympathies of the same constituency. The battle was for the ideological high ground, not for numbers of members, as the Muslim Brethren was a mass organization and Jihad remained a band of secretive, cell-based Islamist cadres.

Jihad's relations with Fatah were close. A number of Jihad's leaders were previously members of Fatah cells in Gaza, and they retained ties to their former colleagues. In fact, "financial and logistical support" from Fatah to Jihad, especially under the direction of Abu Jihad's office in Amman, were essential in the strengthening of Jihad's operations.[47] When the Intifada broke out in December 1987, the Islamic Jihad repaid Fatah by working closely with the PLO's Unified National Leadership of the Uprising. In the year prior to the Intifada—the year of discontent— Jihad's unprecedented assaults on Israel set the psychological stage for the uprising.

The Year of Discontent

While sporadic attacks against Israeli targets by Jihad militants took place prior to October 1986, the great majority occurred in the fourteen months immediately preceding the Intifada. Because of their audacious nature, the Jihad strikes stirred the imagination of many Palestinians, who had so often been the passive recipients of Israeli violence. More than any other political group, Jihad was responsible for breaking the cognitive barrier of fatalism and demonstrating that Palestinian empowerment against Israel was possible. While the grassroots organization-building occurring in the Palestinian lands in the 1980s was a more important form of self-empowerment in many ways, the brazen assaults by Jihad focused attention on the need for immediately confronting the occupation—a position antithetical to that of the old guard of the Muslim Brethren.

The most famous Jihad strike against an Israeli target took place on October 15, 1986, when militants launched a grenade attack against members of the Givati Brigade, an elite army unit, gathered in front of the Western Wall in the Old City of Jerusalem during an initiation rite for new recruits. The attack came on the heels of the slaying of an Israeli civilian in Gaza by Jihad, and resulted in the death of one soldier, with dozens more injured. A wave of arrests muted Jihad for several months before its next action. In May 1987 Jihad staged a jailbreak from Gaza Prison, which freed, among others, six incarcerated leaders of Islamic Jihad. Large prison escapes had been virtually unknown under Israeli occupation, a fact which only enhanced Jihad's standing in the Palestinian community after this jailbreak. Three months later, Jihad militants assassinated an Israeli military police captain in broad daylight on the main square in central Gaza City. Jihad also claimed credit for an attack on an army patrol in Tel Aviv on November 22, 1987. Finally, just days before the Intifada began, Jihad assassinated another Israeli in Gaza.

While Israel abetted the Muslim Brethren as a tool to undermine the PLO and Palestinian nationalism, the militancy of Islamic Jihad—in deed as well as word—was intolerable to Israeli authorities. Therefore, Israel launched a series of strikes intended to eradicate the group. On October 1, 1987, Israeli forces ambushed a group of Jihad militants, killing three. Five days later, a second ambush took place, which killed four more Jihad members (one Shin Bet officer also died in the exchange of gunfire). The crackdown continued in November, when Israel arrested (and eventually expelled) one of the founders of Jihad, Shaykh 'Abd al-Aziz 'Awda from Gaza.

The Intifada led to an intensification of Israeli efforts to liquidate the Islamic Jihad. Three more Jihad leaders—Dr. Fathi Shaqaqi, Ahmad Hasan Muhanna, and Sa'id Barakat—were expelled in the first thirteen months of the uprising. Three Jihad militants with close ties to Fatah were assassinated, presumably by Israeli agents, in Limassol, Cyprus, on February 2, 1988.[48] Jihad's primary liaison in Fatah, Arafat's number two man, Abu Jihad (Khalil al-Wazir), was killed by Israeli forces in Tunis on April 16, 1988. In addition to the expulsions and assassinations carried out by Israel against the Islamic Jihad, a large number of arrests were made. These actions proved to be near-fatal blows to Jihad, as this organization virtually disappeared from the political scene by the fall of 1988. Occasional leaflets, or bayanat, were later issued in Jihad's name on the "inside"—in the occupied territories—but, for the most part, only its deported leaders remained to speak for the Islamic Jihad.[49]

In spite of its eventual demise, Jihad almost alone engineered the psychological breakthrough necessary for Palestinians to actively confront Israel's continuing occupation of their lands (however these lands were defined). The only other act which similarly electrified the Palestinian public on the eve of the Intifada was carried out by a lone hang-glider from Ahmad Jibril's PFLP-GC. On the night of November 25, 1987, a Palestinian hang-glider crossed the border from Lebanon into Israel undetected, landing astride a military camp. The guerrilla killed six Israeli soldiers before being gunned down himself.

Jihad's ideological break with the leadership of the Muslim Brethren had a strong impact on the middle stratum of that organization. Increasingly, there were calls from within this tier for the Brethren to take a more activist role in the Palestinian resistance. As such, Islamic Jihad acted as a catalyst for the deepening divide within the Muslim Brethren. Both Jihad and the Muslim Brethren claimed to be the authentic leadership of the Muslim community, and both claimed jihad, or struggle, to be a central tenet of their ideology. The difference centered on which

elements of jihad were stressed. While the Brethren leadership continued to emphasize the social and personal struggle for betterment—an
interpretation of jihad which has considerable historical legitimacy—
Islamic Jihad and like-minded Brethren cadres stressed the political and
military aspects of the term.

The debate within the Brethren sharpened considerably when the
Intifada began on December 9, 1987. As Jihad acted, pressures mounted
from within and outside the Brethren to put aside its ideological imperative to purify society prior to any confrontation, and to join the uprising.
The realization grew that, if the Brethren did not join in the Intifada, it
would lose completely its political legitimacy within the Palestinian
community.

The overlapping class and ideological fissures—in addition to mount-
ing social pressures—finally resulted in an internal coup by the middle
stratum of the Muslim Brethren against its leaders. The outcome was the
establishment of the *Harakat al-Muqawima al-Islamiya*, the Islamic Resistance Movement: Hamas.

The Birth of Hamas

When the Intifada began, the Muslim Brethren was strong at the local
level, primarily because of the growth of university-educated cadres
who had spent much of the 1980s expanding grassroots Brethren organizations. The national leadership of the Muslim Brethren, however, was
relatively weak because it was still dominated by the old guard: well-to-
do merchants with ties to Saudi Arabia and Jordan. As was argued
above, the Muslim Brethren leadership and the middle stratum cadres
were divided both by class and ideology.

In essence, the formation of Hamas constituted an internal coup
within the Muslim Brethren which brought the middle-stratum cadres
to the fore of the Palestinian Islamist movement and relegated the old
leadership to a more peripheral position.[50]

Not wanting to be left behind by the Intifada, Muslim Brethren cadres
began mimicking their PLO counterparts by distributing leaflets early in
the uprising.[51] Each bayan would discuss recent events with a particular
ideological bent, call for various political undertakings, and announce
strike days and other actions to undertake in the coming period (usually
about two weeks).

The first bayan to be issued which carried the name Islamic Resis-
tance Movement (but not "Hamas," its Arabic acronym)[52] was dated
February 11, 1988. This leaflet had several interesting features.[53] First, the
Intifada was referred to as a blessed Islamic uprising (*al-Intifada al-
Islamiya al-mubaraka*), as opposed to a national one. Reminiscent of the
historiographical battles fought in Iran over whether its revolution was

Islamic (the official discourse) or Iranian (i.e., nationalist), there was an ongoing struggle in the Palestinian community to give the "official" adjective to the Intifada.[54] Second, whereas Hamas had a strong irredentist flavor to its ideology—all of Palestine, not just the West Bank and Gaza, was the stated goal—this first bayan praised Palestinians for their struggles in "all the occupied lands," but then specifically mentioned only those "in Jerusalem, in Ramallah and Nablus, in Tulkarim and Jenin, in Hebron and Gaza, and in all of the villages and [refugee] camps." All of these places are in the West Bank and Gaza, not Israel proper. Third, the bayan ended with the phrase "Khaybir's time has arrived" (qad hanat Khaybir), a reference to a Jewish tribe in the Arabian peninsula which was defeated by the Prophet Muhammad's forces and ultimately expelled by a successor to Muhammad, Caliph 'Umar. The story has come to symbolize "Jewish submission to Islamic rule as long as they accepted it or of their expulsion if they did not."[55]

Hamas began in Gaza, not the West Bank, because the old elite of the Muslim Brethren was principally centered in the West Bank, and thus had more ability to delay and, initially, diminish the rise to leadership of the middle-stratum cadres. The West Bank leadership had strong ties to Jordan—where the Muslim Brethren remained legal and reformist, not revolutionary. In fact, the Muslim Brethren in the West Bank and Jordan constituted a single organization, a vestige of the pre-1967 period. The Muslim Brethren leadership in Gaza, principally Shaykh Ahmad Yasin, did not have a larger organizational link outside of Gaza and was freer to formulate independent policies. Moreover, the Gazan leadership of the Muslim Brethren had class origins much closer to those of the middle-stratum cadres than its West Bank counterparts, making the disruption of the status quo by these "have-nots" more palatable.

While Shaykh Ahmad Yasin was generally considered the leader of Hamas, at least until his arrest and imprisonment, he was not the driving force behind Hamas. Rather, he was a well-respected leader of the Muslim Brethren who was sympathetic to the demands of the middle-stratum cadres to implement jihad against the Israeli occupiers. More important, Yasin gave the cadres a respected titular leader who carried political weight within the larger community, thus expanding the legitimacy and appeal of the rebelling cadres. Yasin, a disabled religious man, had played a large role in the organization-building that dominated Palestinian political life in the 1980s. He was president of the central Islamist collective (Mujamma') in Gaza when he was arrested by Israeli officials in 1984 for having an arms cache. Thus, while it is too simplistic to describe Yasin as merely a front man for Islamist militants within the Muslim Brethren, it would be equally misleading to ascribe preeminent political importance to him.[56]

Even though a number of leaflets signed by the Islamic Resistance Movement appeared in the early months of the Intifada, Hamas was not

"officially" established until August 1988, when it published its covenant (*mithaq*). The covenant is a remarkable document in that it contains many of the ideological ambiguities and contradictions which have
plagued the Islamist movement in Palestine, including the proper response to Palestinian nationalism and nationalist organizations, the
question of political activism versus social transformation, and the role
women should play in the struggle.

The basis of Hamas's claim that not one inch of Palestine can be ceded
to Israel (or any other non-Muslim entity) parallels the argument long
made by the Muslim Brethren: that Palestine is Islamic waqf land, held
in trust for all Muslims.[57] By defining Palestine as waqf, Hamas argued
that Palestine is an inseparable whole, which no temporal being has the
authority to divide (article 11):

> The Islamic Resistance Movement believes that the land of Palestine is an
> Islamic waqf consecrated for future Muslim generations until Judgment
> Day. It, or any part of it, should neither be squandered nor relinquished.
> No Arab country, no king or president, no organization—Palestinian or
> Arab—possesses that right. Palestine is Islamic waqf land consecrated for
> Muslim generations until Judgment Day. This being so, who could claim to
> have the right to represent Muslim generations until Judgment Day?

Palestinian Islamist symbolism had taken on considerable nationalist
overtones in the years leading up to the Intifada, and the Hamas covenant reflected this. Still, the Hamas ideologues also recognized that
nationalist discourse was inherently contradictory to many of the underlying assumptions of Islamism. This ambiguity was manifested in the
covenant. Much of it praised the legitimate role that nationalism has
played in the Palestinian struggle (articles 12 and 14):

> Nationalism,[58] from the point of view of the Islamic Resistance Movement,
> is part of our religion. Nothing in nationalism is more significant or
> important than waging jihad when an enemy treads on Muslim land.
> While other nationalisms are concerned just with material, human, and
> territorial causes, the nationalism of the Islamic Movement has all this in
> addition to the more important divine qualities that give it soul and life.
> The question of the liberation of Palestine is bound to three circles: the
> Palestinian circle, the Arab circle, and the Islamic circle. Each of these
> circles has its role in the struggle against Zionism.

Parallel with its acceptance of nationalism, Hamas also gave due
credit to organizations that espoused nationalism, principally the PLO
(articles 25 and 27):

> The Islamic Resistance Movement respects the Palestinian nationalist
> movements and appreciates their circumstances and the conditions sur-
> rounding and affecting them. It encourages them as long as they do not
> give their allegiance to the Communist East or the Crusading West. The
> Movement assures all the nationalist trends operating in the Palestinian

arena for the liberation of Palestine, that it is there for their support and assistance. The Palestine Liberation Organization is close to the heart of the Islamic Resistance Movement. The PLO counts among its members our fathers, our brothers, our cousins, and our friends, and the Muslim does not estrange himself from his father, brother, cousin, or friend. Our homeland is one, our situation is one, our fate is one, and the enemy is a joint enemy to all of us.

However, Hamas argued that the PLO adopted a secular, nationalist ideology not through informed choice but rather because of "the ideological confusion prevailing in the Arab world as a result of the ideological invasion under whose influence the Arab world has fallen since the defeat of the Crusaders" (article 27). It was only because of the purposeful confusion perpetrated by "Orientalists, missionaries, and imperialists that the PLO adopted the idea of the secular state." While such misperceptions by the PLO can be understood in their historical context, article 27 continued, they cannot be reconciled with the true nature of Islamic Palestine:

> Secularism completely contradicts religious ideology in its attitudes, conduct, and decisions. That is why, with all our appreciation for the Palestine Liberation Organization—and what it can develop into—and without belittling its role in the Arab-Israeli conflict, we are unable to reconcile Islamic Palestine and secularism. The Islamic nature of Palestine is part of our religion. The day the Palestine Liberation Organization adopts Islam as its way of life, we will become its soldiers, and fuel for its fire that will burn our enemies. Until such a day, and we pray that it will be soon, the Islamic Resistance Movement's stand toward the PLO is that of a son toward his father, a brother toward his brother, a cousin toward his cousin: we will suffer his pain and support him in confronting our enemies, wishing him to be wise and well-guided.

Moreover, Hamas addressed the issue for which it had been most criticized by Palestinian political activists, arguing that confrontation with the occupation can be accomplished at the same time as the Islamization of Palestinian society. Hamas stressed that it is "a fighting movement" (article 25) committed to struggle with Israel:

> Leaving the circle of struggle against Zionism is high treason, and all who do so are damned. There is no other way than to concentrate all our powers and energies to face this vicious Nazi and Tatar invasion. The alternative is loss of one's country, the dispersion of its citizens, the spread of vice, and the destruction of religion. The Islamic Resistance Movement considers itself to be the preeminent actor in the circle of struggle with world Zionism. (Article 32)

> There is no solution for the Palestinian question except through jihad. Initiatives, proposals, and international conferences are all a waste of time

and have no hope of success. Since this is the case, the liberation of Palestine is an individual duty for every Muslim wherever he may be. The day our enemies usurp Muslim land, jihad becomes the individual duty of every Muslim. In the face of the Jews' usurpation of Palestine, it is necessary that the banner of jihad be raised. (Articles 13–15)

Yet Hamas was quick to remind its followers that the struggle was not limited to direct confrontation with Israel (articles 30 and 15):

Jihad is not confined to carrying arms and confronting the enemy. The effective word, the good article, the useful book, support and solidarity— all these are elements of jihad. [Jihad] requires the diffusion of Islamic consciousness among the masses, on the regional, Arab, and Muslim levels. It is necessary to instill the spirit of jihad in the heart of the nation.

To emphasize the necessity of social Islamization which should parallel direct action against Israel, Hamas devoted the entirety of article 16 to the means by which a proper Islamic education should be achieved, emphasizing the study of the Qur'an, Muhammad's teachings, and Islamic history and heritage. In addition, Hamas called for students to undertake "a comprehensive study of the enemy, his human and financial capabilities, learning about his points of weakness and strength, and the forces supporting and helping him."

Hamas likewise sent a mixed message regarding the role of women in the struggle against Israel. In article 12, Hamas forthrightly stated that "resisting and quelling the enemy has become the individual duty of every Muslim, male or female. A woman can go out and fight the enemy without her husband's permission." However, in articles 17 and 18, devoted exclusively to the role of women in the conflict, Hamas took the more traditional view that the woman should do her part at home, not in the street, by imparting proper Islamic values to the young. Interestingly, the basis for the argument that women should do their bit at home was not because God willed that it should be so. Rather, the argument was surprisingly utilitarian: that this division of labor maximized the chances for liberating Palestine. For example, when Hamas called on women to, in effect, run the household, it was because household "economy and avoidance of waste in the family budget are requirements in our ability to continue moving forward in the difficult conditions which surround us."

As I have argued, the creation of Hamas represented a revolt by the Muslim Brethren's second-stratum cadres against the Brethren's traditional leadership, a revolt which had both class and ideological overtones. However, Hamas took pains in its covenant not to burn any political bridges, heaping praise on the Brethren and, in fact, calling itself a wing of that organization. In this regard, the covenant turned out to be both a truce between the cadres and the old guard and a brilliant political stroke. Since Hamas claimed to be a wing—but only a wing—of the Muslim Brethren, the Brethren could always disown or discredit Hamas without itself being discredited if the Intifada went badly. This arrangement pleased both the conservatives who stayed in the Brethren and the cadres who formed Hamas, as it led to greater room for political maneuvering for each without a complete divorce.

The views expressed by Hamas in its covenant did not change significantly over the course of the Intifada. Indeed, such ideas were reiterated on a number of occasions by Hamas spokesmen. For example, in an interview given to the Israeli daily *HaAretz* in 1991, Dr. Mahmud al-Zahhar, a leading Hamas figure in Gaza, rejected Israel, criticized Palestinian nationalism, and charged the PLO with corruption.[59] When asked by his Israeli interlocutor if there was any legitimate basis for the establishment of the state of Israel, Zahhar responded:

> If you try to justify the existence of the state by the right of the Jews to return to their homeland, I will ask: Why the right of return to Palestine, and not Spain, for example? I am willing to accept your right of return here after 2,000 years, but then you will have to accept the Palestinian right to return after forty years. The right of return is not a practical argument, because this would raise questions by Australian and American natives, and the whole world would change. The other argument for the establishment of the state could be Jewish suffering. [However,] we are the ones who suffered from the hands of Israel, though we have not carried out any crime against the Jews.

When the *HaAretz* correspondent, Gid'on Levi, questioned "the point of this whole discussion" because "the state of Israel is an irreversible thing," Zahhar replied:

> Who said there is anything irreversible? Only time is irreversible. Nations have come and gone. All issues must be put on the negotiating table. You should remember that you will not be sitting alone at that table. Who, for example, appointed you to select the Palestinian delegation for the negotiations?[60] By the same token, you cannot determine the issues of discussion. Yes, we want to talk about Haifa, Jaffa, and Ramla [predominantly Palestinian cities prior to 1948; now part of Israel proper].

While arguing for the illegitimacy of Israel, Zahhar also heaped scorn on recent Palestinian and Arab national historiography:

> The Palestinians have always been part of a pan-Islamic country. Never in history has there been a state called Palestine, nor were there Syria or Iraq. The borders of the various Arab countries are not ours; they were determined by France and Britain. [Gamal] 'Abd al-Nasir tried to establish a pan-Arab state his way, the secular way, and failed. Now we want to try our way.

Finally, Zahhar condemned the "corruption in the PLO, and [its] misuse of funds," arguing that the PLO collects money in the name of the Palestinian people but then uses it to reward its political friends and punish its political adversaries in the Palestinian community. He concluded his critique of the PLO's strategy by suggesting that if the PLO is unable to get the United States to pressure Israel to at least freeze settlement building in the occupied territories, how can one possibly expect more substantive concessions down the road? "Anyone can see the failure of the secular method." Zahhar was eventually forced into exile by Israel for a year beginning in December 1992.

The Struggle for the Soul of the Intifada

If the two primary fronts in the Intifada were the struggles against Israeli occupation and the notable political elite, then the tertiary front was the Islamists' drive to displace Palestinian nationalists as the hegemonic power—and ideological leaders—in the West Bank and Gaza. The stakes in this struggle were high, reflecting competing Palestinian historiographies and the nature of Palestinian political discourse.

The Islamist movement in the occupied territories had to endeavor to overcome its reputation for cooperating with Israeli occupation authorities. Both before and during the Intifada, Israel supported the Islamist camp as a counterweight to the PLO, believing that the nationalists represented a greater threat to Israeli interests and security. While a number of observers, including the former Israel Defense Forces commander in Gaza, Zvi Poleg, claim that Israel "created" Hamas, such a claim is undoubtedly an exaggeration.[61] Rather, such support came in different forms, but the most important was the political and social space afforded the Islamists that was denied Palestinian nationalists.[62] The Brethren could organize, demonstrate, and speak with little fear of arrest while their nationalist colleagues were punished for similar actions.

Israel's promotion of the Islamist movement as an alternative to the PLO continued during the early part of the Intifada. For example, while the state-controlled Israel Television gave frequent interviews to Islamist leaders during this period, it rarely interviewed nationalist figures.[63] At one point, the IDF helped to enforce a Hamas strike.[64]

Indeed, Israel did not outlaw Hamas until September 28, 1989, nearly two years into the Intifada. In spite of a number of acts of violence for which Hamas members were responsible (they were later convicted), Israeli authorities believed that keeping Hamas legal, if somewhat contained, was preferable to outlawing the organization. This was particularly ironic because, as its own covenant argued, Hamas was an arm of the Muslim Brethren, itself an illegal organization, and had as its goal the destruction of Israel. Israel's change of heart in September 1989 most likely resulted from the fact that Hamas members were increasingly acting on the ideological impulse of its breakaway leaders: that confrontation with the occupation could not wait until societal purification.

Even after the initial 1989 crackdowns on Hamas—which included the arrest of hundreds of Hamas activists, including Shaykh Yasin—tacit Israeli support for the Islamist movement continued for another three years. In a lead editorial entitled "A Historic Mistake," the Israeli newspaper *Hadashot* decried in November 1991 Israel's promotion of the Islamist movement.[65] While the IDF broke up peaceful demonstrations by Palestinians carrying olive branches celebrating the Madrid conference, *Hadashot* reported,

> IDF and Israel police were clearly seen looking the other way when the religious elements rioted against the secular population. Weddings and parties were crashed and shops that carried alcohol were set on fire. In most cases, no one was detained. When construction permits were hardly issued in the West Bank, the Mujamma' built hundreds of mosques where they preached the tradition of the Muslim Brethren.

Israeli support for the Islamist movement did not go unnoticed in the Palestinian community. Even on the eve of the mass arrests and expulsions by Israel of alleged Hamas activists in late 1992, perceptions of collusion persisted. A local leaflet disseminated by PLO activists in November 1992 accused Hamas of complicity in the arrest of "dozens of fighters belonging to the nationalist forces." The leaflet concluded by charging that Hamas activists were "merely misguided provocateurs" and that "many questions crop up about the real reasons that the occupation authorities do not arrest Hamas people or even lay a finger on them on the West Bank and in Jerusalem, but go out of their way to detain fighters from the nationalist movement."[66]

Both the Israelis and the Islamists had their reasons for establishing such an intimate relationship with each other, although the common theme for each was hostility to Palestinian nationalism. For Israel, the Islamist movement represented the best tool to undermine support for the PLO, the largest and strongest political body in the occupied territories. Thus, by supporting the Islamist movement and helping to fragment Palestinian society, Israel was able to more easily maintain social control.

For their part, the Islamists benefited from Israeli assistance in their drive to undermine the PLO and push their own agenda in its place. There was clearly no ideological love lost between Palestinian Islamists and Israel. As the Hamas covenant and various leaflets pointed out, Hamas took an irredentist position on the conflict: not one inch of Palestine could be relinquished. Thus, the cooperation Hamas received from Israel must be considered tactical. In any case, much of this help was not sought by Hamas and was in a form that Hamas could not refuse: space. That Israel refused to outlaw Hamas for nearly two years, or failed to stop anti-PLO violence, or even helped enforce Hamas strikes, cannot be considered decisions taken by Hamas. Thus, Hamas activists could argue, with some justification, that they did not willingly conspire with Israeli authorities.

In fact, some Hamas officials were relatively open about the Israeli connection. In an interview, Muhammad Nazzal, the Hamas representative in Jordan, objected to the idea that Israel "created" Hamas, but admitted that Hamas was given more room to grow than the PLO. He went on to note that Israel was "playing the game of politics, trying to play off groups. But this does not make us its agents. The Israeli mentality is security first, before politics and everything else. It thought its security was enhanced by allowing us to grow, without thinking what might happen down the road."[67]

If Israel did indeed intend to strengthen Hamas at the expense of the PLO, then it created a monster. Successive Israeli crackdowns on Hamas enhanced the credibility of this organization within Palestinian society, helping it to overcome its "tainted" history. As more Islamists were arrested, imprisoned, and put on trial for acts of violence against Israeli targets, the Israeli connection was forgotten or deemed unimportant by most Palestinians. The political bona fides of Hamas—even in the eyes of many nationalists—grew stronger each year.

The real turning point in the relationship between Hamas and the PLO came in November 1988, when the PLO formally accepted a two-state solution to the question of Palestine, explicitly accepting the permanence of the state of Israel. Hamas rejected the PLO's compromise and, from that point on, sought to present itself as a real alternative to the PLO. The widening gap between Hamas and the PLO was reflected on the street in a number of ways, including enhanced competition over commercial strike days. During the first nine months of the Intifada, Hamas only occasionally called for strike days independent of those determined by the UNLU. The strikes that were called by Hamas during that time were observed only in Gaza. Hamas's first successful strike in the West Bank did not come until August 21, 1988, and even then was marred by a number of confrontations between Islamists and PLO activists who did not want the Hamas strike honored.[68]

After the first year or so of the Intifada, virtually all Hamas strikes (as well as UNLU ones) were observed throughout the occupied territories. Resentment and confrontations did occur in the West Bank over some strikes called by Hamas, particularly when they were called on Christian holidays. For example, Hamas called for a strike on Christmas Day, 1989, which resulted in severe criticism from the small Christian community. For the most part, however, even resented strike days were observed, as the penalty for openly disobeying a called strike ranged from a warning to a beating to the destruction of the offending store and its contents.[69] Hamas, like the UNLU, had to be realistic in the number of strike days called or risk criticism and disobedience. On several occasions Hamas rescinded a planned strike day after public protests concerning the number of strike days in a single week. For example, in March 1990, Hamas called for a strike day but canceled it after widespread protests (the UNLU and Islamic Jihad had already called for strikes that week).[70] Also, in response to public pressure, Hamas cooperated with the UNLU in the easing of strike hours announced in bayan 81 (issued April 3, 1992).[71]

Hamas sometimes tried to find clever means to assert its authority while undermining the PLO-affiliated UNLU. For example, UNLU leaflet 45, issued on September 5, 1989, called for a one-minute period of silence and cessation of activity at 10:00 A.M. on September 17, 1989. At that time, all Palestinians were to stop what they were doing and stand still and silent. This type of nonviolent civil disobedience was a common theme in the UNLU leaflets (although not in the Hamas ones). Not wanting the UNLU's ploy to succeed, Hamas then called for a full commercial strike on September 17, effectively clearing the streets of all Palestinians and making the moment of silence inoperable. In fact, in the commercial district of East Jerusalem, there were as many photographers as there were Palestinians on the streets. A local merchant sympathetic to Hamas explained that the UNLU's call was against the tenets of Islam, as complete stillness and quiet were reserved for God alone.[72] More likely, the question was not one of religiosity but of political power.

The choice of strike days reflected the changing historiography and policies of the PLO and Hamas's response to the changes. After the PLO's acceptance in November 1988 of the 1947 United Nations Security Council Resolution partitioning Palestine (UNSCR 181) into Jewish and Arab states—a resolution long anathema to Palestinians—the PLO no longer officially viewed the resolution's passage date as one of mourning and betrayal. Thus, the UNLU did not call for a commercial strike or any other act of protest for November 29, 1989, the forty-second anniversary of the partition.[73] Not accepting the principle of partition, Hamas rejected the PLO's new policy, once again called for jihad to liberate all of Palestine, and announced a strike for November 29. The occupied territories were effectively closed down on that date, as Hamas's strike call was widely observed.[74] Similarly, once the PLO formally accepted partition, it ceased calling for strikes and other forms of rebellion on the anniversary of Israel's 1948 declaration of independence. Hamas would have none of it, and continued to shut down the occupied territories in protest of the declaration.[75]

Events in the year preceding the Oslo Accords showed even more clearly the enhanced power of Hamas and the inroads it was making against the PLO. In response both to harsh measures implemented in the occupied territories after the formation of the Rabin government in July 1992 and to the increased possibility of a diplomatic breakthrough that fall (Rabin had promised an agreement on autonomy within six to nine months of being elected prime minister), Hamas stepped up its attacks on Israeli military and police forces in the West Bank and Gaza. Violence peaked in the week centering on the fifth anniversary of the start of the Intifada. On December 7, Hamas militants killed three IDF soldiers who were on patrol in Gaza. Five days later another soldier was gunned down in a carbon copy attack in Hebron. The day before, on December 11, Issam Barahma, a wanted militant from Islamic Jihad, engaged Israeli soldiers in a gun battle—in which antitank missiles were fired at Barahma—which left Barahma and an Israeli soldier dead and several soldiers wounded. In the most brazen assault during this period, Hamas activists of the relatively new Iz al-Din al-Qassam brigades (the military wing of Hamas, formed in 1990 and named after an Islamist hero killed by the British in Palestine in 1935) kidnapped Nissim Toledano, a member of a Border Police unit which served in the West Bank. Unusually, the kidnapping took place inside Israel proper. After the kidnappers' demand that Hamas leader Ahmad Yassin be set free was rejected, Toledano was killed.

In response to the increased militancy of the Islamist movement, Rabin ordered the biggest crackdown on Hamas since 1989. In a massive sweep, 1,600 alleged Islamist militants were detained in a forty-eight-hour period. In the midst of this campaign, Toledano's body was discovered. Rabin then mandated the expulsion to Lebanon for two years of over 400 Islamists from the West Bank and Gaza, believing such a huge expulsion would break the back of the Islamist movement by decapitating its political head.[76]

The social profiles of those expelled reflect the general political sociology of Islamist cadres noted at the outset of this chapter.[77] As a whole, the expellees were very well educated, with almost half having university degrees or similar diplomas and a smaller number having advanced degrees (the Islamic University in Gaza alone "contributed" its acting president and sixteen faculty members). Indeed, nearly a quarter of the expellees were current faculty, staff, or students enrolled at Palestinian universities. Islamists rarely come from those trained in Islamic jurisprudence; in this case, the 'ulama accounted for only 8 percent of the expellees, numbering fewer than the clerks expelled. The Islamists did not come from the lowest ranks of society: virtually none of the expellees were unemployed or were peasants or farmers. Most were young, with 85 percent in their twenties or thirties. Most of those expelled hailed from cities or large towns, almost a quarter resided in refugee camps, and almost none came from villages. About two-thirds of the expellees came from the West Bank, while Gaza City had the largest share of any town. Many of the leading intellectuals of the Islamist movement were expelled.[78]

In sum, from the creation of Hamas in 1988 to the signing of the Oslo Accords in September 1993, the Islamist movement challenged the PLO for leadership of the Palestinian community and of the Intifada. In spite of its efforts to displace the PLO, however, Hamas did not succeed in gaining political hegemony in Palestine; it remained a potent but minority opposition to the PLO. As discussed in the next section, the relative power balance between Hamas and the PLO—primarily Fatah—remained intact two years after Oslo, in spite of the dramatic wave of terrorist attacks that the Islamists carried out during that period. Hamas had become an umbrella organization which combined cadre activists— the second stratum already discussed—with many other general supporters. In fact, much of Hamas's popular base after Oslo was derivative; that is, it came from among Palestinians who were disillusioned with the accords or their implementation but were not necessarily "true believers."

Symbolic Convergence between Fatah and Hamas

While the rivalry between Hamas and the PLO was real, it would be incorrect to portray their relationship as irrevocably hostile. As noted, Hamas paid a degree of homage to the PLO in its covenant, as it did (to a lesser degree) in its periodic leaflets. The PLO, through the UNLU, generally ignored Hamas in its leaflets, but would occasionally comment on a Hamas activity. For example, in bayan 29 (November 20, 1988), the UNLU criticized Hamas for its call for a three-day continuous strike in Hebron and asked for that call to be rescinded. Conversely, after a series of attacks against Palestinian women in the West Bank—done "under the guise of religion," presumably for "immodest dress"—was condemned by Hamas, the UNLU praised Hamas's action.[79] On a number of occasions after sometimes violent confrontations between Hamas supporters and their counterparts in the PLO, leaders of each camp publicly met in a display of unity. On at least one occasion, in 1990, Israeli troops forcibly prevented a unity meeting in Tulkarim between leaders of Hamas and Fatah, a meeting that had been called to ease tensions between the two groups and to agree on a common strategy.

In a bizarre relationship built more on common tactics than ideological affinity, Hamas and the Marxist PFLP sometimes worked together and occasionally publicly defended each other, particularly after November 1988. The basis of the relationship was their common rejection of the PLO "peace offensive" based on a two-state solution. For Hamas, the rejection was a matter of principle. The PFLP's rejection was more tactical, as it had stated its willingness to come to terms with Israel on a number of occasions. Instead, the PFLP rejected the usual terms of the negotiations (beginning with Israel's April 1989 "peace plan"), which formally banned the PLO, ignored the Palestinian Diaspora, excluded East Jerusalem, and were overseen by Israel's closest ally, the United States.

The oppositional alliances of the PFLP and Hamas strengthened—to the dismay of many in the PFLP opposed to any cooperation with Hamas—after the September 1993 agreement, when these two factions constituted the backbone of the ten "rejectionist" groups based in Damascus. While Oslo and subsequent agreements were based on Israeli recognition of the PLO, which the PFLP had long demanded, the PFLP continued to reject the Oslo process as unjust. In any case, whatever the rationale which led to the PFLP-Hamas working relationship, it is hard to imagine stranger bedfellows.

On a deeper level, there was a growing symbolic convergence between the Islamist movement and Fatah, which belied their often hostile rhetoric and occasional clashes. As noted, Islamic Jihad worked closely with Fatah both before and during the uprising (especially before November 1988). In addition, many senior leaders of Fatah outside the occupied territories had been members of the Muslim Brethren in the 1950s and remained sympathetic with that movement. The increasing convergence between Fatah and Hamas during the uprising was best seen in the use of symbols.

In effect, the Intifada produced a growing Islamization of Fatah and a nationalization of Hamas. Fatah's change in symbolism to a more Islamic flavor could be seen in several areas. First, over the objections of the secular wings of the PLO, Fatah inscribed the common Islamic phrase "In the Name of God, the Merciful and the Compassionate" (*bismillah al-rahman al-rahim*) over the Palestinian declaration of independence of November 15, 1988. While the text of the declaration was replete with secular and national symbols, it ended with a verse from the Qur'an, again to the dismay of activists from the left wing of the PLO. In addition, a large number of the leaflets published by the UNLU began with the same phrase, "In the Name of God." Fatah was clearly trying to strengthen its religious wing against any drift of its members toward its largest competitor, Hamas.

Likewise, activists from Hamas increasingly mixed national and Islamic symbols, even before the group was officially established. As Schiff and Ya'ari note,

> a slow process of "Palestinization" had been at work in the [Islamic] movement, shifting its accent from the broader scope of the "Islamic

nation"and the "community of believers" onto the more narrow concerns of Palestinian nationalism. Some two months before the [Intifada began], Yasin had allowed his people to use the term "national products"at a fair of locally produced merchandise. This was a signal departure, for traditionally he had ruled out any usage that detracted from the inclusiveness of Islam, and he would only distinguish between "believers" and "infidels."[80]

Such concessions to national symbolism became much more pronounced once the Intifada began. The serialized Hamas leaflets would regularly integrate Islamic and national symbols, defining the struggle at one moment as one between Muslims and Jews and at the next moment as one between Palestine and Israel. References to Muslims and the Islamic 'umma, or greater Muslim community, were freely interspersed with mentions of Palestinians and Arabs. Perhaps the greatest indication of the mix between national and Islamic symbolism by Hamas was the widespread use of the Palestinian flag—a national symbol—in its posters and graffiti, often with Qur'anic phrases superimposed. A good example of this dual symbolism was found on a Hamas poster issued in Hebron during the Intifada commemorating the "Martyrs of Hebron" (shuhada' al-Khalil).[81] The Qur'anic symbols incorporated included the phrase "In the Name of God"at the top of the poster, a Qur'an at the bottom, a flag with the Islamic shahada,[82] a picture of the tomb of Ibrahim (or Abraham, Hebron's most famous religious marker for Islam as well as Christianity and Judaism), and the frequent use of the word martyr (shahid).[83] The national symbols employed in the poster included a map of the entirety of Palestine outlined with the colors of the Palestine flag, as well as a separate flag of Palestine. Interestingly, the poster also carried pictures of the "martyrs,"a practice often considered un-Islamic, and listed the dates of death in the Gregorian (i.e., Christian) calendar, not the commonly used Hijra (i.e., Islamic) calendar.

The increasing symbolic convergence between Fatah and Hamas did not lead to friendly relations between the cadres of each. Perhaps in part because Fatah and Hamas were the main competitors for political power within the Palestinian community—with Fatah having the upper hand and Hamas there to step in if Fatah stumbled badly—factional relations were often tense. Thus, even as the parameters of their political discourse narrowed, the relationship on the street between Hamas and Fatah activists was often hostile.

The Islamist Movement and the PLO's "Peace Offensive"

The importance of the nineteenth session of the Palestine National Council, held in Algiers in November 1988, is difficult to overstate.

During this session the PNC (in effect, a Palestinian parliament in exile and the governing body of the PLO) formally adopted U.N. resolutions 181, 242, and 338, among others, explicitly recognizing Israel's existence and its permanence within its pre-1967 boundaries. The PNC called for Israel's withdrawal from the territory it occupied in the 1967 war (the West Bank, East Jerusalem, Gaza, and the Syrian Golan Heights) and for the establishment of a Palestinian state next to Israel. The debate over these resolutions was heated, with the PFLP arguing against their adoption. While the PFLP voted against the resolutions, it committed itself to abiding by the decisions of the council. The other major factions voted for the new policies.

The PLO's change of course had a profound impact on the Islamist movement in the occupied territories.[84] The repercussions from these new policies, widely anticipated in the weeks preceding the conference, were felt even before the PNC met. In October 1988, Islamic Jihad, which had been virtually eliminated by earlier Israeli reprisals, announced that it was breaking from its tacit alliance with the PLO and called for a resumption of armed struggle in direct violation of UNLU directives that the Intifada be unarmed. Then, while PNC delegates were debating the policy changes in Algiers, Jihad issued a leaflet harshly critical of the PNC's impending acceptance of the principle of the partition of Palestine:

> Oh masses of our Palestinian Muslim people! The Movement of the Islamic Jihad in Palestine proclaims in your name, in the name of your struggle, in the name of your sacrifices, that that peace is sacrilegious, that that commitment is null and illicit, that the partition of the homeland with the enemy and the recognition of its legitimacy go against the divine order.[85]

Hamas likewise repudiated the PNC's imminent acceptance of Israel, and sent an appeal to Algiers:

> The Islamic Resistance Movement (Hamas) has committed itself to [a] comprehensive jihad until the liberation of the whole of Palestine. We condemn all the attitudes calling for ending jihad and struggle, and for establishing peace with the murderers, and the attitudes which call for the acceptance of the Jewish entity on any part of our land. Our people offered sacrifices to protect the pride and dignity of the nation and to destroy the cancerous Jewish entity, which tries to spread its hegemony over our area. We believe that Palestine belongs to the Muslim generations until the Day of Judgment.[86]

Hamas followed up its appeal to the PNC by issuing a leaflet within the occupied territories on November 25, 1988, once again rejecting the PLO's two-state solution.[87] In this bayan, Hamas referred to partition as "a dark idea" which had plagued Palestinians ever since the 1937 Peel

Commission Report proposed partition as the optimal solution to the problem of Palestine.[88] Much of the rest of the leaflet constituted an Islamist historiography of the Palestine question, harshly criticizing both Israeli acts (e.g., the 1967 war, the 1981 bombing of the nuclear reactor in Baghdad, the bombardment of PLO headquarters in Tunis, and the assassination of Abu Jihad) and the capitulation of Arab leaders, principally Anwar al-Sadat, to Israel. Part of the failure to liberate Palestine, Hamas argued, comes as a result of the continuing attack on Islam by Arab regimes, which persist in "waging war against, imprisoning and killing" Islamist activists.

Following the 1988 PNC meeting in Algiers, the political differences between Palestinian factions became more pronounced. Factions pursuing a negotiated settlement which would represent, at base, a two-state solution were Fatah, the PCP, and the 'Abd Rabbu faction of the DFLP, while those that rejected partition were the Islamist groups, the PFLP, and the Hawatma faction of the DFLP.[89] As the Intifada wore on, each grouping became more committed to its own solutions. Thus, once the PNC decision was made, each faction acted in the diplomatic arena in a manner consistent with the position it adopted in November 1988.[90]

Under pressure from Washington to respond diplomatically to the Intifada, Israeli Prime Minister Yitzhaq Shamir unveiled his April 1989 political initiative days before he was due to arrive in the United States. The Shamir plan eventually evolved into a "ten-point" plan advocated by Hosni Mubarak of Egypt, then into U.S. Secretary of State James Baker's "five-point" plan. The PLO, in particular Fatah, gave its blessing to the proposed Cairo negotiations between Israel, Palestinians, Egypt, and the United States, even though the PLO *qua* PLO was explicitly excluded from the negotiations.

Hamas issued a leaflet in October 1989 "rejecting all political initiatives to resolve the Palestinian problem, specifically the five points of Secretary of State Baker."[91] Refusing to take no for an answer, Egypt and the United States pushed Hamas to join the discussions as part of the Palestinian team. Certain Hamas leaders gave a conditional acceptance of the proposal, provided that Hamas be given approximately one-third of the team's delegates.[92] Shortly thereafter, Hamas reiterated its rejection of the proposal.[93] All of the discussions were to no avail, as in March 1990 Prime Minister Shamir rejected his own initiative, leading to the collapse of the Israeli government. The right-wing coalition government which was subsequently formed under Shamir's leadership—dubbed a "war cabinet" in the Arab media—had no interest in reviving the proposals.

The conclusion of the Gulf war of 1990–91 and the collapse of the Soviet Union prompted further U.S. efforts to resolve—or at least attenuate—the Arab-Israeli conflict. The October 1991 Madrid conference came about as a result not only of intense U.S. lobbying but also of drastically changed regional and international circumstances—subjects which are beyond the scope of this study. What is relevant here is that the PLO's decision to support the Madrid conference further deepened the political cleavages set in motion by the 1988 PNC meeting while enhancing Hamas's stature as a real alternative to Fatah. Hamas was invited to attend the twentieth session of the PNC, convened in Algiers one month before the Madrid conference, but refused after its demand for up to 40 percent of the PNC's seats was rejected by the PLO. However, representatives of Islamic Jihad did attend as independents.

Refusing to attend either the PNC conference or the Madrid talks, Hamas issued an extended leaflet condemning the peace talks as nothing less than a capitulation to Israel and the United States, helped along by the PLO and certain Arab states. The leaflet is quoted at length here because it represented well Hamas's views on the peace talks in addition to its larger political ideology:

> In these difficult circumstances which have followed the Gulf crisis and war, and under which the United States has become the sole leader of the world and has imposed a new world system founded in part on entrenching weakness, division, and subservience in our Arab and Islamic nation—in this circumstance, the United States is seeking to convene a peace conference whose main objective is to liquidate the Palestinian cause. The most important objective of this [conference] is to get the Palestinian people, the victim, to recognize the right of the Zionist entity, the aggressor, and to confiscate [the Palestinian] presence, sacred lands, and right to freedom and independence. Thus, this is a conference for selling Palestine, all of Palestine with its blessed soil, its holy al-Aqsa Mosque,[94] and its venerable Jerusalem. [The PLO is] left with nothing to cede as a result of the chain of Arab and Palestinian concessions and retreats. They moved from demanding the full and undiminished liberation of all Palestine from the [Jordan] river to the [Mediterranean] Sea and rejecting peace, recognition, and negotiation to demanding the territories occupied in 1967 and dropping all the no's. Now they [the PLO] have ended up accepting the current U.S.-Zionist conditions. which do not secure minimal Palestinian rights. What is required now at the U.S. and Zionist level is to bestow Palestinian legitimacy on the unjust U.S.-Zionist solution. We are all required to sell this legitimacy and to sign our own death warrant, with nobody among our people and nation daring to swerve from the U.S.-Zionist will, to demand Palestine, or fight for Palestine. Hamas has tried to stop the chain of concessions, and has warned the PLO leadership of their dangers, demanding that the leadership reject them in part and parcel, and unite with the Palestinian people in their struggle and resistance against the occupation. To accomplish this objective, Hamas expressed its willingness to enter the PNC if it is formed by election, if Hamas is represented according to its true weight. Hamas did all this in an endeavor to stop the deterioration in the official Palestinian position, to drop the

settlement and recognition program adopted by the PNC's nineteenth session, held in November 1988, and to try and adopt a struggle and political program which emphasize our people's right to all of Palestine and to Jerusalem in order to stem the current condition of collapse and capitulation. The "conference to sell Jerusalem" is intended to bless the capitulationist steps taken by some Arab regimes and PLO leaders. We declare with utter clarity that in its current structure, the PNC does not represent all the influential forces that lead the bloody daily struggle against the occupation and its instrument of suppression, that it is not eligible or empowered to make a decision representing the Palestinian people and that nobody whomsoever, be it a council, an organization, a state, or an individual, is entitled to cede or relinquish any part of Palestine, regardless of the condition and circumstances. Jerusalem belongs to us, and so do Haifa, Jaffa, Lod, al-Ramlah, Hebron, Nablus, and Gaza. They all belong to us.[95]

On October 21, just a week before the opening of the Madrid conference, Hamas, the PFLP, and a wing of the DFLP issued a joint statement from Tunis opposing the Madrid conference: "We proclaim our categorical rejection of the American liquidation project, and we rise up to combat it."[96] The statement came just three days after Yasir Arafat had obtained a majority vote in a meeting of the PLO's Executive Committee in favor of proceeding to Madrid.

Hamas continued to reject the Madrid conference and the subsequent talks in Washington. Hamas and Islamic Jihad, in addition to a number of smaller factions, participated in a Tehran conference on the Islamic Intifada in December 1991; it condemned the dialogue and called for enhanced confrontation. The deported leader of Islamic Jihad, Shaykh 'Abd al-Aziz 'Awda, addressed the conference, saying that Islamic law forbade making peace with Israel and that all Islamic forces should unite to foil any U.S. plan for a regional settlement.[97] Several days later Hamas, along with Islamic Jihad, the PFLP, and a host of smaller factions, issued a statement in Beirut, once again rejecting "all the proposed capitulationist plans" and calling on those Palestinians participating in the talks to "abandon this conspiracy and return to the trenches of resistance and the masses."[98]

Hamas's condemnation of the talks was not limited to proclamations issued in foreign capitals. Following the Madrid conference and the first round of talks in Washington, PLO activists actively campaigned in the occupied territories to explain the goals of the talks. A number of formal debates were also held between supporters and opponents of the ongoing dialogue. Hamas activists disrupted several of the rallies and debates, such as one in Tulkarim at the end of December 1991, where Hamas supporters pelted Faysal al-Husayni and other Fatah representatives with stones and bottles. The informational rally was stopped after only a few minutes.

The talks in Washington continued through 1992 without bearing fruit; in fact, after Yitzhaq Shamir's defeat in the June 1992 election, he admitted that his policy had been to drag out the negotiations for "ten years," during which time he would try to fill up the occupied territories with Jewish settlers. Faced with such intransigence on the Israeli side, Hamas supporters had little difficulty in portraying the negotiations as a mistake. Lording it over the PLO, Mahmud al-Zahhar of Hamas remarked in August 1992 that "since the Madrid conference, we said that those who have followed that path would not gain anything. We even used a Palestinian proverb that says, 'You will not get even one drop of oil from a stone.'"[99] Accusing the PLO of "psychological and moral retreat," a Hamas official in Jordan, Ibrahim Ghuwsha, drew the conclusion that

> the U.S.-Zionist plan does not satisfy any sovereignty or independence requirement, notably self-determination and the right of return after liberation. It is limited to self-government for the residents only and leaves security, foreign affairs, and settlements under the jurisdiction of the Zionist occupation. It leaves Jerusalem and natural resources, including water resources, outside of the plan. It also leaves the door wide open for Jewish immigration from the former USSR, financed by the United States and Europe. Barbarism and Zionist arrogance will only increase if a peace settlement is reached, God forbid.[100]

Because of the stalemated talks, the PLO strategy of a negotiated settlement came under severe criticism in the occupied territories throughout 1992. Hamas (and the PFLP) reaped the benefits of Fatah's failures, leading to a further deterioration of relations between the two largest political factions in the West Bank and Gaza. In fact, throughout the spring and summer of 1992, violence between Hamas and Fatah cadres increasingly complemented their mutually harsh rhetoric (Hamas publicly denounced certain Fatah activists as "fugitive dogs").[101] The violence included assassinations and attempted assassinations of each others' cadres, as well as pitched street battles between hundreds of rival supporters.

Seeking to stem both the political violence with Hamas and an upsurge in the killing of collaborators—primarily by Hamas—Arafat urged the UNLU to adopt a "pact of honor"(*mithaq al-sharaf*) with Hamas.[102] A short-lived eleven-point agreement between Hamas and the UNLU was reached which called for an end to intra-Palestinian violence, a curbing of collaborator killings, and joint coordination of Intifada activities. Almost as quickly as it had signed the honor pact, Hamas renounced it, reflecting the schisms within that organization.[103] Hamas's volte-face made relations with Fatah go from bad to worse. More clashes ensued, culminating in a public letter from Hamas accusing Fatah of "hatching an evil scheme to assassinate some Islamic leaders in the Gaza Strip" and darkly "reminding" Fatah that "bullets will be answered with bullets."[104] In response, all the major factions of the PLO issued a joint statement condemning Hamas and charging it with "putting narrow sectarian interests before the public interest."[105]

Under intense pressure and following widespread accusations that it was destroying national unity, Hamas agreed to end its attacks on Fatah. This newest "cease-fire," initialed on July 10, was also only briefly observed. Within a week Hamas accused Fatah of shooting seven Hamas activists in Gaza. Moreover, in a leaflet which condemned Fatah for the new violence, Hamas referred to itself as the "sole legitimate representatives of the Palestinian people," a designation long reserved for the PLO. Needless to say, Hamas's declaration did not sit well with PLO officials.[106]

The shock of the mass expulsion of Hamas activists in December 1992 briefly returned a degree of unity to the PLO and Hamas. For the first time since before the Madrid conference in October 1991, all factions of the PLO and Hamas met together in Tunis in order to discuss the expulsions. However, the December meeting did not produce the desired result for Hamas, the PFLP or the Hawatma wing of the DFLP—i.e., withdrawal from the Washington negotiations. In spite of their remaining differences, Hamas and the PLO factions issued a joint communiqué promising unity in the Palestinian ranks. Follow-up talks in Khartoum explored the possibility of Hamas formally joining the PLO, something Hamas agreed to do "in principle."[107]

The hostility eased in the occupied territories as well. For the first time ever, representatives from Hamas, Fatah, the PFLP, and the DFLP appeared together in a special solidarity rally in the Hakawati theater in East Jerusalem on December 20. Also for the first time, a joint bayan was issued by Hamas and the UNLU in a bid to close ranks and coordinate policy in the West Bank and Gaza. In addition, Hamas went out of its way in this period to state that it was not an alternative to the PLO, that it did not seek to supplant the PLO, but instead believed in joint action.

Again, peace between Fatah and Hamas did not last long. In particular, Arafat's decision to return to round nine of the Washington negotiations while the 400 expellees were still in exile was denounced by Hamas and received with incredulity in the West Bank and Gaza. To express his opposition to the decision to return to Washington, the head of the negotiating team, Haydar 'Abd al-Shafi', briefly resigned. In addition, the Palestinian People's Party, one of three factions participating in the talks, refused to return to Washington for round nine. Most seriously, the negotiators themselves received death threats. The threats were taken so seriously by Fatah that it issued a special statement warning of "the most severe punishment" to any individual or party which attacked the negotiators.[108] For its part, Hamas denied it made the threats.

What was not known then was the real reason for Arafat's order to return to Washington: to protect the secret negotiations then taking place in Oslo between Israel and the PLO.[109] Arafat chose to continue the negotiations in Washington in order to divert attention from the Oslo talks and to "float" ideas arrived at in Oslo (such as the "Gaza-Jericho first" plan) to the Palestinian public. Round nine, therefore was merely a sideshow; as might be expected, it failed.

The ostensible failure of round nine left Hamas free to charge Fatah with betraying the Palestinian cause for no benefit. Hamas's accusations rang true to a great number of Palestinians in the occupied territories. More than anything else, the expulsion issue had provided Hamas with the political bona fides that it had previously lacked, while undermining Fatah's political standing.

Oslo and the Limits of Power for Hamas

In a number of articles published after the first year of the Intifada, Western and Israeli observers pushed the notion that Hamas was on the verge of replacing Fatah and the PLO as the preeminent political power in the occupied territories. Their argument was based on several points. First, critics and proponents alike acknowledged the evident ability of Hamas to enforce its agenda in the Intifada, particularly its strike days. Second, Hamas was the logical political repository for large sections of the Muslim Brethren as well as for students who supported the Islamist blocs in university elections prior to the Intifada. In other words, there was a history of Islamist political support and activism in the West Bank and Gaza independent of the PLO. Third, and most important, it was assumed that as the Intifada wore on without any significant diplomatic breakthroughs, support would naturally drift from those who supported political settlement to those who rejected such compromises. It was thought that Hamas (and the PFLP) would be the major beneficiary of such a polarization.

Certain events contributed to the perception that Hamas had emerged—or was on the verge of emerging—as the dominant actor in the occupied territories. The strength of Islamist parties in the outside Arab world, principally in Jordan and Algeria, raised expectations that Palestinian Islamists would do as well given free elections. In Jordan, for example, the Islamist bloc won a plurality of seats in the parliamentary elections of November 1989, leading one commentator to suggest that "if really free elections were held in the [occupied] territories, the fundamentalists would win more seats than the PLO."[110]

In the two years preceding Oslo, there was a good deal of evidence to bolster such an argument. In particular, candidates linked to Hamas enjoyed widespread electoral success in local races. For example, Hamas swept a number of chambers of commerce elections, including those in Hebron and, surprisingly, in Ramallah, and gained 45 percent of the vote in Nablus. In student body elections at Palestinian universities, Hamas won all seats at both Hebron University and its sister school, Hebron Polytechnic, while remaining in power at the Islamic University and doing well elsewhere. Even in a stronghold of Palestinian nationalism, the Jerusalem Electric Company, Hamas candidates won a majority five of the nine board seats.

The point is not that Fatah and the PLO were disappearing politically. PLO candidates did well in a number of other local elections, especially in Gaza, the heartland of Hamas. Fatah remained the largest political movement in the occupied territories in spite of the competition offered by Hamas. Yet Hamas was able to capitalize on discontent spawned by the PLO's lack of real diplomatic gains. While the PLO was seen as making a series of concessions at Madrid and Washington—agreeing to exclude itself and the large Palestinian Diaspora from the process, for example—and getting little in return, Hamas was seen increasingly as the vehicle for continuing the Intifada. Much of Hamas's newfound strength in the early 1990s was derived from the failures of Fatah rather than from its own intrinsic appeal, and could be seen largely as a "protest vote."

Hamas's potential for recruitment was large but not unlimited. The organizational framework established by the PLO throughout the 1980s provided an ongoing political socialization process which linked the provision of social goods to nationalist ideology. This social infrastructure continued its work in the West Bank and Gaza, even after the near-bankruptcy of the PLO in Tunis following the Gulf war, in which it had supported Iraq. While the Islamist movement attempted a parallel mobilization, it lacked the widespread institutional framework that the PLO enjoyed. Mosques were by no means strictly in the political domain of Hamas. Just as important was the nationalists' long history of direct struggle against the occupation—a struggle the Islamist movement had only recently assumed.

Palestinian Islamists, like all Palestinians, were taken by surprise in August 1993 when it was suddenly revealed that the PLO and Israel had been negotiating in Oslo for months and were close to agreement both on mutual recognition and on a document outlining the principles governing an interim autonomy period for the West Bank and Gaza. Hamas immediately rejected the Oslo Accords (or Declaration of Principles), as it had rejected the 1988 PNC declarations, the 1991 Madrid conference, and the subsequent Washington talks.

Reflexive rejection of the accord aside, the actual impact of the agreement on Hamas was complex. The agreement both strengthened and weakened Hamas. The organization was strengthened insofar as it became a political home for Fatah members and others disenchanted with the accords. Moreover, overnight Hamas became the largest Palestinian political opponent of Israel, Fatah having relinquished this role when it signed the accord with Israel. More important, however, Hamas was politically weakened by its inability to frame its opposition in a coherent and unified manner. Like the PLO, Hamas had become an umbrella organization with vastly different sets of class and ideological constituencies. The accords effectively split Hamas along its own seams.

The confusion in Hamas's ranks was seen on several issues. An early subject of contention within Hamas was the question of participation in elections for a Palestinian legislative council charged with overseeing the interim period. It would be the highest Palestinian elected body in the West Bank and Gaza for up to five years. While criticizing the PLO-Israel accord, Shaykh Yasin promised that Hamas would participate in the elections for the council, because Hamas "wanted to have an influence on the daily lives of Palestinians in the territories." Abd al-Aziz Rantisi, the expellees' spokesman in southern Lebanon, quickly countermanded Yasin, saying that Hamas would "not take part in any self-rule institutions."[111] Mahmud al-Zahhar then split the difference by creatively claiming that Hamas would participate "in any elections to choose the Palestinian people's representatives" but would not participate "in any legislative or executive institution linked to self-rule."[112]

A second issue of contention was how to deal with Palestinians, primarily from Fatah, who supported the agreement. Within days of the PLO-Israel agreement, Fatah and Hamas issued a joint statement renouncing any intra-Palestinian violence, basically agreeing to disagree on the accord. Initially this pact was honored. However, as the PLO-Israel agreement stagnated—particularly after the December 1993 deadline for the start of the Israeli pullout from Gaza and Jericho was missed—Hamas cadres urging confrontation became more emboldened in their opposition to Fatah and initiated several skirmishes with accord supporters.[113] In short, Hamas was divided over whether it should be a "loyal opposition" to Fatah or should actively seek to undermine the agreement, including through the use of force.

The accord also brought into sharper focus the incongruity of the alliances between Hamas and the secular left wing of the PLO, principally the PFLP and the DFLP. In seeking a common format of opposition to the PLO-Israel accords, these factions (with seven other small groups), meeting in Damascus, could not agree on much of anything, with the exception of rejecting the accords. The factions twice had to postpone issuing a statement, in large part because they could not agree on what to call themselves (Islamic, national, Arab, etc.), could not agree on whether to refer to "international legitimacy" (e.g., U.N. resolutions), and could not agree on whether a Palestinian state should be phased in or not. The latter two points, pushed by the PFLP and DFLP, would imply recognition of Israel, which Hamas officially rejected.[114]

Part of the problem Hamas and other "rejectionist" factions faced was the lack of a real alternative to the agreement, save more hardship and the continuation of the Intifada. Responding to the question of alternatives, a Hamas spokesman answered in a way indistinguishable from the PFLP and DFLP:

> We have been asked what is the alternative to the Gaza-Jericho agreement. We have chosen, declared, and explained the alternative. The alternative is jihad, the struggle, and more jihad. Struggle, then, is the alternative chosen by any people whose land is occupied, from which it is expelled, and whose sons are imprisoned. Whoever said that a fair agreement can be signed under the imbalance in power? Such an agreement would be one of submission and capitulation, as is happening now.[115]

In sum, while Hamas's official position was to reject the agreement, its extant response could be better characterized as hedging its bets. Hamas wanted it both ways: to reject Oslo, but not so completely as to be left out of the emerging political order the agreement established. Oslo could not simply be wished away as though it had never happened, as many in Hamas wanted. Nor did it have to be accepted *in toto*. Rather, it established a new political reality in the West Bank and Gaza and had to be dealt with as such. If Oslo worked in some significant way, Hamas risked marginalization by being too rejectionist. Conversely, if the accords failed, as most Islamists predicted, Hamas did not want to be tainted by having accepted it.

The twin realities of Hamas in the post-Oslo era—a powerful and occasionally deadly opposition force, but one with an inability to form a coherent and consistent response to the PLO-Israel deal—will be dealt with further in chapter 7.

In the preceding discussion, I have argued that Hamas came into being in the opening months of the Intifada largely as a result of a revolt by middle-stratum cadres within the Muslim Brethren against their traditional leaders. Social emergencies, such as the uprising, by their very nature undermine more traditional leaders who rely on routine as the central pillar of their position and put a premium on new leaders with different types of skills. In many ways, Islamic Jihad laid the groundwork in the year preceding the Intifada for Hamas activism during the uprising.

The Islamist palace coup, as it were, had strong class and ideological overtones. The new Hamas cadres came from lower classes than the old elite of the Muslim Brethren and had a more activist ideology, which emphasized the dialectical relationship between confronting the occupation and purifying Palestinian society. In the latter years of the Intifada, Hamas lost its organizational distinctiveness, moving from a cadre-based organization to a large umbrella movement. Much of its expanded support, however, was derivative, based on the perceived failures of Fatah.

Commentators have often taken the erroneous view that all Islamist movements, by definition, are antimodern—a sort of revolt by traditional or semitraditional segments of society which are being "left behind." Like most Islamist movements, Hamas did not warrant this characterization. The Hamas cadres, like the PLO activists, came from what Halpern once called a modern, new middle class. Each was rooted in modern society and neither represented the more traditional segments of Palestinian society. The differences between the two sets of cadres were grounded in ideological cleavages. However, the symbolic expressions of these ideological differences increasingly converged during the Intifada, even while the animosity between the competing elites persisted.

7

The Logic of Palestinian State-Building after Oslo

Palestinian state-building in the post-Oslo period has not been as haphazard as it might appear. Characteristics of this process have included authoritarianism in decision-making, the anti-institutional personalization of power, and the pervasiveness of violence in the system. I argue in this chapter that these political characteristics are the function of the dominant domestic political task facing Yasir Arafat and the Palestinian Authority: to undermine the power and position of the new elite that had emerged in Palestine in the 1980s. In order to consolidate their own power, Arafat and the other PLO "outsiders" had to create a political process that was the antithesis of the politics of the new elite. This is the logic of Palestinian state-building after Oslo. Devolved authority not only had to be recaptured by the center, but it had to be captured by an elite that was absent during the Intifada.

Three general issues are covered in this final chapter. First and most important, I discuss the process of Palestinian state-building by expanding on the themes just noted, including the necessity for the "outside" PLO to construct an alternative political base, and the logic of the authoritarian and personalized politics plainly visible in Palestine. Second, I deal with the most pressing domestic issues of self-rule: the Islamist challenge and the 1996 Palestinian elections. Finally, I speculate on the characteristics of the future Palestinian state by noting the political issues and processes which will continue to shape it in the coming years.

The Oslo Context

The September 1993 Oslo Accords (formally known as the Declaration of Principles) between Israel and the PLO set in motion a process by which this decades-old conflict could end. The Oslo Accords outlined the principles which were to govern relations between the PLO and Israel for a five-year interim period, during which final arrangements for ending the conflict over Palestine would be negotiated. Plagued by problems and delays, the details of the interim arrangements took two years to be fully concluded. An initial agreement signed in Cairo in May 1994 gave Palestinians autonomy in most of Gaza and in the West Bank town of Jericho. A full interim agreement, negotiated in Taba, Egypt, was finally signed in September 1995.[1] Oslo II gave the Palestinians, in addition to Gaza and Jericho, direct control of about 7 percent of the West Bank (known in the agreement as area A), and shared control over another 24 percent (area B). Israel retained absolute control over approximately 69 percent of the West Bank (area C), with three future undefined withdrawals from area C anticipated.

The Oslo Accords shaped the Palestinian state-building process—that is, provided the context for the "logic" of Palestinian state-building—in three fundamental ways. First and most obviously, Oslo made the possibility of actual Palestinian statehood much more likely. Indeed, one of the most consistent features of the Oslo process was recognition by both the political right and the left in Israel that a Palestinian state would be the end product (although they greeted that prospect in very different ways).

Second, the Oslo process—including the Oslo, Cairo, and Oslo II Accords—focused exclusively on interim arrangements. All of the major contentious issues—Jerusalem, Jewish settlements in the West Bank and Gaza, the right of Palestinian refugees to return to the area, and eventual Palestinian sovereignty—were left for future negotiations. By ignoring these key issues, Oslo increased Palestinian opposition to the process, not only by Hamas and PFLP supporters but also by mainstream politicians and former peace negotiators. In fact, the former chief negotiator during the Washington peace talks, Haydar 'Abd al-Shafi', led a 1994 petition campaign and then formed a political movement to oppose the direction in which the Oslo process was heading. His stance found a receptive response, as 'Abd al-Shafi' received more votes than any other candidate in the January 1996 Palestinian elections. His electoral success was especially remarkable, given that he was elected in Gaza City, the "capital" of the Palestinian Authority.

Third and most important, Oslo revived a fiscally bankrupt and politically dying PLO in Tunis and put in power in Gaza and the West Bank a political elite quite removed from the realities of modern Palestine. At base, Palestinian state-building after Oslo has been a process by which an outside political elite has tried to consolidate its political power in the West Bank and Gaza. The PLO's self-defeating decision to back Iraq during the 1990–91 Gulf war led directly to its bankruptcy. Its major financial donors, Kuwait and Saudi Arabia, cut off all financing of the PLO as a result of its Gulf war positions. Without major sponsors, the PLO was unable to pay its own personnel regularly or in full. Deep cuts in spending led to the closure of a number of PLO offices and the cessation of many of its functions. Significantly, the PLO's economic crisis prompted the virtual ending of financial assistance to the families of "martyrs" or prisoners in the occupied territories; this program had been a major source of both political patronage for the PLO and financial survival for dependent families. In spite of its efforts to remain economically viable, the PLO in Tunis was broke by the end of 1992 and had no prospects for correcting its slide into oblivion.

Political prospects were likewise bleak for the PLO in Tunis prior to Oslo. The end of the Cold War and the demise of the Soviet Union had left the PLO without a superpower patron, thus marginalizing it internationally. The Gulf war was politically (as well as economically) disastrous for the PLO, marginalizing the organization even within the Arab world. A large bloc of Arab states, in implicit alliance with Israel, had supported the U.S. effort to reverse Iraq's occupation of Kuwait. When the PLO allied itself against this effort, it guaranteed itself political hostility from much of the Arab world. Prospects for a political resurgence for the PLO were slim at best.

Thus, the Oslo process saved the PLO in Tunis from permanent obscurity or worse. The PLO's reasons for joining the process are obvious—any organization's first imperative is to survive. For the top echelon of the PLO the Oslo process was a minor miracle: in a matter of months these men went from political oblivion to center stage in Palestine. Accepting terms that they had previously rejected as wholly inadequate was the price they paid for their weakness. Israel's reasons for saving the PLO are more complex. However, recognizing that a solution to Palestine can only ultimately be arrived at politically, not militarily, a weak, dependent negotiating partner is far superior to no partner at all. After all, Oslo was not an agreement negotiated between political equals.

In sum, while Oslo greatly enhanced the possibility that a Palestinian state would be created, it simultaneously shaped the outline of the state-building process by focusing only on near-term issues, thus guaranteeing strong opposition, and by putting into power a political elite geographically and politically removed from the realities of post-Intifada Palestine. The principal political task for the PLO as it returned to Palestine from Tunis was to consolidate its power over a population with whom it shared many emotional bonds but with whom it had no practical political experience. In order to consolidate its own power, the returning PLO had to undermine, through coercion, co-optation, and marginalization, the new elite which had emerged during the Intifada. In other words, the first job of the "outside PLO" was to neutralize the "inside PLO" in order to assert its own authority.

Constructing a Political Base

When a revolution comes to power, the new regime brings with it a political base born of the upheaval itself. Rarely does a revolutionary regime have to scramble to construct the social forces upon which it will base its rule. It is essential for a revolutionary regime to have such social support in order to survive politically, given the usual chaos and lack of adequate coercive power that follows these new regimes into power. After the successful conclusion of the Iranian revolution, for example, Khomeini's regime based its power on a coalition of radicalized urban students, the bazaari merchant class, and the 'ulama. Its coercive capabilities, outside of armed, self-appointed, and undisciplined neighborhood watchdog groups (*komitehs*), took months to develop. New Leninist regimes—in China, Cuba, and elsewhere—similarly had extant powerful social forces supporting them after their rise to power.

The Palestinian Authority (PA) under Yasir Arafat enjoyed none of the advantages of other regimes brought to power following a social revolution. To begin with, the Intifada remained politically and socially incomplete at the time the Oslo Accords were negotiated. Politically, Israel had contained the Intifada to a level it could live with, although it could not completely rid itself of Palestinian collective action. Thus, while the Intifada continued, in a way, right up to Oslo, it had long since become clear that it would never be capable of directly ending Israel's occupation. Socially, the new elite was not able to fully consolidate its own position in Palestinian society. The level of social transformation promised by the Intifada was not completed—and could not be completed without the new elite's actually taking the reins of political power.

In any case, the elite that actually took power in Palestine after Oslo was not the same political elite which produced the Intifada. Put bluntly, the PLO in Tunis successfully captured political power in the West Bank and Gaza not because it led the revolution but because it promised to end it. The PA had to construct its own political base, which would diminish the position of the new elite inside the West Bank and Gaza while consolidating its own power.

The political base of PA authority in Palestine consists of four groups: security forces, "state" bureaucrats, the notable social class, and a reconstructed Fatah cadre system. Because of their coercive capabilities, the various police and security forces are a cornerstone of PA rule. In Gaza and Jericho in 1994 and in the other urban areas in the West Bank in late 1995, these forces preceded the political leadership's arrival in order to secure the areas. Several relevant points about these forces should be noted. First is the sheer size of the police force: at the time of the signing of Oslo II in September 1995, the PA employed 22,000 police in Gaza and Jericho, with plans to recruit an additional 8,000. The number of police during the interim period may eventually reach 40,000.[2] Second, the regular police are just one of a handful of police and security services (the exact number is in some dispute, with estimates ranging from four to ten separate services employing up to 9,000 people). The most notorious of these is the West Bank's Preventative Security Forces, headed by Colonel Jibril Rajub. Even when Rajub's forces were supposed to be confined to Jericho alone, they would often take actions against Palestinians elsewhere in the West Bank. In spite of the fact that technically none of these security forces (with the exception of the regular police) is allowed to exist under the Oslo agreements, cooperation between Palestinian and Israeli security forces has been routine. Third, the heads of the various police and security forces—nearly all PLO "outsiders"—report directly to Arafat, enhancing the personalized nature of PA rule. Their legal basis for reporting to Arafat, whether as head of the PA or of Fatah, is not clear; there is no functioning chain of command. Such fragmentation is purposeful, preventing the emergence of a strong and unified security apparatus which might pose political problems for Arafat in the future.

Moreover, the police and security forces form the largest segment of a large PA bureaucracy. This bureaucracy constitutes a second pillar of PA power, based on an old-fashioned political patronage machine. In Gaza, for example, the PA employs a total of 40,000 Palestinians (of whom nearly half are policemen) to run its affairs. By contrast, the Gazan civil administration under Israeli occupation employed 5,000 Palestinians.[3] Total PA employment at the end of 1995 approached 60,000 people, divided roughly equally between police/security personnel and civilian bureaucrats.[4] When the families of the civil servants are included, more than one-quarter of all Gazans are directly dependent on the PA for their livelihood. While the patronage machine is not as flagrant in the West Bank, the political logic of constructing a bloated PA bureaucracy throughout the territories is clear. Important political support for the PA is thus derived from the distribution of state jobs in Gaza and the West Bank.

Third and most interesting from the perspective of the argument offered in this book, Arafat has recruited members of the old notable elite into the PA's political fold. Examples of notable appointments abound. For instance, mayors appointed by Arafat prior to municipal elections[5] have often come from the old landowning class, including the

Shawwa family in Gaza and the Natsche family in Hebron. More than half of the PA's cabinet ministers in the lead-up to the 1996 elections came from the landowning class.[6] The PA's embrace of the old notable class was not limited to the distribution of posts but was also reflected in policy actions. One noteworthy example was Arafat's dismissal of the mayor of Jericho, Munther Irshayd—himself an Arafat appointee— based on a complaint to Arafat by Khader Maslamani, a local landowner. The mayor, acting upon the city council's recommendation, had ordered a more equitable distribution of local water supplies to Jericho farmers, much to the chagrin of Maslamani, the largest user of the water source in question.[7]

The political logic of embracing the notable class was impeccable. As noted earlier, the position of the notables had been eclipsed so much in recent decades—and particularly during the Intifada—that this class no longer had an autonomous base of power from which to oppose PA authority. Since notables owed their newfound political positions directly to Arafat, it was to Arafat personally that their loyalty was given. At the same time, given their long political history and their still respectable resources, notables could confer upon the PA a certain political respectability. Thus, recruiting notables to the political base enhanced the standing of the PA without significant political risk. Notable inclusion had the added benefit of sending a clear signal to members of the new elite as to the political and social direction the PA was taking. Rolling back the partial gains of the Intifada brought added security to Arafat's own position; there was no better symbol of this than making the notable social class a bedrock of PA power.

The final pillar of PA rule in the West Bank and Gaza is the Fatah political faction of the PLO—Arafat's own. In order to solidify his hold on power, Arafat has had to partially reconstitute Fatah's cadre system. As the largest single faction of the PLO, Fatah contained many activists and institution-builders who had helped mobilize Palestinian society before and during the Intifada. It was clear during the Intifada that Tunis did not have complete control over a number of its own members (from Fatah and other PLO factions) on the ground. These cadres, like other members of the new elite, did not formally break with Tunis. Rather, decisions were often taken in the field and institutions run with regard to the local context. As part of their larger task of neutralizing the new elite in the West Bank and Gaza, Arafat and the returning members of Fatah had to deal with locally popular and partially autonomous Fatah cadres. Put briefly, loyalist cadres—numbering in the thousands—were retained, while those with some autonomy were removed from decision-making positions and replaced.

The Fatah housecleaning began shortly after the signing of the Oslo Accords. In November 1993, Arafat appointed Zakharia al-Agha as the

Fatah head in Gaza, prompting the immediate resignation of a number of leading Fatah cadres. Agha comes from the notable class and had not been involved in the Intifada. One local cadre who resigned in protest, Zakharia Talmas, was bitter about this and other recent appointments: "The leadership has shoved aside the people who have struggled, who have sacrificed for the cause. We refuse to have leaders who have lived in five-star hotels eating fish and chocolate while our people starve. The real leaders are those who are in the fields and not in hotels, those who got their education in prison."[8] Sara Roy characterized the appointment of "traditional, old-guard types no longer seen as representative of the collective interest" in this way:

> Such appointments are at the expense of Gaza's younger Fatah activists, who enjoy substantial grassroots support and who are seen as having paid their dues through long years in prison. Many believe that Arafat's aim in making such appointments—beyond the loyalty factor—is to marginalize Fatah's younger political leadership so as to diminish the challenge they inevitably present.[9]

As Roy points out, in addition to replacing Fatah political leaders with notables and more loyalist cadres, Arafat appointed a number of individuals "who lack credibility or legitimacy within the community, who are distrusted and hated, and, in some instances, [were] even perceived as collaborators" during the Intifada. The appointment of one collaborator to a political posting by Arafat prompted a joint protest letter from local Fatah, PFLP, and PPP cadres. The candidate and Arafat held their ground, and the appointment went through.[10] Locally popular Fatah cadres who have resisted marginalization have sometimes been met with violence. A prominent local Fatah leader, As'ad Saftawi, was assassinated in Gaza by assailants widely believed to have been sent by Arafat or, more likely, one of his deputies.

The clearest example of the restructuring of Fatah by Arafat came in the weeks prior to the January 1996 Palestinian elections. Regional Fatah councils held informal primaries throughout the West Bank and Gaza, producing candidate slates. Most often the top candidates in each district were popular cadres, active in the Intifada, and members of the new elite. The primaries, however, only constituted recommendations for candidate lists. When presented with various lists, Arafat invariably replaced a number of the most popular Fatah cadres with his own choices, usually people without a local following. When presented with the Gaza city primary results, for example, Arafat dismissed the nominees and the process which elected them with a curt "this is child's play" and substituted his own very different list.[11] Many of the most popular Fatah cadres ran as independents in the elections—and won.

The rooting out of local autonomous Fatah leaders was not limited to the political side but was also seen in the military wing of Fatah. The leader of the Fatah Hawks in Nablus, Ahmad Tabuk, spent much of the fall of 1995 engaging in a game of verbal chicken with Arafat's closest advisors, especially Jibril Rajub. Tabuk had a passionate following among a number of Fatah militants in Nablus, although he was far less popular among local businessmen, from whom he demanded "taxes." The former deputy commander of Fatah in Nablus and a leader of the Fatah-allied Black Panthers for a period, Tabuk claimed that both his protection racket and the Fatah Hawks' continued killing of alleged collaborators (eight during 1995) had the approval of the Fatah command at the highest levels. The war of words finally came to a head in December 1995 as the PA assumed control of Nablus and arrested Tabuk and forty of his followers after a long standoff in the Nablus casbah.

In sum, as an outsider distrustful of the local PLO leadership which had come to the fore during the Intifada, Arafat's first task in the West Bank and Gaza was to construct a political base which did not include members of the new elite. The political base had four pillars: the security forces, a patronage network of new PA bureaucrats, members of the old notable social class, and his own Fatah cadres (except those too independent to control adequately). A strategy of fragmenting the new elite was adopted: some were co-opted into positions of authority, others were intimidated, and most were marginalized by being prevented by the PA from actively participating in the political process. The distribution of authority downward during the Intifada was in conflict with the needs to centralize power during the state-building process.

L'état c'est Arafat: Authoritarianism and Personalized Power

The basic tension between the reality of devolved authority in Palestine and the centralizing impulse of the PA informed all aspects of post-Oslo Palestinian politics. The most obvious indications of the discord between the Intifada-driven distribution of authority and the attempts to centralize power by the PA have been the resort to authoritarianism by the PA and its anti-institutional personalization of power. Authoritarianism and personalism, in this case, were not the natural results of some teleological political culture or even the by-product of the psychology of Yasir Arafat. Rather, these two intertwined phenomena were the result of the political logic of state-building in the unusual circumstances of Palestine. Ruling by decree limited the necessity of "doing politics" in Gaza and the West Bank—that is, directly engaging a vibrant civil society—a task which the "outsiders" were little prepared to undertake and at which they may not have been terribly successful. At the same time, the personalization of politics directly undermined the core political strength of the new elite, which was collective action through institution-building. Rather than play into the strength of the "inside" PLO, the PA changed the rules of the game, emphasizing personalism, demobilization, and deinstitutionalism instead.

The authoritarian political style of the PA and of Arafat in particular has been widely noted by observers in and out of Palestine. A few examples here should make the point. First, the PA has openly intimidated the Palestinian press to the point that self-censorship is now the norm, much as it was under Israeli occupation. The largest Palestinian daily, *al-Quds*, has on occasion been denied distribution when it carries mildly anti-Oslo views on its opinion page. A pro-Jordanian paper, *al-Nahar*, was closed in July 1994 and allowed to reopen only when its editorial direction was changed. *Al-Quds* was prevented from carrying the story of *al-Nahar*'s closure and was compelled to fire columnist Daoud Kuttab, who had protested the closure. A pro-Islamist newspaper, *al-Watan*, was likewise closed for months because of its views. Carrying negative stories about the PA was not the only grounds for punishment. In December 1995, *al-Quds* carried a flattering story on Arafat, who then had the editor, Mahir al-Alami, detained because the story was not put on page one. In such an atmosphere, editors routinely practice self-censorship in order to avoid closure or arrest. As Khalil Shikaki notes, *al-Quds* has "refrained from publishing stories about torture in Palestinian jails, reports by human rights organizations on press freedom, and opinion polls showing widespread opposition to PA restrictions."[12]

The authoritarian impulse is also seen in the establishment of a number of overlapping security and intelligence services to monitor and control dissent. The various forces include the General Intelligence Service, headed by Brigadier General Amin al-Hindi; the Preventive Security Force, under Colonel Rajub in the West Bank and Colonel Muhammad Dahalan in Gaza; the Presidential Guard/Force 17, under Colonel Faysal Abu Shira in Gaza and Colonel Ikhmat Barakat in the West Bank; and the Special Security Force, under General AbuYusuf al-Wahidi. The principal goal of this last force is believed to be intelligence gathering on the other forces.[13] The paramount job of all these forces is to monitor and control all internal opposition, militant or political. Rajub's forces in particular have been known to kidnap Palestinians from territories outside PA control and bring them to Jericho for questioning or worse. When human rights workers take note of PA abuses, the workers themselves are sometimes arrested, as was the case (briefly) for both Bassam Eid, a Palestinian working for B'tselem, and Iyad Sarraj, a leader of the Palestinian Independent Commission for Citizens' Rights.

Adopting a characteristic feature of authoritarian states, the PA established security courts in April 1995, following two suicide bombings which killed seven Israeli soldiers and one civilian in the Gaza Strip. Ironically, the courts were established under the 1945 Emergency Regulations of the British Mandate, a law which was used by Israel to justify some of its harshest measures of occupation and which the Palestinians had argued for years had become null and void with the end of the Mandate. The security courts provide a quick and dirty means for responding to pressure from Israel and the United States to crack down on Hamas militants. Held at all hours, lasting sometimes only a few minutes, and usually occurring without legal representation for the accused, security trials always end in conviction, frequently with long prison sentences. For accused militants, making it as far as the security courts can be a good sign—a number of detainees have died during security interrogations. Interrogators have also been responsible for widespread torture of detainees, employing techniques learned from their Israeli occupiers.

While rampant abuses by security forces are an easy target, a more troubling sign of growing authoritarianism is the manner in which political decisions by the PA have been made. The PA rules by decree, not consensus, and the arbitrariness of the decree process has been alarming. Examples from two sectors—law and NGOs—demonstrate the point. First, the potential for rule of law in the Palestinian entity is made difficult for a host of reasons, including, most importantly, vastly different legal codes in place in the West Bank and Gaza. The legal system employed in the West Bank is derived from the Napoleonic tradition which was imposed on the West Bank by Jordan following its annexation of the territory. West Bank law today is largely the same as Jordanian law of the 1950s and 1960s. Conversely, the legal system in Gaza is based on the Anglo-Saxon common law tradition. It dates from the British Mandate period and was left largely unchanged by Egyptian and Israeli occupiers. Thus, British Mandate law, referred to by Gazans as "Palestinian law," continues to operate today in the autonomous areas of the Gaza Strip.

The process of integrating the legal systems has been marked by arbitrary decree. The most conspicuous example of this involved a case in Jericho where a former politician had both criminal and civil charges filed against him by Palestinian prosecutors. Under West Bank law, once charges are filed they cannot be withdrawn without cause. This contrasts with Gazan law where, under article 59, filed criminal charges can be withdrawn at the discretion of the prosecutor. Wanting to save a political ally of Arafat's, the Palestinian attorney general Khalid al-Qidre dropped the criminal charges by decree in December 1995, citing article 59 of Gazan law. Such disregard of West Bank legal traditions enraged the West Bank legal community. The Jericho affair came only days after an earlier decree had been issued by the attorney general (and signed by Arafat) which placed prosecution responsibilities for Jenin, newly under PA control, in Gaza, effectively making West Bank prosecutors and West Bank law irrelevant.

Nor was the issuance of decrees in this sector limited to the attorney general's office. For his part, the chief justice of Gaza, Qusay al-Abadla, regularly issued decrees for the West Bank, including one for the formation of a judicial council to nominate judges. This particular decree was posted in a Jericho courthouse in the early fall of 1995 and was not discovered by the rest of the West Bank legal community until November 1995. Rule by decree has become the chosen method of decision-making in light of the structural problems faced by the legal community.

The PA's handling of Palestinian NGOs is another example of the authoritarian nature of the fledgling regime. NGOs are a key aspect of Palestinian society, and a principal reason for optimism that a liberal political order can be built in Palestine. However, as was made clear earlier in this book, NGOs are an institutional home of the new Palestinian elite and, as such, have been treated with suspicion by the PA from the outset of its rule. Even before the Oslo Accords had been signed on the White House lawn, Fatah was directing foreign donors to divert contributions from Palestinian NGOs to its own "shadow ministries." This was a clear attempt to financially strangle the institutional base of Fatah's opposition within the PLO. After the PA was established in 1994, this process of diverting funds away from NGOs intensified, with Western donors usually complying with the PA's request to give the money directly to it for further distribution. Often these donors openly admitted that they would no longer support projects of NGOs associated with political factions opposed to Oslo or its implementation. Ironically, it was precisely the non-Fatah NGOs that provided the best development services to Palestinian society. For the PA, the political calculus of consolidating its power over society, including the NGO sector, took priority over the interests of Palestinians helped by these NGOs.

The PA then moved from indirect financial strangulation of NGOs to a bid for direct control of this sector. Dismissing without comment a draft law put forward by the semiofficial development agency PECDAR for NGO governance, the PA instead drafted a highly restrictive law. More accurately, three individuals from the PA drafted this law without consulting any NGOs.[14] The law, based on its Egyptian counterpart—itself the most repressive NGO law in the Arab world—gave the PA the right to dissolve or merge together NGOs without their consent and to appoint members of the boards of directors, and placed prohibitive restrictions on the handling of NGO finances. In short, the draft law gave the PA, and not members of civil society, the right to determine if an NGO should exist or not. It was another example of the PA's fundamental distrust of the society over which it ruled.

The NGO draft law produced a firestorm of criticism, not just from the NGOs but also, and more importantly, from a number of international donors. Initially the PA tried to quiet the criticism by making slight modifications to the draft law. Embarrassed by such criticism at donor meetings in Europe and elsewhere, the PA has apparently dropped the NGO draft law and will draw up a new one. It should be clear, however, that the decisive impetus in this matter came from abroad and that without strong international pressure, the PA would have been able to resist internal criticism. Other sectors of Palestinian society do not have the benefit of foreign patrons.

The PA's distrust of Palestinian society was likewise seen in the manner in which individual members of NGOs were treated by the PA. Leaders of NGOs, particularly those associated with non-Fatah factions, have been routinely summoned to appear before security officials, most often from Force 17. Those summoned have not been given any explanation as to why their presence was needed at these offices. Another security force, the General Intelligence Service, distributed a questionnaire to employees of Palestinian NGOs in which they were required to give details of their personal life and political history. Recipients were asked, for example, the names, addresses, and occupations of all their relatives and "three important friends." Political questions on the questionnaire included: Have you ever belonged to any Palestinian organization? Have you ever been a member in a political party? Has any family member been charged with spying? Do any of your family members belong to a political party? Have you ever been imprisoned for political reasons? Other reasons? It is likely that there was no coordination between the various security forces or with the Ministry of Social Affairs on this matter. What it demonstrates is that the first inclination of those with power in the PA is to distrust the NGOs and intimidate their leaders. Rather than being a well-thought-out policy, this kind of intimidation is more likely a reflection of what is diffusely understood to be a primary political objective of the PA: to suppress any potential political opposition, with institutions more than individuals being the primary targets.

Leaders of charitable societies, however, were not subject to this kind of intimidation. Charitable societies are led primarily by notable and politically conservative elements, and therefore are seen by the PA as areas of natural political support. Relations between NGOs and charitable societies are not particularly good, as they have "entirely different visions of the development process and their roles in it."[15]

Concomitant with its political need to demobilize Palestinian society in order to rule over it, the PA has nourished an atmosphere of political personalism, with a cult of personality constructed around Arafat himself. Cults of personality, unlike charisma, do not spontaneously generate from within society but are constructed from the top down in order to personalize the political order when an institutional process is undesirable.

The Palestinian polity has come to be viewed as synonymous with Arafat himself. For internal consumption, Gaza and the West Bank have been plastered with pictures of Arafat and, to a much lesser degree, Abu Jihad, the late PLO official. In Ramallah, for example, the town was plastered with posters and pictures of Arafat and graffiti singing his praises virtually overnight during November 1995. In Bethlehem in the days before Christmas, 1995, a three-story-high banner with a drawing of Arafat's head was hung from Manger Square, dominating its surroundings. In Gaza, two years after Oslo was signed and a year and a half after the PA took power there, pictures of Arafat were everywhere. While some individuals undoubtedly hang pictures of "Abu 'Ammar" out of genuine support, it is clear that Fatah cadres do most of the actual placing of posters and banners.

In this atmosphere of personalized politics around Arafat, individuals and groups seeking redress must solicit intervention from Arafat himself. Institutional process is irrelevant. For example, in the case cited earlier in which the attorney general applied Gazan law to free a political ally in the West Bank, lawyers and judges had no institutional means to appeal. Instead, over 400 West Bank lawyers and judges signed a petition to Arafat concerning this matter and virtually had to corner him on his first visit to Nablus in nearly three decades to raise the issue.

The equation of Arafat and the PA extends to the image projected abroad as well. The best example of this came when donors at first demanded greater accountability for the $2.4 billion in aid promised to the Palestinians over a five-year period. Donors wanted the monies handled institutionally (through PECDAR, for example), with normal accounting procedures applied. Arafat wanted the monies just handed over to the PA without real accountability, arguing, in effect, that there was no difference between the PA and Arafat—that demanding accountability was a personal affront to Arafat. Arafat had faced similar charges from within the ranks of the PLO in previous years and had responded similarly: that he *was* the PLO. In both cases Arafat largely prevailed.

The personalization of politics in the PA goes well beyond the attempts to construct a cult of personality around Arafat. In fact, the PA has deliberately nurtured an atmosphere of confusion in the West Bank and Gaza so that proximity to key individuals defines the distribution of power. Whom one knows is more important than any process in decision-making. The key bit of evidence to suggest that such confusion is deliberate and not just the by-product of creating a new polity is the sustenance of ambiguous lines of authority throughout the PA. "Who decides?" and "who reports to whom?" are commonplace questions. Two primary examples of this policy have already been mentioned. First, the various (and technically illegal) security forces have no clear and formalized role, nor is there any chain of command within the security community. They operate solely at the pleasure of Arafat. Second, within the legal community the delineation of roles and responsibilities between the minister of justice, the chief justice in Gaza, the chief justice in the West Bank, and the attorney general are nonexistent. When the chief justice in Gaza pressed Arafat to make clear the differences between his duties and the duties of the minister of justice, Arafat muddied the waters further by granting quasi-cabinet stature to the chief justice, but without commenting on the actual distribution of authority. The ambiguity in their roles was thereby magnified.

Personalized political atmospheres tend to attract corruption, as legality is seen to be based in the individual making the action, not in an impersonal standard of behavior. That is, in the minds of those with power, politically connected individuals cannot commit corrupt acts virtually by definition. For these people, the distinction between private and public goods is not clear. Palestine has been rife with corruption, or at least questionable behavior, under the PA. Some examples are well known, others less so. In one case, a powerful individual sold poor quality building cement to the PA and pocketed the extra profit. The PA had to act on the scam in this case because of the obvious results: structures were collapsing. More systematically, the business group Team International has been awarded numerous contracts by the PA and has had the inside position on innumerable profit-making ventures. Team International is owned by Nabil Sha'th, a leading Arafat advisor and one of the principal Palestinian architects of the Oslo process.

In another example, subsidized Travinour intravenous solution destined for Gaza regularly was sold at unsubsidized black market rates in the West Bank. It is believed by West Bank doctors that someone at or very near the top of the Palestinian Health Ministry has been responsible for diverting the solution and pocketing the difference.[16] Jibril Rajub has likewise gotten a piece of the action, buying a gas station in Jericho (on a meager PA salary), then having local roads diverted to pass directly by his new station.

The point here is not to suggest that all these—and many, many other—actions are illegal, as legality itself implies the implementation of an impersonal standard. Rather, it is to argue that this is policy—that by encouraging such behavior the PA accomplishes two goals. First, Arafat can reward personal loyalty on the part of his lieutenants: it is an example of pure political patronage. Second, such corruption further reduces the role of institutions in Palestinian society, showing plainly that personal status and loyalty, not merit and standards, govern behavior.

It must be stressed that such authoritarianism and personalism constitute regression in Palestinian politics, as neither the PLO in Tunis nor the "inside PLO" took decisions quite in this way. While the PLO in Tunis could never be mistaken for a democracy, it had a form of liberalism in decision-making. Put bluntly, Arafat was not (and could not have been) a dictator of the PLO. The Palestine National Council was the principal decision-making body of the PLO, and all Palestinian factions were represented in it. An example of the intensity of debate in the PNC over policy changes is the 1988 resolution adopting formally a "two-state" approach (i.e., recognizing and accepting the permanence of Israel). The resolution was hotly contested, with, for example, the PFLP voting against it. While Arafat prevailed in the end, it was because of political wrangling, not decree making. Within the PLO, Arafat was always seen as a political animal who could mediate, persuade, and co-opt, but who did not rule over the PLO with an iron hand. He did not rule with an iron hand precisely because he could not so rule and expect the PLO to follow him. Importantly, Arafat had to largely bypass the PNC and the PLO's Executive Committee in order to carry out the Oslo process, which is one reason for its unpopularity in the diaspora.

Institutional process was important not only for the PLO abroad but also within a host of Palestinian institutions in the West Bank and Gaza. It has become something of a cliché, but no less true as a result: Palestinian politics were the most liberal in the Arab world. This was not because of some primordial political culture; rather, liberal politics were an integral part of the ideology of the new elite, so political discourse became more liberal as this class assumed more influence. Democratic elections were routinely held at a number of levels, including at universities, chambers of commerce, professional associations, and labor unions. Internal political debate in Palestine was usually open and vigorous.

By continuing the tradition—either abroad or at home—of a relatively liberal political process characterized by institutions more than personalities, Arafat and the PLO may well have failed in their endeavor. While Oslo I had mixed Palestinian support, the Cairo agreement (Gaza-Jericho) was universally unpopular. In August 1995, for example, as the final details of Oslo II were being hammered out, 60 percent of all Palestinians did not believe the process would lead to a lasting peace with Israel, a figure that increased to 69 percent among Palestinians with a university degree.[17] Since Arafat would likely not have won majority support in either the PNC or a general election for many, if not all, of the agreements signed with Israel, nor could he have easily withstood opposition if formal processes of decision-making were respected, the logical political option was to adopt authoritarian methods under which institutional process is ignored. In this case, Palestinian politics under the PA has been a function of the political need of its rulers to effect social control over a society which they do not fully trust.

The Islamist Dilemma

One of the most important issues of the self-rule period has been the role of the Islamist movement, particularly Hamas. The political dynamics of the Oslo process effectively painted Islamists into a corner. Either they could participate in the political process—Palestinian Council elections, for example—and gain certain leverage with the PA, but in so doing legitimate a process they rejected, or they could refuse to participate and be marginalized from political decision-making and patronage resources. Since no social movement would voluntarily accept marginalization, the use of violence to destroy the peace process and create a different reality was always a danger. This situation led to numerous dilemmas for all three parties. Israel's dilemma centered on how to deal with Hamas in order to decrease violence but without putting so much pressure on the PA that it would be seen as an Israeli puppet. The PA's dilemma focused on how to co-opt Hamas on favorable terms so that it would not be able to kill the Oslo process through violence from outside the system or through politics from inside the system. Given its weakness under the terms of self-rule, Hamas's dilemma was perhaps the most acute of the three: how to survive the interim period organizationally and ideologically.

As the principal target of Islamist acts of violence, Israel was particularly keen on eliminating Hamas. Given Israel's central role in the strengthening of the Islamist movement in the 1980s, it was ironic that Hamas had become the most threatening Palestinian opposition to Israel in the 1990s. Israel knew from firsthand experience that eliminating Islamist violence was impossible, and it hoped that the PA would be better at it than Israel was. In fact, this was a fundamental tenet of Israel's Oslo policy: that the PA could enhance Israel's security better than Israel itself could by more effectively controlling and suppressing anti-Israel opposition in the West Bank and Gaza. Yitzhaq Rabin, then prime minister, was quite open about Israel's desire to see the PA do Israel's "dirty work":

> The Palestinians will be better at it than we were because they will allow no appeals to the Supreme Court and will prevent the Israeli Association of Civil Rights from criticizing the conditions there by denying it access to the area. They will rule by their own methods, freeing, and this is most important, the Israeli army soldiers from having to do what they will do.[18]

From Israel's standpoint, the Palestinians failed to adequately control Hamas during the first two and a half years after Oslo, in spite of security courts, arrests without charge, imprisonment without trial, multiple security forces, and general autocratic rule. Islamist acts of violence against Israeli targets continued sporadically during this time; these acts included two clusters of bus bombings. The first group of suicide attacks occurred on the eve of the PA's assumption of power in Gaza and Jericho in the spring of 1994, while Israel was still in control of the territories. These attacks, which included deadly bus bombings in the Israeli towns of Afula and Hadera, did not, as was feared by many, stop the handover of Gaza and Jericho. Hamas claimed responsibility for them, indicating that they were in retaliation for the earlier massacre of Palestinians by an Israeli settler in Hebron.

A second, more deadly, cluster of suicide attacks occurred in late February and early March 1996, when four buses were blown up in the span of nine days, killing over sixty Israelis. Hamas claimed that these bombings were in retaliation for the Israeli assassination of Yahya Ayyash in Gaza in January 1996.[19] Ayyash, known as the "Engineer," was the leading Hamas bomb-maker, and was killed in an area controlled by the PA, leading to charges that the PA may have acquiesced in Israel's assassination effort. The wisdom of Israel's move was questioned by many who noted that there had been no attacks at all between August 1995 and February 1996. The assassination reversed Hamas's move toward accommodation with the PA, which had included a cessation of violence against Israel.

These attacks led immediately to a wave of arrests of Islamists by both Israel and the PA, and to the closing off of the territories. It also led Israel to impose a virtual curfew over all Palestinian villages where Israel and the PA share security responsibilities (area B), and the sealing and demolition of family homes of the dead terrorists. The scheduled withdrawal from parts of Hebron was put on hold, as was any discussion of the three undefined future withdrawals. The ramifications of these attacks are still unfolding as of this writing.

While Israel pushed the PA to crack down hard on Hamas throughout this period—demanding that the PA join in Israel's self-declared "war on Hamas"—it was only this last, most deadly cluster of attacks that prompted Israel to rethink its security equation under Oslo. Israel sought to enhance its own security by relying on the PA to contain Hamas. However, Israel could not be perceived by Palestinians to be dictating the internal policies of the PA. In other words, Israel sought to rule (as far as security matters were concerned) indirectly through the PA. Even when it did not believe the PA was doing enough, Israel had to lie low in order to bolster the PA's legitimacy and independence in the eyes of its own people. By reverting to a more direct security policy both in terms of its own work in area B and in terms of directing the PA forcefully and publicly to crack down on Hamas, Israel threw open the future direction of its security policy in the West Bank and Gaza.

Hamas likewise posed a dilemma for the PA, both externally and internally. Externally, Hamas was the single biggest threat to the PA's delicate relationship with Israel. With its violence, Hamas could undermine months of negotiation and work between the PA and Israel overnight. Since the PA's existence, not to mention the political future of Arafat himself, was so closely tied to making the Oslo formula succeed, the PA had every incentive to contain Hamas in order to placate Israel.

In the same vein, the Clinton administration in Washington further encouraged an iron fist approach to Hamas by the PA. Washington did not raise serious objections to widespread human rights abuses under the PA, including the creation of the security courts where sham "trials" of Hamas activists took place. Washington further implicitly linked aid to the PA with success against Hamas. Vice President Al Gore made this link very clear to Arafat when they met in Jericho in 1995, saying that the United States would be "more generous with the PA if it took tougher measures to combat the enemies of peace"—a clear reference to the Islamists.[20]

The PA's problem, of course, was that by pleasing its foreign partners and crushing Hamas, it would undermine its fragile standing within Palestinian society. By trying to crush a popular social movement, the PA risked launching a civil war. Hamas's lowest ranking in opinion polls stands at 17 percent support, which represents a following of tens of thousands of adults. Supporters rise to over 100,000 if teenagers are included. The tenuous legitimacy of the PA would come into question if such a move were taken.

On the other hand, Hamas embarrassed the PA by showing the world—and Palestinian society—that the PA did not really control the autonomous areas. By demonstrating the actual weakness of the PA, Hamas invited a show of force against it. The first of these occurred in Gaza in November 1994 when the PA used live ammunition to break up a Hamas anti-Oslo rally, killing sixteen people and injuring more than 200.

Not surprisingly, different factions within the PA argued over the appropriate strategy vis-à-vis Hamas. The Preventive Security Forces, made up largely of "insider" Palestinians, viewed Hamas cadres more sympathetically and argued for a policy of co-optation and dialogue. In fact, Rajub's refusal to arrest Hamas political leaders following the March 1996 bombings led to his forced (temporary) resignation. Other security forces, especially those made up of "outsider" PLO members, took a much harsher line, arguing that Hamas needed to be crushed. It was the "outsider"-led forces that killed the sixteen Hamas supporters, further discrediting the outsiders' position in society.[21]

In the end, Arafat opted for a carrot-and-stick approach. The crackdown was undertaken by "inside" Fatah cadres throughout the first half of 1995, with scores of Hamas activists arrested and imprisoned. Those arrested were primarily from the autonomous military wing of Hamas, the Iz al-Din al-Qassam brigades. The establishment of the security courts was likewise part of the general get-tough policy on Hamas. After pummeling Hamas for months, Arafat opened an ongoing dialogue with the political arm of Hamas, which continued right up to the January 1996 elections. The dialogue sought to ease Hamas into the political process, including participation in the elections, while cementing Hamas's cessation of violent attacks.

At base, what Arafat sought to do was to split Hamas so that the military wing could be more easily crushed while the political wing could be a partner in the political process. Arafat was largely successful in this project, as all Hamas attacks ceased in August 1995, and Hamas entered into a vigorous internal debate about participating in the Council elections. The dialogue exposed numerous fissures in Hamas, and not just between the military and political sides of the organization. Even within the political camp, there was little agreement as to the extent of political participation in the PA. While Hamas as an organization did not participate in the elections, it did encourage its supporters to register for the elections and a number of Hamas individuals did run for office as independents. Hamas pledged to participate fully in the 1996 municipal elections.

A new center of Palestinian politics was slowly emerging as a result of Arafat's policy of splitting Hamas and co-opting its political arm. The new center would likely be composed of Fatah and the Muslim Brethren wing of Hamas, with a leftist and Islamist "loyal" opposition. All of this came to a sudden halt with the Israeli assassination of Ayyash and the retaliatory bombings in Jerusalem, Tel Aviv, and Ashkelon.

Hamas's dilemma was the most acute because it dealt with questions of political survival for the Islamist movement. Oslo began a process which redefined the viability of political groupings. Fatah and its allies in the PLO now had the weight of Israel, the West, and much of the Arab world behind them in establishing the PA. For Hamas to ignore this new reality risked oblivion, as it would be outside all decision-making structures. However, the terms of the Oslo Accords were considered wholly inadequate by most Hamas members, and participation by the organization in the PA would be an implicit recognition of the legitimacy of the Oslo process. Thus, barring a sudden collapse of the whole process, Hamas's conundrum was to participate at the loss of its convictions or to not participate at the loss of its viability over the long run.

For some in Hamas, of course, the purpose of undertaking violence was exactly to avoid having to make such a historic decision: bombing buses could lead to the sudden collapse of the Oslo process. The closer the process came to fruition, the more desperate—and violent—some grew.

Hamas's dilemma led to the exposure of a number of fissures within the organization. Hamas, like the earlier PLO, had become an umbrella organization, home to many kinds of factions and individuals who opposed the Oslo Accords. While the original "second stratum" leaders remained in Hamas, they no longer had significant organizational discipline owing to the sheer size of the organization and the necessity of a loose structure. Four faultlines were most important: political-military, inside-outside, intrapolitical wing, and intramilitary wing.

The political and military wings of Hamas had, years before Oslo, become independent of each other in order to preserve the vulnerable political decision-makers. The military wing came to resemble the earlier Islamic Jihad organization: secretive, small, and cell-based. While there was clearly communication between these two wings, it was also clear that neither side controlled the other. The cracks between these two wings became apparent as the political side debated the pros and cons of participating in the political process. Arafat's carrot, held out in mid-1995, clearly tempted a number of Hamas's political figures, while the Iz al-Din al-Qassam brigades were being hunted down by the PA's security forces. The January elections, in which members of Hamas participated as independents and which demonstrated clearly that there would be no return to the pre-Oslo reality, further separated the military wing from the political. The March bombings, criticized by a number of Islamist politicians, can be viewed, in part, as a last gasp of a marginalized force.

A second fissure was brought into the open by the move toward accommodation with the PA: that between the "inside" and "outside" of Hamas. Like the PLO, Hamas had a popular following both inside Palestine and among the Palestinian Diaspora. Also like the PLO, Hamas had leaders both inside and outside the occupied territories. During the Intifada, the different interests of these two constituencies were not important. However, as the Oslo process unfolded the differences in goals between these two communities became apparent. For those on the outside, the Oslo process is seen as leading directly to the political annihilation of the Palestinian Diaspora. It is a process for the benefit, if any, of only those living in the West Bank and Gaza. Quite naturally, the diaspora leadership is more hardline on the issue of accommodation with the PA or Israel. As such, it has been the diaspora leaders that have generally been the strongest supporters of the Iz al-Din al-Qassam brigades. The closer the inside political leadership came to doing a deal with the PA, the more intransigent the "outside" became.

A third crack could be seen within the political wing of Hamas. It was this fissure that prompted the greatest debate over participation in the Palestinian Council elections in January 1996. After the signing of Oslo I and the Gaza-Jericho agreement, Hamas's political leadership was confident that the whole process would fall apart by itself, and thus showed few signs of dissent in its opposition to Oslo. However, as the PA gradually consolidated its position in Palestine, the easy dismissal of the process as inherently doomed gave way to a debate within Hamas as to its appropriate action if the process continued. By the summer and fall of 1995—when it was clear both that the PA was not going away and that important Palestinian elections would be held early in 1996—a wide-ranging debate began in earnest within Hamas. The elections were the focus of debate. Should Hamas participate in the elections? Should it boycott them? Is the future of Hamas that of a loyal opposition within the PA or a strident opposition outside the political process? Could it participate at some level yet maintain its ideological opposition to the system?[22]

Hamas activists who argued for participating in the election, such as Imad Faluji, the editor of *al-Watan*, took a pragmatic view of the situation. He argued that there is a new reality in Palestine, like it or not, and to boycott the elections would be self-defeating. The alternative to participation was further marginalization. As Faluji noted, Hamas "cannot let Fatah win all the seats in the Council" for the sake both of Hamas's own interests and the future of Palestine.[23] As the only opposition voice strong enough to challenge Fatah's hegemony, it was Hamas's duty to take part. The discourse from this camp was in part about pushing the PA on issues of democracy and human rights abuses. In addition, supporters of participation noted that, as Israel withdrew from Palestinian urban areas during November and December 1995, the PA was riding a crest of support from the population. Since elections were scheduled to take place while this wave was high, the possibility of complete Fatah domination in the elections was real. Hamas had to get involved to prevent this from happening, the argument went. For his part, Faluji ran for and won a seat on the Palestinian Council.

Opponents of participation continued to argue against taking any steps that would legitimate what they considered an illegitimate process. For them, once Hamas took steps that implicitly supported the PA and Oslo, the game would be over and lost. Some opposed participating in any structure under the PA. More common was the call to boycott only the Council elections which were called for specifically under the Oslo Accords, but to participate in all other elections: municipal, professional, student, and others. These elections, it was pointed out, were independent of the Oslo process. For many of these people, employment in the PA's bureaucracy was also acceptable for Hamas members.

In the end, the debate was never fully settled. Just prior to the election, it appeared that Hamas had created a "front" party that would run in the election under a separate name. Its announcement was called off at the last minute because of further dissent. While Hamas did not formally take part in the elections, a number of Hamas supporters ran in the elections as independents, with four winning seats. The Hamas independents seemed to run with the approval of many in the organization. The debate within Hamas will continue for some time, the likely result being a formal split between different political elements, with one side opting to participate in the political process.

A fourth line of fissure within Hamas could be seen in the military units. At least two autonomous military wings came to the surface with the March 1996 bombings. In addition to the Iz al-Din al-Qassam brigades, a splinter group appeared, naming itself "The Cells of the Martyr the Engineer Yahya Ayyash—the New Pupils." After one of the bombings, the Ayyash cells issued a communiqué claiming credit in their name, not in the name of the Iz al-Din al-Qassam brigades. When both Hamas political leaders and leaders of the Qassam brigades disavowed the attack but promised a cease-fire anyway, the Ayyash cells issued a further communiqué ordering that their "brothers" not speak for them.[24] The Ayyash cells are seemingly more hardline than the Qassam brigades, and may be linked to diaspora Hamas leaders.

Ironically, Hamas's bombing campaign may have brought to fruition Arafat's strategy of dividing and conquering his Islamist opposition. The political leadership of Hamas was taken by surprise by the bombings, lending more support to those within it who argue for accommodation with the PA at the expense of military activities. Just as the Madrid and Oslo process ripped apart the umbrella organization of the PLO, it seems likely that coming to terms with the new Palestinian reality will likewise fragment Hamas—but not without violence. Arafat will then be free to pick up the pieces he chooses through a policy of co-optation.

The 1996 Palestinian Elections

The January 20, 1996, Palestinian elections for an eighty-eight-member legislative Council and for the *Ra'is*, or president, of an Executive Authority were a seminal event in the interim period.[25] The importance of the elections, however, was not that they represented a democratic retreat from PA authoritarianism. Rather, the elections were designed to consolidate the political power of Arafat and the PA. The elections had more to do with consolidation than democratization. In this regard, they were largely successful.

The elections were constructed in such a way as to lead to a predictable outcome. In particular, they were designed to lead to an overwhelming victory by Fatah and its conservative notable and tribal allies. They further guaranteed a poor showing by members of Fatah's opposition, at least those that chose to participate. The key to this structure was adopting a district-based, winner-take-all electoral system, instead of a unitary, proportional representation (PR) system. Gaza and the West Bank were divided into sixteen electoral districts, with each district electing between one and twelve representatives depending on its population size. By taking a geographic area about the size of many congressional districts in the United States and dividing it into sixteen smaller districts, the electoral system tilted the scales in favor of large families and tribes which have a local presence in this or that town but no national constituency. Conversely, any of the smaller PLO parties that enjoy a national following of up to about 10 percent (and thus would win seats in a PR system) would likely be shut out in this system because in any single district they would not be able to gain sufficient votes. For example, in a unitary PR system, the PFLP—had it chosen to participate—would likely have won five to six seats in the Council. In the system actually adopted, it likely would not have won a single seat—a factor that, along with its ideological rejection of the Oslo process, influenced the PFLP to boycott the elections.

By contrast, Israel—a state with three times the population and four times the size of the entire West Bank and Gaza—employs a single district, proportional representation system, allowing for a diverse number of parties to win representation in the Knesset. The proliferation of tiny parties has arguably hurt Israeli politics over the years, but it is a problem easily solved by adopting a higher threshold level of the national vote to qualify for representation. In fact, Israel has debated adopting such a threshold in recent years. The point is, however, that by refusing to adopt a more democratic unitary PR system, the PA demonstrated that it sought a certain kind of electoral outcome.

The electoral structure did not go unnoticed by Palestinians or foreign observers. Even before the formal adoption of the current system, the Palestinian Independent Electoral Commission presented Arafat with a detailed PR system which would include symbolic votes from the diaspora community as well as Palestinians in the West Bank and Gaza. Arafat rejected it out of hand.[26] In addition, a number of foreign institutions concerned with democratic process, including the International Commission of Jurists, publicly called on the PA to change to a PR system, calling it more democratic. One official foreign election observer best summed up the electoral system chosen by the PA. After recounting to me a number of small abuses that had occurred in the run-up to the elections, he said, "You know, 90 percent of the abuses in elections occur well before the election itself and take place in full public view."[27]

The elections were not just about electing a Fatah slate with sympathetic conservative allies but also about who in Fatah was to be elected. Specifically, the election campaign provided Arafat with the opportunity to further undermine popular Fatah cadres and replace them with more compliant and less autonomous members. As noted, Fatah held informal primaries in each of the sixteen districts to produce an electoral list. After each primary, the list was presented to Arafat, who then replaced, at his own discretion, a number of Fatah winners with candidates of his own choosing. Usually it was the most popular and independent Fatah cadres who were removed and marginal Fatah members (or, in some cases, non-Fatah individuals) that Arafat substituted in their place.

To argue that the elections were about consolidating power, not democracy, is not to dismiss the level of enthusiasm they generated among familial and local groups, as well as within Fatah itself. While some of the most important Palestinian political elements did not participate—Hamas, the PFLP, Islamic Jihad, the DFLP—a great number of previously nonpolitical people did. In fact, 676 candidates ran for the eighty-eight available seats (which included seven religious quota seats),[28] and many of them clearly took to the whole process. Voter turnout was likewise impressive, with three-quarters of all Palestinians registered to vote actually casting ballots (although voter turnout in Jerusalem and the city of Hebron was only half the overall number). Interestingly, 42 percent of voters were women, as were twenty-eight of the candidates (five of whom won seats).[29]

The elections produced, in large part, the Council that they were designed to produce. Fatah candidates won fifty of the eighty-eight seats, giving the party an outright majority. Winning Fatah candidates included members of Fatah's traditional leadership, notables and business elites (which overlap considerably), a small handful of Arafat's handpicked Fatah representatives, and tribal representatives who were put on Fatah's slate. Moreover, many of the sixteen nonaligned independents fall into this last category, and will likely vote with Fatah on any important issue. Thus, the elections produced a Council in which two-thirds to three-quarters of the members can be counted on to support Arafat on any major issue. The Council will effectively give its stamp of legitimacy to Arafat and his Executive Authority, further consolidating their power.

Running virtually unopposed for the position of president, Arafat won 88 percent of the vote. Samiha Khalil, a woman from al-Bira who has run the In'ash al-'Usra charitable society for years, won a surprising 12 percent.

If there was any surprise in the Council elections it was the number of independent members elected, given the electoral structure and the opposition's boycott. Sixteen popular and autonomous Fatah cadres snubbed by Arafat ran and won as independents. Moreover, four Hamas supporters ran and won as independents as well. The single largest vote getter in the entire election was Haydar 'Abd al-Shafi', a senior statesman who has been outspoken in his opposition to Arafat's authoritarianism. In fact, one-quarter to one-third of the Council members will likely resist Arafat's authoritarian impulse on a number of issues—not enough to stop certain decisions outright, but enough to raise questions in the mind of the general public.

The Future Palestinian State

I have argued that the PA's politics are, in effect, the antithesis of the politics of the new Palestinian elite in the 1980s. This is not coincidental, as the primary political task of the returning PLO was to neutralize the institutional power base of the new elite, itself largely part of the "inside" PLO; only by so doing could the PA establish its authority. Such is the logic of Palestinian state-building under Yasir Arafat.

That an actual Palestinian state will emerge from this process is likely, but not guaranteed. The question becomes, then, what will this new state look like? I argue in this final section that the future Palestinian state will remain authoritarian, as it will be shaped by three reinforcing dynamics. The first dynamic is simple political inertia. The Palestinian polity is currently being built along certain lines, and as those lines become sharper and more consolidated, it is less likely they will be dramatically changed. Second, I suggest that the imbalance of power between Israel and Palestine will impact the final status issues—in particular, it is unlikely that the PA will be able to win significant concessions from Israel on the issues of Jerusalem and settlements—so that the Palestinian regime will be compelled to tighten its authoritarian grip domestically. Finally, I note that the PA will likely continue to be a rentier regime—its revenues coming from outside aid, not domestic taxation— and therefore will be better able to withstand societal pressures to liberalize.

The preeminent lesson from state-building enterprises throughout the ex-colonial world in the past few decades is, in the words of Shibley Telhami, "how you start significantly determines how you finish." That is, "many well-meaning officials in emerging states rationalized early excesses as necessary, or emergency, compromises that would be corrected in the future, only to discover that these mistakes often become permanent features" of the new states, with their own bureaucratic defenders.[30]

Patterns of political and institutional behavior established during the interim period will likely be reproduced in whole or in large part after a state is created. Thus, there is no reason to believe, a priori, that the authoritarianism and political personalism visible now will suddenly end at the turn of the millennium. Nor should we expect that the level of violence (abuses by security forces, arbitrary arrest, imprisonment without trial, security trials, etc.) which permeates the system—indeed, supports the system—will vanish.

The PA finds itself in charge of a geographically fragmented area. The West Bank in particular under Oslo II is a crazy patchwork of distributed control. Even assuming that a final arrangement consolidates Palestinian control of large areas of the West Bank, it is likely that the Palestinians will end up with three geographically noncontiguous parts to their state: the northern West Bank, the southern West Bank, and Gaza. Supporters of the agreement are already referring to "cantons," while opponents use the less generous "bantustans" to describe this fragmentation. Looking at the Oslo II map of the West Bank one can see clearly a second logical, political reason for the PA's authoritarianism, besides the distrust of a society it barely knows: the PA would not likely win an open, democratic debate on the terms of Oslo II and its map.[31]

The terms of the deal with Israel will not likely improve for the PA in the future, making the PA's willingness to open up the political system even more remote. All of the major issues of the conflict still have to be negotiated at precisely the time when Palestinian leverage is at a low ebb. Two particularly problematic issues remain for the PA, even assuming that Palestinian statehood is achieved: Jerusalem and Jewish settlements. On neither of these issues is it likely that the PA will succeed. On the issue of Jerusalem, Israel routinely rejects any hint of compromise on permanent Israeli control over all of Jerusalem. While a number of creative plans of shared sovereignty or dual sovereignty have been devised which satisfy the main interests both parties have in Jerusalem, the PA has little leverage with which to push its interests.

The bulk of Jewish settlements, particularly in the West Bank, will likely also remain, to the PA's discredit. Even discounting settlements in East Jerusalem, there are well over 120,000 Jewish settlers in the occupied territories, with the vast majority in the West Bank. The Labor government elected in 1992 has been unwilling to relocate even the most problematic settlements, such as those in downtown Hebron, and no Israeli government will have the domestic political support necessary to remove over one hundred thousand settlers. The Rabin government seemed to recognize this, and rather than diminishing the number of settlers, it instead built a series of bypass roads to lessen friction between settlers and Palestinians in the West Bank. The expansion of settlements and the concomitant land confiscations continued in the post-Oslo period. So while there may be some consolidation of settlements by Israel and even dismantling of the most problematic ones, it is highly unlikely that more than a handful of settlements will be removed. Again, the PA has little leverage with which to compel Israel to dismantle or abandon these settlements.

Palestinian capacity to adequately solve these issues—never great—is on the decline. The PA may discover in a couple of years, when final status negotiations are under way, that it has lost the little leverage it used to have. By agreeing to Oslo, the PLO opened the door for other Arab states—notably Jordan—to make their own peace with Israel. It is quite possible that all "frontline" states will be at peace with Israel by the time discussions of Jerusalem and settlements begin between the Palestinians and Israel. Without any viable leverage, Palestinian rights in these crucial areas will likely be ignored. Given this probable outcome, in addition to its geographically fragmented polity, the PA will most likely be compelled to sustain its current authoritarian structures in order to maintain social control.

The characteristics of a future Palestinian state, then, emerge not only from inertia in the present political system but also from a recognition of how fundamental issues currently unresolved will likely impact the political structure. The question that then arises is whether the Palestinian regime has the capacity to withstand inevitable societal pressures. Strong opposition to the PA will likely emerge, because of both its authoritarianism and its probable failures in the final status negotiations. Briefly put, the PA will likely be able to survive such social pressure simply because of the lack of leverage (i.e., taxes) society will have on the regime. Palestine is an emerging rentier state. That is, the PA is now, and will be well into the future, disproportionately dependent for its revenues on external sources of rent. In this case, the rent is not from the sale of oil, as is the common form of rentierism in the Middle East, but from government-to-government transfers, i.e., aid. As has been noted by numerous authors, heavy external rents free a state from the process of political bargaining with its own society. Under more usual circumstances, a state must raise revenues from its own population through taxation, leading to some form of political deal between state and society: taxation for representation. Freed from the burden of requiring resources directly from its own society, the PA need not be particularly responsive to its needs.

Given its autocratic present, its troubled future, and its structural ability to withstand societal pressures to reform, the Palestinian state will likely be authoritarian well into the future.

NOTES

1. The Traditional Notable Elite in Palestine

1. The "politics of notables" approach in Middle East studies was initiated in the works of Ira Lapidus, especially his *Muslim Cities in the Later Middle Ages* (Cambridge: Harvard University Press, 1967). Albert Hourani and a number of his students then refined and expanded the paradigm. For Hourani's definitions, see his chapter "Ottoman Reform and the Politics of Notables," in William R. Polk and Richard L. Chambers, *Beginnings of Modernization in the Middle East* (Chicago: University of Chicago Press, 1968). A student of Hourani's, Philip Khoury, has also used the concept with success. See his *Urban Notables and Arab Nationalism: The Politics of Damascus 1860–1920* (Cambridge: Cambridge University Press, 1983) and *Syria and the French Mandate: The Politics of Arab Nationalism 1920–1945* (Princeton: Princeton University Press, 1987). For notable politics in the transition from Ottomanism to Arabism, see C. Ernest Dawn, *From Ottomanism to Arabism: Essays on the Origins of Arab Nationalism* (Urbana: University of Illinois Press, 1973), and his essay "Pan-Arab Ideology in the Interwar Years," *International Journal of Middle East Studies* 20, no. 1 (February 1988).

2. For more detailed accounts of early Palestinian notables and their politics, see Muhammad Y. Muslih, *The Origins of Palestinian Nationalism* (New York: Columbia University Press, 1988), and Issa Khalaf, *Politics in Palestine: Arab Factionalism and Social Disintegration 1939–1948* (Albany: State University of New York Press, 1991).

3. Ian Lustick, *Arabs in the Jewish State: Israel's Control of a National Minority* (Austin: University of Texas Press, 1980).

4. David D. Laitin, *Hegemony and Culture* (Chicago: University of Chicago Press, 1986), and "Hegemony and Religious Conflict: British Imperial Control and Political Cleavages in Yorubaland," in Peter B. Evans et al., *Bringing the State Back In* (New York: Cambridge University Press, 1985).

5. Joel S. Migdal, *Strong Societies and Weak States* (Princeton: Princeton University Press, 1988).

6. Hourani uses the term *a'yan* specifically for the secular landed notables. However, since religious, military, and administrative roles often overlapped, e.g., in the Husayni family, I have chosen to use the term *a'yan* to refer to all three.

7. Haim Gerber, *The Social Origins of the Modern Middle East* (Boulder: Lynne Rienner, 1987), p. 56.

8. Y. Porath, *The Emergence of the Palestinian-Arab National Movement, 1918–1929* (London: Frank Cass, 1974), p. 9.

9. Ibid., p. 12.

10. Gerber, *Social Origins*, p. 72.

11. Muslih, *Palestinian Nationalism*, p. 22.

12. Gerber, *Social Origins*, p. 72.

13. Porath, *Emergence*, p. 11.

14. Ann Mosely Lesch, *Arab Politics in Palestine, 1917–1939* (Ithaca: Cornell University Press, 1979), p. 27.

15. Joel S. Migdal et al., *Palestinian Society and Politics* (Princeton: Princeton University Press, 1980), p. 29.

16. See Philip Mattar, "The Mufti of Jerusalem and the Politics of Palestine," *Middle East Journal* 42, no. 2 (Spring 1988).

17. Nels Johnson, *Islam and the Politics of Meaning* (London: Kegan Paul, 1982), p. 17.

18. Ibid., p. 19.

19. It was this preacher who became the namesake a half century later for Hamas's military wing, the Iz al-Din al-Qassam brigades.

20. The Arab headdress, or *kafiya*, as a symbol of political resistance dates to the 1935–39 revolt. It replaced the *fez*, or *tarbush*, in urban areas in order that rebel peasants—who already wore the kafiya—would be less noticeable in towns; see Ted Swedenburg, "The Role of the Palestinian Peasantry in the Great Revolt (1936–1939)," in Edmund Burke III and Ira M. Lapidus, eds., *Islam, Politics and Social Movements* (Tauris, 1988), p. 192.

21. Donna Robinson Divine, "The Dialectics of Palestinian Politics," in Migdal, *Palestinian Society*, p. 222.

22. Johnson, *Islam*, p. 52.

23. Khoury, *Urban Notables*, and Dawn, *From Ottomanism to Arabism*, pp. 158–74.

24. Migdal, *Palestinian Society*, p. 30.

25. Ibid., p. 22.

26. The information and quotes used in this brief overview of Israeli policy are drawn from Lustick, *Arabs in the Jewish State*, pp. 201–205.

27. Shaul Mishal, "Conflictual Pressures and Cooperative Interests: Observations on West Bank–Amman Political Relations, 1949–1967," in Migdal, *Palestinian Society*, p. 170.

28. These are just some examples. For a more complete list, see Mishal, ibid., pp. 174–78.

29. Ibid., p. 172.

30. Benny Morris, *Israel's Border Wars, 1949–1956* (New York: Oxford University Press, 1993).

31. William Quandt, in William Quandt, Fuad Jabber, and Mosely Lesch, *The Politics of Palestinian Nationalism* (Berkeley: University of California Press, 1973), p. 68.

32. Ibid.

33. Migdal, *Palestinian Society*, p. 49.

34. Emile Sahliyeh, *In Search of Leadership: West Bank Politics since 1967* (Washington, D.C.: Brookings Institution, 1988), p. 34.

35. Ibid., p. 21.

36. Migdal, *Palestinian Society*, p. 46.

37. Moshe Ma'oz, *Palestinian Leadership on the West Bank: The Changing Role of the Mayors under Jordan and Israel* (London: Frank Cass, 1984), p. 135.

38. Sahliyeh, *In Search of Leadership*, p. 47.

39. Ma'oz, *Palestinian Leadership*, pp. 136–37.

40. Sahliyeh, *In Search of Leadership*, p. 47.

41. Ma'oz, *Palestinian Leadership*, p. 151.

42. Ibid., p. 144.

43. Sahliyeh, *In Search of Leadership*, p. 61.

44. Ibid., p. 71.

45. Divine, "Dialectics," pp. 227–28.

46. Quandt, *The Politics of Palestinian Nationalism*, p. 83.

47. For an excellent discussion of land policy, see Raja Shehadeh, *Occupier's Law: Israel and the West Bank* (Washington, D.C.: Institute for Palestine Studies, 1985; revised 1988), esp. part 1 and the epilogue.

48. Joost R. Hiltermann, *Behind the Intifada: Labor and Women's Movements in the Occupied Territories* (Princeton: Princeton University Press, 1991).

49. See chap. 3.

50. See chap. 2.

51. Emile Nakhleh, "The West Bank and Gaza: Twenty Years Later," *Middle East Journal* 42, no. 2 (Spring 1988), p. 221.

2. The Rise of a New Political Elite in the West Bank and Gaza

1. Initially, Palestinian Communists were organizationally part of the Jordanian Communist Party. In 1982, a fully independent Palestine Communist Party (PCP) was formed.

2. While the Communists had joined the PNC in 1968, they did not hold a seat on the crucial PLO Executive Committee until 1987.

3. Sahliyeh, *In Search of Leadership*, p. 118.

4. Jerusalem University consists of the Nursing College in al-Bira, the Scientific Institute in Abu Dis, and the College of Religious and Islamic Studies in Bayt Hanina.

5. Lisa Taraki, "Mass Organizations in the West Bank," in Naseer Aruri, ed., *Occupation: Israel over Palestine*, 2d ed. (Belmont: AAUG Press, 1989), p. 454.

6. Sahliyeh, *In Search of Leadership*, p. 123.

7. Both Sahliyeh, *In Search of Leadership*, p. 121, and Taraki, "Mass Organizations," p. 455, make this point.

8. Sahar Khalifeh, *Wild Thorns* (New York: Olive Branch Press, 1991), p. 123.

9. This last point was especially relevant in devising ways to detect and deal with informers routinely integrated by the Israeli jailers into prisoner cells. For an interesting fictionalized account of this process, see ibid., esp. pp. 127–35.

10. *Catholic New York*, February 9, 1989.

11. Office of Student Affairs, Bethlehem University.

12. A 1986 opinion survey found that a scant 3.3 percent of Palestinians in the West Bank and Gaza viewed King Husayn as their preferred leader. Most of the king's support came from those who were illiterate or over the age of forty. By contrast, 72.2 percent supported the PLO leadership. Mohammed Shadid and Rick Seltzer, "Political Attitudes of Palestinians in the West Bank and Gaza Strip," *Middle East Journal* 42, no. 1 (Winter 1988), pp. 22–23.

13. Information on recruitment comes from a number of interviews with current and former students. However, due to the sensitive nature of the subject, few respondents were willing to speak in great detail. I am particularly grateful to two graduates of Bir Zeit University who provided many of the details found in this section. I have respected their requests for anonymity. The interviews were conducted in 1989 and 1990.

14. Interview, East Jerusalem, December 1, 1989.

15. *Jerusalem Post*, November 20, 1991.

16. Sahliyeh, *In Search of Leadership*, p. 106.

17. Land that periodically lay fallow was particularly vulnerable to confiscation.

18. Jim Lederman, "Interpreting the Intifada," *Foreign Policy*, no. 72 (Fall 1988), pp. 232–34. The figure does not include the hundreds of thousands of Palestinians who left or were driven out by Israel in the immediate aftermath of the 1967 war.

19. Taraki, "Mass Organizations," p. 452.

20. Lisa Taraki, "The Development of Political Consciousness among Palestinians in the Occupied Territories," in Jamal R. Nassar and Roger Heacock, eds., *Intifada: Palestine at the Crossroads* (New York: Praeger, 1990), p. 59.

21. Taraki, "Mass Organizations," p. 456.

22. Identifying the refugee camp population is not without its difficulties. For example, a number of camps abut towns—Shu'fat and East Jerusalem, 'Askar and Nablus, are two examples—so those environments are partially urban. In many ways, Gaza is a continuous, partially urbanized refugee camp. Yet, for obvious reasons, the life experiences of refugee camp residents remain quite distinctive.

23. Interview with Musaddiq al-Masri, al-Najah University, February 14, 1990.

24. Bir Zeit University remained closed throughout the 1991–92 academic year, while the other Palestinian universities were allowed to reopen in the fall of 1991.

25. Council for Higher Education, *Statistical Guidebook to Palestinian Universities, 1987/88–1988/89* (in Arabic) (Jerusalem, n.d.), p. 31.

26. Ibid., p. 33.

27. Jad Isaac, "A Socio-economic Study of Administrative Detainees at Ansar 3," *Journal of Palestine Studies* 18, no. 4 (Summer 1989), pp. 102–109.

28. Interview, December 1, 1989.

3. The Professional Middle Class

1. Numerous works deal with this theme. For an excellent overview, see the collection of essays in George T. Abed, ed., *The Palestinian Economy: Studies in Development under Prolonged Occupation* (New York: Routledge, 1988). For more recent assessments, see Sara Roy, *The Gaza Strip: The Political Economy of De-Development* (Washington, D.C.: Institute for Palestine Studies, 1995), and the series by the World Bank entitled *Developing the Occupied Territories* (Washington, D.C., 1993).

2. Now known as the Palestinian People's Party (PPP).

3. The figures come from Mustafa Barghouti and Ibrahim Daibes, *Infrastructure and Health Services in the West Bank: Guidelines for Health Care Planning; The West Bank Rural PHC Survey* (Ramallah: Health Development Information Project, 1993); *An Overview of Health Conditions and Services in the Israeli Occupied Territories*, written by the Union of Palestinian Medical Relief Committees (Jerusalem, August 1987); World Bank, *Developing the Occupied Territories, Volume 6: Human Resources and Social Policy* (Washington, D.C., 1993); and the Palestinian Central Bureau of Statistics, *Health Statistics in the West Bank and Gaza Strip* (Ramallah, 1995). Exact figures vary from source to source, but a general consensus exists for most. Infant mortality is the most disputed; most reports agree that the rate by 1992 was approximately 45 per 1,000. Whether this figure represented an improvement based on the enhanced primary health care services discussed in the chapter or had remained relatively unchanged for years is a matter of dispute.

4. Anne Elizabeth Nixon, *The Status of Palestinian Children during the Uprising in the Occupied Territories*, Excerpted Summary Material of Part I (Jerusalem, January 1990), p. 5.

5. Barghouti and Giacaman's arguments are drawn from their chapter "The Emergence of an Infrastructure of Resistance: The Case of Health," in Nassar and Heacock, *Intifada*, as well as individual interviews with Rita Giacaman and Mustafa Barghouti in 1989, 1990, 1992, and 1994.

6. Information on the UPMRC comes primarily from interviews with Mustafa Barghouti, head of the UPMRC, in East Jerusalem, October 16, 1989, and in Bayt Hanina, May 5, 1994.

7. Formerly known as the Popular Committees for Health Services, or PCHS.

8. Information on the UHWC comes from multiple interviews with Ahmad Maslamani, Na'im Abu Tayr, Majid Nassar, and other UHWC officials in 1990, 1992, 1994, and 1995.

9. According to the HDIP survey, this ratio had increased so that by 1992, 86 percent of the rural West Bank population had access to one of the 523 rural clinics.

10. UHWC Annual Activity Report, 1989.

11. See Sara Roy, "The Political Economy of Despair: Changing Political and Economic Realities in the Gaza Strip," *Journal of Palestine Studies*, no. 79 (Spring 1991), p. 64.

12. Interview with Ahmad Maslamani, then head of the UHWC, Shu'fat, January 14, 1990, and the UHWC Annual Activity Report, 1989.

13. Interviews with Na'im Abu Tayr, head of the UHWC, Shu'fat, April 1994, and Majid Nassar, vice-chair of UHWC, Bayt Sahur, October 1995.

14. The DFLP-affiliated Women's Action Committee was founded in 1978.

15. Interview with Muhammad Jadallah, secretary-general of the Union of Health Care Committees, East Jerusalem, January 10, 1990. Further interviews were conducted with Jadallah in 1992 and 1994, providing much of the information on UHCC activities.

16. Ibid. For its part, UHCC has encouraged a policy of spacing, arguing that no woman should be pregnant before age twenty or after age thirty-five and all women should have at least two years between births. If these guidelines were followed, rural birthrates would decline.

17 Ibid.

18. Program and Internal Platform, Union of Health Care Committees in the West Bank and Gaza Strip (n.d.), p. 12.

19. I would like to thank Dr. Anis al-Qaq for clarifying the issue of volunteerism and related matters in a personal communication, June 26, 1993.

20. Interview, East Jerusalem, May 5, 1994.

21. Barghouti and Daibes, HDIP survey, p. xvi.

22. Interview with Rita Giacaman, Ramallah, September 13, 1989.

23. Interview with the secretary-general of the UHCC, East Jerusalem, January 10, 1990.

24. Interview with UPMRC officials, East Jerusalem, October 16, 1989.

25. Ibid.

26. *Al-Quds*, August 12, 1989.

27. Interview with Hisham Awartani, East Jerusalem, December 14, 1989.

28. Interview with Labib Nashashibi, East Jerusalem, May 29, 1992.

29. For a fuller discussion of Palestinian agriculture prior to the Intifada, see Hisham Awartani, "Agricultural Development and Policies in the West Bank and Gaza," in Abed, *The Palestinian Economy*.

30. Meron Benvinisti, *The West Bank Data Base Project* (Washington, D.C.: AEI, 1984), p. 13, and World Bank, *Developing the Occupied Territories, Volume 4: Agriculture* (Washington, D.C., 1993), p. xi.

31. Awartani, "Agricultural Development," p. 143.

32. World Bank, *Developing the Occupied Territories, Volume 4: Agriculture*, p. 84.

33. PARC, *Agricultural Development and the Uprising* (Jerusalem, May 1988), p. 4.

34. Ibid., p. 5.

35. *The Palestinian Agricultural Relief Committee* (Shu'fat: n.d.), p. 3.

36. Interview with PARC officials, Shu'fat, February 7, 1990.

37. Interview with Ismail Da'iq, head of PARC, Bayt Hanina, May 1, 1994.

38. Interview with PARC officials, Shu'fat, February 7, 1990.

39. Interview with TCAS officials, Hebron, January 7, 1990.

40. Central Bureau of Statistics, *Statistical Abstract of Israel*, no. 40 (1989). The figure was derived from chart 27/24.

41. Interview, East Jerusalem, December 5, 1989.

42. Interview with PARC officials, Shu'fat, September 21, 1989.

43. PARC, 1989 Annual Report, pp. 7–8.

44. UAWC, Activity Report, 1988–89, p. 1.

45. Interview with PARC officials, Shu'fat, September 21, 1989. PARC Annual Report for 1989, pp. 10–12.

46. UAWC, Activity Report, 1988–89, p. 1.

47. Interview with Dr. Faras Sawalha, director of the Rural Research Center at al-Najah University, Nablus, January 10, 1990.

48. Interview with TCAS officials, Hebron, January 7, 1990.

49. Interview with a leading member of the popular committees, Nablus, September 24, 1989.

50. Interview with Mazan al-Risha, Nablus office of the Israeli Ministry of Agriculture, Nablus, December 23, 1989.

51. Interview, Salfit, October 12, 1989.

52. Figures come from TCAS officials, interview, Hebron, January 7, 1990.

53. These examples come from *Bitter Harvest: Israeli Sanctions against Palestinian Agriculture during the Uprising* (Jerusalem Media and Communication Centre, May 1989), pp. 5–8. Similar examples can be found in materials published by B'tselem, al-Haq/Law in the Service of Man, and the Palestine Human Rights Information Center (PHRIC).

54. *Al-Fajr* (weekly), December 18, 1989, and interview with TCAS officials, Hebron, January 7, 1990.

55. Reports of the incident were in a number of newspapers at the time. The figures for losses come from TCAS, Hebron, January 7, 1990.

56. Interview, Ministry of Agriculture (Nablus branch), December 23, 1989.

57. Interview, East Jerusalem, December 14, 1989.

58. Figures derived from Israel's Central Bureau of Statistics, *Statistical Abstract of Israel*, no. 40 (1989), table 27/30.

59. World Bank, *Developing the Occupied Territories, Volume 4: Agriculture*, p. 63.

60. Ibid., p 78.

61. Central Bureau of Statistics, *Statistical Abstract of Israel*, no. 40 (1989), table 27/29.

62. Interview with Hisham Awartani, East Jerusalem, December 14, 1989.

63. Interview, al-Bira, February 26, 1990.

64. Interview, East Jerusalem, December 5, 1989.

65. Interview, East Jerusalem, December 5, 1989.

4. Abu Barbur: Elite Conflict and Social Change in Bayt Sahur

1. *Jerusalem Post*, September 29, 1989.

2. Interview with Khader Muslih, January 5, 1990, Bayt Sahur.

3. Ibid.

4. Much of the information on Bayt Sahur during the early months of the Intifada comes from a lengthy interview with Jad Ishaq, East Jerusalem, November 20, 1989. Dr. Ishaq, an early leader of the self-sufficiency movement, was imprisoned at Ketziot/Ansar III without charge or trial for five months because of his Intifada activities.

5. Interview with community activist, Bayt Sahur, January 16, 1990.

6. Interview with Jad Ishaq, East Jerusalem, November 20, 1989.

7. Interview with community activist, Bayt Sahur, January 16, 1990.

8. Interview with Ibrahim Jabbar, Bayt Sahur, February 27, 1990.

9. Interview with Jad Ishaq, East Jerusalem, November 20, 1989.

10. Interview with Khader Muslih, Bayt Sahur, January 5, 1990.

11. Rapid communication—often in the form of gossip—is legendary in Bayt Sahur. Bayt Sahur contains Shepherd's Field, from where, Christian lore tells us, local men took a bright star above Bethlehem as evidence for the coming of the Messiah. The unofficial Bayt Sahurian version of this story is that it was necessary for God to give the sign specifically to Bayt Sahurians in order for the word of Jesus' birth to spread as quickly as possible. Otherwise, nobody might have known.

12. Interview with Majid Nassar, Bayt Sahur, March 11, 1990.

13. The information on early clan histories in Bayt Sahur comes from Tuma Banura, *The History of Bethlehem, Bayt Jala, and Bayt Sahur* (in Arabic) (Jerusalem: Matb'a al-Ma'arif, 1982), as well as an interview with Dr. Banura, conducted in Bethlehem, February 17, 1990. Other respondents from Bayt Sahur vouched for the veracity of Dr. Banura's history: the book is based on family records made available during his research.

14. The Ishaqs date their arrival in Bayt Sahur to 1635. See Glenn Frankel, *Beyond the Promised Land* (New York: Simon & Schuster, 1994), p. 51.

15. There is presently a branch of the Murajda clan in the primarily Muslim village of 'Aqraba outside Nablus. The story goes that a member of the Murajdas in Bayt Sahur insulted a Bedouin shaykh in the early nineteenth century. Afraid for his life, the man moved to Shu'fat, near Jerusalem, until he spotted the same shaykh some time later, at which point he moved north to 'Aqraba. Returning temporarily to Bayt Sahur a few years later in order to find suitable marriage partners for his sons and daughters, the man was refused because he lived in a Muslim area. He returned to 'Aqraba, married his children to local Muslims (presumably the sons had to convert to Islam), and that branch of the Murajdas has been Muslim ever since. Banura, *History*, p. 220, and interview with Dr. Banura, Bethlehem, February 17, 1990.

16. Interview with Ghassan Andoni, Bayt Sahur, February 12, 1990.

17. Interview with Jad Ishaq, a founding member of the Agricultural Committee, East Jerusalem, November 20, 1989. See also F. Robert Hunter, *The Palestinian Uprising: A War by Other Means* (London: Tauris, 1991), p. 137.

18. Interview with Jad Ishaq, Bayt Sahur, February 5, 1990.

19. Interview with PARC officials, Shu'fat, February 1990. See also PARC's 1989 Annual Report, p. 13.

20. Interview with Jad Ishaq, East Jerusalem, November 20, 1989.

21. Interview with a member of the cooperative nursery—a pharmacist in Bethlehem—in Bayt Sahur, June 13, 1992.

22. The information on Bayt Sahur's cows comes from an interview with a cooperative member in Bayt Sahur, June 13, 1992. See also *New Outlook*, September–October 1989, p. 25, and the *San Francisco Examiner*, December 9, 1990.

23. According to sources in Bayt Sahur, an Israeli commander once passed around a photograph of one of the "wanted" cows with its branded number showing and asked residents if they had seen it. This incident precipitated a running joke about how the cows, when milked, cried "PLO." Interview, Bayt Sahur, June 13, 1992.

24. Ibid.

25. Interview with Majid Nassar, Bayt Sahur, February 27, 1990. Dr. Nassar is

the founder of the clinic. Most of the information about the clinic comes from him in a series of interviews from 1990 to 1995.

26. Ibid.

27. Interview with Rifa't al-Qassis, Bayt Sahur, June 13, 1992.

28. Ibid.

29. Interview with Jad Ishaq, Bayt Sahur, February 5, 1990.

30. Interview with Elias al-Rishmawi, Bayt Sahur, February 1990.

31. Interview with Ghassan Andoni, a member of the Sulha committee, Bayt Sahur, February 12, 1990.

32. Interview with Majid Nassar, Bayt Sahur, March 11, 1990.

33. A more accurate, if less refined, translation is "father of snot."

34. A copy of this letter can be found in *Uprising in Palestine: The First Year* (Chicago: Database Project on Palestinian Human Rights, 1989), p. 275.

35. Witnessed by the author.

36. Interview with Majid Nassar, head of the clinic, Bayt Sahur, May 29, 1992.

37. Frankel, *Beyond the Promised Land*, p. 53.

38. The Sulha committee was known formally as the General Committee for Coordination between Institutions in Bayt Sahur (*al-lajna al-'ama l'il-tansiq al-mu'sisaat fi Bayt Sahur*).

39. Interview with Khader Muslih, a member of the Sulha committee, Bayt Sahur, January 5, 1990.

40. Interview with Ghassan Andoni, Sulha member, Bayt Sahur, February 12, 1990.

41. Ibid.

42. There is some disagreement among my respondents over the level of actual Sulha involvement in this episode. It seems likely the Sulha was involved behind the scene in this case, allowing local factional activists to take the lead.

43. Salim Tamari, "Israel's Search for a Native Pillar: The Village Leagues," in Aruri, ed., *Occupation*, p. 617.

44. Interview with Ghassan Andoni, Bayt Sahur, February 12, 1990.

45. Ibid.

46. Interview with Khader Muslih, Bethlehem, June 2, 1992.

47. One may have been arrested for non-Sulha reasons.

48. The figures vary from $50 million to $150 million. Figures in excess of $100 million include those presented by Hanna Siniora, "An Analysis of the Current Revolt," *Journal of Palestine Studies*, no. 67 (Spring 1988), p. 6; Lisa Hajjar et al., in *Intifada: The Palestinian Uprising against Israeli Occupation*, ed. Zachary Lockman and Joel Beinin (Boston: South End Press, 1989), p. 104; and Azmy Bishara, *Middle East Report*, no. 157 (March–April 1989). Meron Benvinisti uses the more conservative figure of $50 million annual tax profit for Israel from the occupied territories (quoted in Hunter, *The Palestinian Uprising*, p. 127). For further discussion on this issue, see Sara Roy, *The Gaza Strip Survey* (Jerusalem: West Bank Data Project, 1986), and Raja Shehadeh, *Occupier's Law: Israel and the West Bank* (Washington, D.C.: Institute for Palestine Studies, 1988).

49. See al-Haq, *Punishing a Nation: Human Rights Violations during the Palestinian Uprising December 1987–1988* (al-Haq, December 1988), p. 396, and Frankel, *Beyond the Promised Land*, p. 54.

50. For an excellent overview of household income and related data in the West Bank and Gaza, see Marianne Heiberg and Geir Øvensen, eds., *Palestinian Society: A Survey of Living Conditions* (Oslo: FAFO Report 151, 1993).

51. Quoted in Frankel, *Beyond the Promised Land*, p. 63.

52. *Al-Fajr* (weekly), February 19, 1990.

53. Interviews with a number of store owners in both East Jerusalem and the West Bank.

54. Al-Haq, *Punishing a Nation*, p. 397.

55. Cited in the *Jerusalem Post*, February 27, 1990.

56. Al-Haq press release no. 31 (September 28, 1989). Petty fines were also rampant and were used as an instrument of harassment and control. Two types were common: fining a driver for not wearing a seat belt (regardless of whether or not he was) and fining the drivers of shared taxis for having the Arabic sign for "no smoking" placed above its Hebrew counterpart on the dashboard. The author personally witnessed both types.

57. These figures come from noted economist Hisham 'Awartani, cited in *al-Fajr* (weekly), December 11, 1989.

58. *Jerusalem Post*, September 29, 1989.

59. From a leaflet dated November 5, 1989, and signed "People of Bayt Sahur."

60. Interview with Elias al-Rishmawi, Bayt Sahur, February 12, 1990.

61. Ibid.

62. *New Outlook*, September–October 1989, p. 25.

63. *Al-Fajr* (weekly), October 2, 1989.

64. Press release no. 31 (September 28, 1989)

65. *Jerusalem Post*, October 5, 1989.

66. *Jerusalem Post*, October 11, 1989, and *al-Fajr* (weekly), October 16, 1989.

67. The vote was 140 to 2, with only Israel and the United States voting against it. All 12 members of the European Community supported the resolution.

68. Leaflet addressed "To the People of Bayt Sahur" and signed by the Commander of the Israel Defense Forces in the Area (no date). A copy of the leaflet can be found in Jibra'il al-Shumli, *al-Tajriba al-'Asiyaniya fi Bayt Sahur* (The Disobedience Campaign in Bayt Sahur) (Jerusalem: Markaz al-Zahra, 1991).

69. Official Israeli estimate.

70. *Jerusalem Post*, November 1, 1989.

71. Ibid.

72. *Al-Fajr* (weekly), November 6, 1989.

73. *Jerusalem Post*, November 1, 1989.

74. *Jerusalem Post*, November 6, 1989.

75. *Abu Ita et al. v. Customs Commissioner of Judea and Samaria et al.* and *Kansas et al. v. Customs Commissioner, Gaza Strip Command et al.*

76. Personal communication from Majid Nassar, July 28, 1995.

77. Interview with Ghassan Andoni, Bayt Sahur, May 29, 1992.

78. Ibid.

79. Interview with Khader Muslih, Bethlehem, June 2, 1992. The military governor was referring to the traditional apolitical reconciliation aspects of sulha, done usually by community elders. Muslih was not among those arrested.

80. Interview with Ghassan Andoni, Bayt Sahur, May 29, 1992.

5. Popular Committees in the Intifada

1. Interview with Tuqua activist, Bayt Sahur, February 5, 1990.

2. Interview with member of Rafadiya popular committee, September 24, 1989.

3. *Jerusalem Post*, August 19, 1988.

4. Much of the information on the UNLU comes from an extended interview with Muhammad Khalid, a member of the UNLU in 1989–90. Khalid had been a colleague of my wife at Save the Children in East Jerusalem concurrent with his (then unknown) UNLU activities. After his arrest in March 1990, Khalid spent three years in prison, including a year at Ansar 3. The interview for this book occurred May 3–4, 1994, in al-Bira.

5. The PFLP used two different members in the fourth group.

6. Local production and labor absorption were strongly encouraged, so big industries received special dispensations regarding hours and other issues.

7. Interview, May 3, 1994, al-Bira.

8. Ibid.

9. Dated May 13, 1988.

10. Dated June 8, 1988.

11. The Arab world's equivalent of the SAT examination in the United States.

12. Andrew Rigby, *The Intifada: The Struggle over Education* (East Jerusalem: PASSIA, July 1989), p. 8.

13. *Palestinian Education: A Threat to Israel's Security?* (East Jerusalem: Jerusalem Media and Communication Centre, n.d.), p. 41. Hereafter cited as JMCC.

14. Stanley Cohen, "Education as Crime," *Jerusalem Post*, May 18, 1989.

15. JMCC, p. 44.

16. Interview with Munir Fasheh, professor and dean at Bir Zeit University and founder of the Tamer literacy program, East Jerusalem, September 25, 1989.

17. Ibid.

18. Information on Salfit was gathered by the author during a series of interviews in that town on October 12, 1989.

19. *Jerusalem Post*, August 19, 1988, as quoted in "The Criminalization of Education," a report from Bir Zeit University.

20. Al-Haq, *Punishing a Nation*, p. 423.

21. *Jerusalem Post*, May 18, 1989.

22. A copy is in the author's possession.

23. Interview with Hiyam Zakhriya, one of the principals of the project, al-Bira, June 1, 1992.

24. Jad Isaac and Ghassen Andoni, "A Model for Continuing University Education in the Occupied Arab Territories in Light of the Uprising," a paper presented at the First Educational Conference of the Union of Educational Sectors, East Jerusalem, May 5, 1989, p. 1.

25. "University Closures," Council for Higher Education, East Jerusalem, 1987 (in Arabic).

26. The average age of those people killed in the uprising was twenty-four years.

27. Bir Zeit University Newsletter, no. 18, March 1989.

28. See the course listings for the 1989 Summer Session, the Registrar, Bir Zeit University.

29. The campus was actually allowed to open for one day, February 1, 1989, but by 8:40 P.M. that same day the military governor had, once again, closed the campus "until further notice." No incidents had occurred on campus that day, but the military accused Bethlehem University students of participating in "incidents in the town during the day." See "Closure by Military Authority of Bethlehem University February 1, 1989," in the "Intifada file" of Bethlehem University. Much of the information on Bethlehem University comes from this file, maintained by the university to document its history during the uprising. I was allowed to study the file periodically during the 1989–90 academic year.

30. Interview with the Registrar, Bethlehem, September 11, 1989.

31. Ibid.

32. The missing two students were in prison at the time.

33. "Report on the Return of Students," Maria Homberg, March 2, 1989, Intifada file.

34. See the August–September 1989 schedule.

35. Bethlehem University memorandum, September 4, 1989, Intifada file.

36. See the August–September 1989 schedule.

37. An experiment used to separate components from a mixture.

38. Interview with Professor Adnan Shqueir, Dean of the Faculty of Science, Bethlehem University, Bethlehem, September 11, 1989.

39. Notes from the academic meeting on December 2, 1988, Intifada file.

40. Faculty meeting notes, August 22, 1989, Intifada file.

41. Letter written by Brother James, June 25, 1989, Intifada file.

42. Ibid.

43. Quoted in the *National Catholic News Service*, February 6, 1989.

44. Interview with Mona Rishmawi, lawyer with al-Haq, Ramallah, October 27, 1989.

45. An overview of the B'tselem report can be found in the *Jerusalem Post*, December 6, 1989.

46. Ibid. Frequently, the punishment far exceeded the crime. The military courts handed down particularly severe sentences, often sentencing juveniles to long prison terms for relatively minor offenses. Moreover, judicial inequality rose precipitously during the uprising. As B'tselem points out, Israelis charged with the killing of Palestinians were usually sentenced to several months of public service or imprisonment, while Palestinians charged with killing Israelis were given life sentences and their homes were demolished. Mona Rishmawi contends that the military court system during the Intifada was a real learning experience for the tens of thousands of Palestinians who went through it. Palestinians "can feel much more tangibly the injustice [of the occupation] by just one experience in the military courts." Without these experiences, she maintains, "people may not have believed" the stories of injustice coming out of the courts. In short, the structured injustice of the military courts during the uprising enhanced Palestinian solidarity by infuriating all who went through it. Such anger was shared by the Palestinian lawyers who had to represent their clients in the system. While relations between Palestinian lawyers and the Israeli military courts were never good, the Intifada led to marked increases in Israeli "hostility, racism, and sexism" toward Palestinian lawyers. Interview, Ramallah, October 27, 1989.

47. Amnesty International, "Israel and the Occupied Territories," July 1991. Cited in *Palestine Monitor*, September–October 1991.

48. Interview with Raja Shehadeh, a lawyer and co-founder of al-Haq, Ramallah, December 21, 1989.

49. The divorce rate during the first two years of the Intifada was down significantly—as much as 70 percent in Nablus, for example—because, in part, men could not afford the price of a new bride.

50. Interview with Raja Shehadeh, Ramallah, December 21, 1989.

51. Interview, East Jerusalem, February 13, 1990. See chapter 4 for a discussion of the Sulha, a mediation committee in the town of Bayt Sahur.

52. Information regarding the early involvement of the merchants in the Intifada comes from Salim Tamari, "The Revolt of the Petite Bourgeoisie: Urban Merchants and the Palestinian Uprising," in Nassar and Heacock, eds., *Intifada*, pp. 159–73.

53. *HaAretz*, April 22, 1989. Reported by Tamari, "The Revolt," p. 159.

54. According to Shimon Levy, then Israeli chief of police in Gaza, as reported in *The Middle East*, April 1989, p. 25. In a number of cases of theft, documented by al-Haq, soldiers arrested Palestinians investigating the incident rather than the thieves themselves. They were charged with being members of popular committees. Many such thefts in the first two years of the Intifada were carried out by collaborators as a means of disrupting the Intifada.

55. Bayan 9, March 2, 1988.

56. Bayan 44, August 15, 1989.

57. Interview with a popular committee member in the Rafadiya quarter of Nablus, September 24, 1989.

58. Ibid.

59. *Jerusalem Post*, February 13, 1990.

60. *Jerusalem Post*, December 27, 1989.

61. *Jerusalem Post*, March 15, 1990.

62. *Jerusalem Post*, January 16, 1990.

63. *Jerusalem Post*, March 15, 1990.

64. *Jerusalem Post*, March 13, 1990.

65. This account is taken from the *Jerusalem Post*, November 10, 1989.

66. See B'tselem's excellent report *Collaborators in the Occupied Territories* (Jerusalem, 1994), pp. 137–38 for other examples.

67. Ibid., p. 30.

68. The exact number of undercover collaborators recruited since 1967 has never been revealed. B'tselem estimates that the number is in the "tens of thousands" (*Collaboration in the Occupied Territories*, p. 10). For a discussion on the use of notables for social control, see chapter 1.

69. The civil administration is an administrative arm of, and answerable to, the military government. Thus, the sharp distinction drawn by some writers between the military government and the civil administration is unwarranted.

70. This episode was recounted in the Tel Aviv newspaper *Ha'ir*, September 11, 1987. It is similar to many other stories of collaborator recruitment.

71. This type of familial response is not unique to the Arab world. The "comfort women" of World War II—Korean girls coerced into prostitution by the Japanese military—were usually shunned by their own families at the war's end (*New York Times*, January 27, 1992).

72. *Ha'ir*, September 11, 1987. The Mattar house of prostitution was well known in the Bethlehem area (where Bayt Jala is located). Four years into the uprising, Nina Mattar was badly beaten by fellow Palestinians for her activities, and the house in question was destroyed.

73. B'tselem, *Collaborators in the Occupied Territories*, p. 143.

74. *New Outlook*, November–December 1989, p. 29.

75. Salim Tamari, "Israel's Search for a Native Pillar: The Village Leagues," in Aruri, ed., *Occupation*, p. 609.

76. Interestingly, the Village Leagues heads in Ramallah and Bethlehem—perhaps the areas of greatest educational achievement among Palestinians in the West Bank and Gaza—were both illiterate. Yusuf al-Khatib of Ramallah was eventually assassinated, while Bishara Qumsiya of Bethlehem renounced his collaboration during the Intifada. Ibid., p. 610.

77. B'tselem, *Collaborators in the Occupied Territories*, pp. 26–27.

78. Ibid., p. 33.

79. Ibid., p. 27.

80. Bayan 8, February 19, 1988.

81. *Christian Science Monitor*, April 22, 1988.

82. Ibid.

83. *Jerusalem Post*, September 10, 1989.

84. *Jerusalem Post*, December 18, 1989.

85. B'tselem, *Collaborators in the Occupied Territories*, p. 82.

86. *Jerusalem Post*, September 26, 1989.

87. Daoud Kuttab, "A Profile of the Stone Throwers," *Journal of Palestine Studies*, no. 67 (Spring 1988).

88. Interview with Sa'id Kan'an, a notable from Nablus, February 18, 1990.

89. *New York Times*, September 23, 1989, and *Jerusalem Post*, September 26, 1989.

90. For details on these units and their activities, see B'tselem, *Activity of the Undercover Units in the Occupied Territories* (Jerusalem, 1992); Palestine Human Rights Information Center, *Targeting to Kill: Israel's Undercover Units* (Jerusalem, 1992); and Amnesty International, news release, January 3, 1990.

91. The number is in some dispute. The Israeli government uses the highest figure, eighteen, while other sources halve this figure. From the beginning of the Intifada through November 1993, the Associated Press counted 771 killings on suspicion of collaboration.

92. Bayan 40, issued May 22, 1989.

93. Bayan 44, issued August 15, 1989.

94. *Jerusalem Post*, February 22, 1990.

95. *Jerusalem Post*, December 1, 1989.

96. B'tselem, *Collaborators in the Occupied Territories*, pp. 152–53.

97. *Jerusalem Post*, October 22, 1989.

98. Information on collaborator villages comes from B'tselem, *Collaborators in the Occupied Territories*, pp. 193–95, and Haitham Hamad, "Palestinian Snitches Live in Uneasy Limbo," *San Francisco Chronicle*, June 2, 1994.

99. B'tselem, *Collaborators in the Occupied Territories*, p. 108.

100. *Jerusalem Post*, November 24, 1989.

101. *Jerusalem Post*, December 3, 1989.

102. *Jerusalem Post*, December 4, 1989.

103. Ibid.

104. I was living in the West Bank during this period and make this assessment based on my own discussions with Palestinians following the interview.

105. *Jerusalem Post*, December 4, 1989.

106. Frantz Fanon, *The Wretched of the Earth* (New York: Grove Press, 1963). See esp. pp. 35–95.

107. Interview with Sari Nusayba, East Jerusalem, February 5, 1990.

108. Interview following a fire bombing in East Jerusalem, February 25, 1990. *'Araq*, or *arak*, is a licorice liqueur popular in the Levant.

109. *Jerusalem Post*, February 18, 1990.

110. *Jerusalem Post*, March 11, 1990.

111. *Al-Fajr* (weekly), December 4, 1989, and *Jerusalem Post*, November 24, 1989.

112. *Al-Fajr* (weekly), December 4, 1989. The quote comes from the leaflet issued on November 27, 1989, as cited by *Al-Fajr*.

113. *Jerusalem Post*, December 29, 1989.

114. *Jerusalem Post*, January 17, 1990.

115. B'tselem, *Collaborators in the Occupied Territories*, pp. 109–10.

116. *Jerusalem Post*, September 10, 1989.

117. Interview with Sari Nusayba, East Jerusalem, February 5, 1990.

118. B'tselem, *Collaborators in the Occupied Territories*, p. 106.

119. Bayan 45, September 5, 1989.

6. Hamas and the Islamist Mobilization

1. Michael Walzer, "A Theory of Revolution," *Marxist Perspectives* 2, no. 1 (Spring 1979), p. 31.

2. The information on Jihad comes from Nemat Guenena, *The Jihad: An Islamic Alternative in Egypt*, Cairo Papers in Social Science 9, no. 2 (Cairo: American University in Cairo Press, Summer 1986). See also Hamied N. Ansari,

"The Islamic Militants in Egyptian Politics," *International Journal of Middle East Studies* 16 (1984), and Saad Eddin Ibrahim,"Anatomy of Egypt's Militant Islamic Groups: Methodological Note and Preliminary Findings," *International Journal of Middle East Studies* 12 (1980).

3. There is some evidence to suggest that in Egypt in the 1990s the profile of a typical radical Islamist changed somewhat to a younger, less-educated individual. According to the Ibn Khaldun Center's (Cairo) statistics of arrested Islamists, the "typical" Islamist has gotten younger (the median age going from the upper twenties to the lower twenties since the 1970s), less educated (four out of five Islamists in the 1970s went to university; only one out of five in the 1990s did), and less urban (55 percent from large cities in the 1970s; only 15 percent in the 1990s).

4. Manfred Halpern, *The Politics of Social Change in the Middle East and North Africa* (Princeton: Princeton University Press, 1963), p. 52.

5. For the most provocative work on this subject, see Fouad Ajami, *The Arab Predicament: Arab Political Thought and Practice since 1967* (Cambridge: Cambridge University Press, 1981; reissued in 1992).

6. Sahliyeh, *In Search of Leadership*.

7. For a good general survey of the Palestinian Islamist movement, see Ziad Abu-Amr, *Islamic Fundamentalism in the West Bank and Gaza: Muslim Brotherhood and Islamic Jihad* (Bloomington: Indiana University Press, 1994). This is a translation of his original work of the same title in Arabic ('Akka: Dar al-'Aswar, 1989). See also Hisham H. Ahmad, *Hamas, from Religious Salvation to Political Transformation: The Rise of Hamas in Palestinian Society* (Jerusalem: PASSIA, 1994).

8. Mohammad K. Shadid, "The Muslim Brotherhood Movement in the West Bank and Gaza," *Third World Quarterly* 10, no. 2 (April 1988), p. 663.

9. Ibid., p. 672.

10. All sources agree that the number of mosques in Gaza at least doubled during this period, but they do not agree on the numbers. Ze'ev Schiff and Ehud Ya'ari, *Intifada: The Palestinian Uprising—Israel's Third Front* (New York: Simon & Schuster, 1990), p. 225, cite an increase from 77 to 160. Don Peretz, *Intifada: The Palestinian Uprising* (Boulder: Westview, 1990), p. 103, uses similar numbers: from 75 to 150. *The Middle East*, no. 169 (November 1988), p. 15, states that the number of Gazan mosques during this period went from 200 to 600!

11. Schiff and Ya'ari, *Intifada*, p. 225.

12. The shari'a college formed the basis of what later became Hebron University.

13. Emile Sahliyeh,"The West Bank and Gaza Strip," in Shireen Hunter, ed., *The Politics of Islamic Revivalism: Diversity and Unity* (Bloomington: Indiana University Press, 1988), p. 92.

14. Ibid. According to Schiff and Ya'ari (p. 226), one such committee in Nablus, run by the Muslim Brethren, "controlled the allocation of welfare to 10,000 needy families, granting loans and scholarships, hiring lawyers for detainees, paying compensation for property damaged by the army, and running orphanages, homes for the aged, and even an independent high school."

15. Sahliyeh, *In Search of Leadership*, p. 144.

16. Abu-Amr, *Islamic Fundamentalism in the West Bank and Gaza*, p. 16.

17. Ibid., p. 16.

18. Interview with Ziad Abu-Amr, Ramallah and Jerusalem, January 20, 1990.

19. Evidence for this proposition includes the results of the 1987 student body elections at the Islamic University in Gaza. Whereas the actively confrontational Islamic Jihad garnered 11 percent of the male vote, it received only 4 percent of the female vote. Conversely, the more quietist Muslim Brethren received 75

percent of the female vote and 60 percent of the male vote. See *al-Fajr* (weekly), December 6, 1987.

20. This observation was made to me by Dr. Ali Jarbawi, a professor at Bir Zeit University, in an interview, Ramallah, September 27, 1989.

21. The results can be found in Mohammad Shadid and Rick Seltzer, "Political Attitudes of Palestinians in the West Bank and Gaza Strip," *Middle East Journal* 42, no. 1 (Winter 1988).

22. Shadid, "The Muslim Brotherhood," p. 660.

23. Sahliyeh, "The West Bank and Gaza Strip," p. 98.

24. Shadid ("The Muslim Brotherhood," p. 671) notes the emergence of an "Islamic theater" in the occupied territories in the 1980s, which dealt with political issues. Often the shows were satires of the activities and the ideology of the Palestinian nationalist camp.

25. Ibid., p. 663.

26. Ibid., p. 671.

27. The results of the survey can be found in Iyad Barghouti, "Religion and Politics among the Students of the Najah National University," *Middle Eastern Studies* 27, no. 2 (April 1991). The results had been published earlier in Arabic in *Shu'un Akadimiya*, no. 5 (Summer 1989).

28. Defined as those who answered "always" or "sometimes" to the question of religious observance, instead of "rarely" or "never." Ibid., p. 205.

29. See Sahliyeh, *In Search of Leadership*, p. 142.

30. The principal text for the early history and organizational makeup of the Muslim Brethren is Richard P. Mitchell, *The Society of Muslim Brethren* (London: Oxford University Press, 1969).

31. The ideological arguments for such views were most famously articulated by Sayyid Qutb in a book entitled *Ma'allim f'il-Tariq* (Signposts on the road), which indirectly called for the overthrow of Nasir's regime. Qutb, who sought to take the Muslim Brethren in a very different and more confrontational direction than it was then heading, was hanged for his views.

32. While its charter called exclusively for social and cultural activities, the Brethren in Jordan was clearly a political organization as well. The Brethren was used as a counterweight by the regime against both pan-Arabists and more radical Islamists.

33. Shadid, "The Muslim Brotherhood," p. 660.

34. Ibid., pp. 660–61.

35. Ibid., p. 672.

36. Interview with shaykh from the Hizb al-Tahrir al-Islami, Hebron, August 26, 1989.

37. Shadid, "The Muslim Brotherhood," pp. 680–81.

38. Ibid., p. 666.

39. Ibid., p. 665.

40. Ibid., p. 666.

41. Peretz (*Intifada*, p. 103) has suggested that there were eight offshoots of the Muslim Brethren in the 1980s in Gaza alone.

42. Interview with Ziad Abu-Amr, East Jerusalem and Ramallah, January 20, 1990.

43. Schiff and Ya'ari, *Intifada*, p. 215.

44. Jean-François Legrain, "The Islamic Movement and the Intifada," in Nassar and Heacock, *Intifada*, pp. 176–78.

45. Ali Jarbawi, *The Intifada and the Political Leadership in the West Bank and Gaza Strip* (in Arabic) (Beirut: Dar al-Tali'a, 1989), p. 102. For a more sensationalist version, see the *Jerusalem Post*, October 21, 1987.

46. Shadid, "The Muslim Brotherhood," p. 678.

47. Legrain, "The Islamic Movement," p. 178.

48. Those killed in Cyprus have variously been called Fatah activists with close ties to Jihad and Jihad activists with close ties to Fatah. The former interpretation is offered by Schiff and Ya'ari (p. 228) and the latter by Legrain (p. 180) and the *Jerusalem Post*, April 17, 1988.

49. Jihad carried out sporadic acts of violence after Oslo. While it never fully recovered from the earlier crackdown, it was enough of a problem for Israel that Rabin had its leader, Fathi al-Shaqaqi, assassinated in Malta in 1995.

50. There is some debate over interpreting the creation of Hamas. Abu-Amr, in *Islamic Fundamentalism in the West Bank and Gaza*, argues that the formation of Hamas did not represent a break in the Muslim Brethren, but was rather a logical continuation of Brethren policy, made by long-time Brethren leaders (passim, but esp. pp. 67–68). His analysis denies the kinds of internal pressures which had built up in the Brethren, in part because of the changing nature of its recruitment in the 1980s. At the same time, Abu-Amr admits that a radicalization of the Islamist movement occurred (p. 134), but gives no sociological explanation for such radicalization. The model employed in this chapter corrects this deficiency.

51. Hamas was accused of inflating the numbers of their leaflets to give the impression that Hamas had issued more leaflets—and started them earlier—than the UNLU. For example, Hamas bayan 24, issued on June 26, 1988, was really Hamas's fifteenth leaflet, according to Legrain (p. 184). In this way, Hamas tried to claim the preeminent leadership role in the Intifada, giving the impression that the UNLU was just mimicking Hamas, not the reverse.

52. The acronym "Hamas" by itself constitutes an Arabic word meaning "ardor" or "zeal." Hamas also has the sense of "steadfast" or "unflinching" based on its relation to other Arabic words (i.e., *hamis* and *ahmas*). This should not be confused with the word usually used for steadfastness, *sumud*.

53. The leaflet is in the author's possession.

54. Naming the uprising was also debated, with the DFLP's choice, Intifada, quickly gaining currency. Intifada means "shaking off," like a wet dog would shake off water.

55. The interpretation of the Khaybir story comes from Raphael Israeli, "Islamic Fundamentalism among the Palestinian Arabs," *Survey of Arab Affairs*, August 15, 1989, p. 6.

56. This view of Yasin's role was confirmed by a number of observers, including Muhammad Nazzal, then Hamas spokesman in Jordan. Interview, April 13, 1994, Amman.

57. Historically, waqf lands are lands endowed to the religious hierarchy, often in perpetuity, for the benefit of the Muslim community. Depending on the lands, the Islamic clergy either maintained daily control (as with the Haram al-Sharif in Jerusalem) or, in the case of agricultural areas, leased them back to their owners and used the profits to sustain its activities. Landowners would benefit from endowing their lands in terms of both ideal interests (supporting the Muslim community) and material ones. Waqf lands were generally excluded from both taxes by the state and division through inheritance laws. In this way, large waqf landholdings remained intact.

58. Hamas uses the Arabic *wataniyya*, not *qawmiyya*. The former is usually employed in Arabic to represent state-based nationalism (e.g., Egyptian nationalism), while the latter has a communal or ethnic sense and is used in the phrase "Arab nationalism" (*al-qawmiyya al-'Arabiyya*).

59. *HaAretz*, August 23, 1991, as cited in Foreign Broadcasting and Information Service (FBIS), August 27, 1991.

60. This was a reference to Israel's demanding a veto over Palestinian representation at Madrid and the Washington talks. Israel wanted to exclude Palestinians from the Diaspora and East Jerusalem, symbolically denying both the right of return and the occupied status of East Jerusalem.

61. Poleg served as commander of the IDF in Gaza from July 1988 to March 1990 and was later elected mayor of Natanya. In a December 1994 interview he stated: "Hamas was set up by us, in the mid-1980s, as a competitive movement to the PLO. The idea was that Hamas would carry out cultural, educational, and humanitarian activities. Within a few months the movement became more militant, and began leading the violent resistance, including the use of guns against the IDF." *Mideast Mirror*, December 15, 1994, pp. 5–6. Marwan Muasher, Jordan's first ambassador to Israel and former spokesman for Jordan's delegation to the Washington peace talks, likes to tell the story of his delegation's meeting with President Bush. A member of the delegation commented that Israel "created" Hamas. Surprised, Bush turned to advisor Dennis Ross and asked if this were true. Ross replied simply "yes." Interview with Marwan Muasher, April 11, 1994, Amman.

62. Funding Islamists also occurred, as David Shipler pointed out in *Arab and Jew: Wounded Spirits in a Promised Land* (New York: Times Books, 1986), p. 177. Michel Sela, a respected Israeli journalist, reported that assistance also included arming certain Islamists, although this was certainly a less common form of support. See her article "The Islamic Factor," *Jerusalem Post*, October 25, 1989.

63. Lisa Taraki, "The Islamic Resistance Movement in the Palestinian Uprising," in Lockman and Beinin, eds., *Intifada*, p. 171.

64. IDF soldiers reportedly detained and confiscated identification cards of Ramallah merchants who did not comply with the Hamas strike of September 9, 1988; see *Middle East*, no. 169 (November 1988), p. 16. Yehuda Litani's article in the *Jerusalem Post*, September 8, 1988, outlines further measures Israel took to support the Islamists early in the Intifada.

65. *Hadashot*, November 6, 1991, as cited in FBIS, November 6, 1991.

66. Reported in *HaAretz*, November 9, 1992, as cited in FBIS, November 10, 1992.

67. Interview with Muhammad Nazzal, Amman, Jordan, April 13, 1994.

68. *Jerusalem Post*, August 22, 1988.

69. Many stores in heavily touristed areas, such as East Jerusalem, devised clandestine means to stay open during strike days or hours, especially after the first year of the uprising.

70. *Jerusalem Post*, March 19, 1990.

71. *Middle East International*, May 1, 1992, p. 8.

72. Interview, East Jerusalem, September 18, 1989.

73. UNLU bayan 48 covered the events of late November and early December 1989 and did not include a strike day for November 29.

74. *Jerusalem Post*, November 30, 1989.

75. One other competing historiography is worth mentioning. The exact beginning of the Intifada was disputed, and thus could not be honored with a single strike day. While Hamas and the UNLU called a strike on the ninth of every month (dating the Intifada from December 9, 1987), Islamic Jihad dated the Intifada from December 6, 1987, so called for a strike on the sixth of each month.

76. The actual expulsion was held up about twenty-four hours while an emergency appeal on behalf of the expellees was being heard before the Israeli High Court of Justice. The security forces took advantage of this delay by

returning 35 Palestinians for various reasons and "replacing" them with 32 others, making the total number of initial expellees 415. A journalist from Gaza whom Israel had tried to silence on a number of occasions, Tahir Shritah, was among those initially taken to Lebanon but was later returned under heavy international pressure from the Western media. A small number were returned within a few weeks because of failing health, leaving just under 400 behind. The High Court has never reversed a military government's expulsion order, even though nearly 2,000 Palestinians have been expelled in clear violation of the Fourth Geneva Convention. In this case it ruled, in effect, that while mass expulsion was illegal, if individual expulsion orders were drawn up for each of the 400 Palestinians then the expulsions could proceed. This legal stretch was labeled by jurist and human rights activist Raja Shehadeh as "a joke, a cruel joke"; *al-Fajr* (weekly), February 1, 1993.

77. Data for the expellees were gathered from B'tselem, *Deportation of Palestinians from the Occupied Territories and the Mass Deportation of December 1992* (Jerusalem, June 1993); *Middle East International*, January 8, 1993; *al-Fajr* (weekly), December 28, 1992; *HaAretz*, December 21, 1992, as cited in FBIS, December 21, 1992; and other documentation provided to me by al-Haq, B'tselem, and the Palestine Human Rights Information Center.

78. Interestingly, the relatively poor relations between Hamas and the Islamic Jihad (having been historically closer to Fatah than the Muslim Brethren) were reproduced in Lebanon during the year most expellees resided in the border encampment. In fact, for several months, each group had its own spokesman: Abd al-Aziz al-Rantisi for Hamas and Shaykh Abdallah Shami' for Islamic Jihad.

79. Bayan 43, July 25, 1989.

80. Schiff and Ya'ari, *Intifada*, pp. 221–22.

81. A picture of the poster can be found in the newspaper *Sawt al-Haq w'al-Hurriya*, December 15, 1989. *Sawt al-Haq* is associated with the views of the Muslim Brethren.

82. "There is but one God and Muhammad is His Prophet." Bearing witness (the meaning of the word *shahada*) to this is one of the five duties incumbent on all Muslims.

83. *Shahid* (pl. *shuhada'*) is an expressly Qur'anic term which was fully adopted by secular forces as well to indicate those who died as a result of the Intifada. The use of the word *shahid* was itself evidence of the blurring of national and Islamic symbolism in the Intifada.

84. Some observers have argued that the November 1988 decision was not so much a policy reversal as a sharpening of a policy which had evolved since 1974, when the PLO declared its intent to establish an independent Palestinian state on "any inch" of liberated Palestine, effectively establishing a two-state solution. While this argument has some truth to it, the heated tone of the PNC debate in Algiers suggested that the Palestinians themselves believed they were making a landmark decision. Certainly the Islamist opposition recognized it as such.

85. Legrain, "The Islamic Movement," p. 181.

86. Quoted in Ziad Abu-Amr, "The Politics of the Intifada," in Michael Hudson, ed., *The Palestinians: New Directions* (Washington, D.C.: Center for Contemporary Arab Studies, Georgetown University, 1990), p. 9.

87. Hamas bayan 32.

88. The Royal Commission of Inquiry, or Peel Commission, was sent by Britain to Palestine in November 1936 in order to collect information and then recommend to London the best solution for Palestine's future. Initially, Arab Palestinians boycotted the committee hearings, but eventually did testify against parti-

tion. In spite of Arab objections, the committee recommendations, contained in a 400-page report issued in July 1937, called for partition. The Peel report foresaw an Arab state in what is today roughly the West Bank, Gaza, the Negev (Naqab) desert, and an enclave around Jaffa. The Jewish state would occupy the coastal strip from, roughly, Ashkelon to the Lebanon border in addition to the Galilee region. International enclaves would be found around Nazareth and in a strip from Jerusalem to the Mediterranean Sea.

89. The origins of the 1991 split in the DFLP are found in the 1988 PNC resolutions, with Hawatma opposed to and others supportive of the new policies. Ideologically, the 'Abd Rabbu offshoot ('Abd-Rabbu was the chief Palestinian negotiator during the short-lived U.S.-PLO dialogue) of the DFLP, known as FIDA, viewed itself as coming to terms with the collapse of the USSR, while Hawatma and his faction "remained Marxist-Leninist even after 1989—never reconsidering their program [in light of the Soviet collapse]." Interview with Salih Ra'fat, FIDA representative in Jordan, April 18, 1994, Amman.

90. Such consistency remained through Oslo, and only began to unravel over the 1994 Cairo accord when the PPP (formerly PCP) and FIDA openly opposed Arafat's concessions.

91. *Jerusalem Post*, October 29, 1989.

92. *Jerusalem Post*, December 14, 1989.

93. Instead, Hamas activists went on a concerted graffiti campaign to discredit any possible negotiations. Seemingly, their favorite graffito took the form of a rhyming couplet:

na'm l'il-muqawama	Yes to the Struggle
alf la' l'il-musawama	A thousand no's to bargaining

94. Al-Aqsa is the most important mosque in Palestine, located on the Haram al-Sharif, or Noble Sanctuary (the Temple Mount), in the Old City of Jerusalem. It ranks behind only Mecca and Medina in importance in the Islamic world.

95. The Hamas statement was issued on September 23, 1991, and is reproduced in FBIS, October 17, 1991. The statement that no "council, organization, state, or individual" is entitled to cede any part of Palestine was a reference to, respectively, the PNC, the PLO, Jordan, and Yasir Arafat.

96. *New York Times*, October 22, 1991.

97. Tehran Voice of the Islamic Republic of Iran (in Arabic), December 24, 1991, as reported in FBIS, December 26, 1991.

98. *Al-Nahar*, December 28, 1991, as reported in FBIS, January 3, 1992.

99. *Al-Sharq al-Awsat*, July 14, 1992, as cited in FBIS, August 26, 1992.

100. *Al-'Ahd* (Beirut), October 30, 1992, as cited in FBIS, November 19, 1992.

101. *Jerusalem Post*, March 2, 1992.

102. *Jordan Times*, May 23–24, 1992, as cited in FBIS, May 28, 1992.

103. Middle East News Agency, Cairo, June 12, 1992, as cited in FBIS, June 16, 1992.

104. *AFP*, Paris, June 28, 1992, as cited in FBIS, June 29, 1992.

105. *Voice of Palestine* (in Arabic), Algiers, July 9, 1992, as cited in FBIS, July 10, 1992.

106. See the PLO Executive Committee statement of July 22, 1992, which accused Hamas of betraying the Palestinian cause. *Voice of Palestine* (in Arabic), Algiers, July 23, 1992, as cited in FBIS, July 24, 1992. In November 1992 Iran recognized Hamas as the official representative of the Palestinians.

107. The Ten-Point Agreement can be found in *al-Dustur*, January 12, 1993, as cited in FBIS, January 12, 1993.

108. Reported by Israel Television Network (Arabic service), April 21, 1993, as cited in FBIS, April 22, 1993.

109. There has been speculation Arafat told 'Abd al-Shafi' about the Oslo talks and that is what led to his return to Washington. 'Abd al-Shafi', however, denied any knowledge of the secret Oslo talks and, in hindsight, viewed the return to Washington as a mistake. Interview with 'Abd al-Shafi', May 7, 1994, Gaza City.

110. *Jerusalem Post*, November 10, 1989.

111. *Middle East International*, October 22, 1993, p. 6.

112. *Al-Quds*, January 5, 1994, as cited in FBIS, January 7, 1994.

113. Disillusionment was not limited to Hamas supporters. In response to both the continuing occupation and several assassinations by undercover Israeli forces of their colleagues, some Fatah cadres returned to armed struggle against Israeli targets briefly during this period.

114. See the interview with Hamas spokesman Ibrahim Ghuwsha in *al-Diyar*, November 27, 1993, as cited in FBIS, December 8, 1993.

115. Ibid.

7. The Logic of Palestinian State-Building after Oslo

1. The interim agreement is alternately known as Oslo II or the Taba Accords.

2. Graham Usher, "The Politics of Internal Security: The PA's New Intelligence Services," *Journal of Palestine Studies* 25, no. 2 (Winter 1996), p. 23.

3. Ibid.

4. Some 27,000 were employed in the civil bureaucracy, 22,000 were policemen, and about 9,000 were security personnel.

5. Scheduled for late 1996.

6. *Economist*, April 1, 1995.

7. *New York Times*, August 7, 1994.

8. *Monterey County Herald*, December 28, 1993.

9. Sara Roy, "'The Seed of Chaos, and of Night': The Gaza Strip after the Agreement," *Journal of Palestine Studies* 23, no. 3 (Spring 1994), p. 86.

10. Ibid.

11. Interview with a leading PLO cadre, Gaza, December 15, 1995.

12. Khalil Shikaki, "The Peace Process, National Reconstruction, and the Transition to Democracy in Palestine," *Journal of Palestine Studies* 25, no. 2 (Winter 1996), p. 10.

13. Usher, "The Politics of Internal Security," pp. 23–24.

14. This information comes from a talk by Dennis Sullivan on Palestinian NGOs, given at PASSIA, East Jerusalem, November 1, 1995.

15. This observation comes from numerous interviews held by the author with members of each group during the fall of 1995. The quote comes from an interview with Rana Bishara, the coordinator for a network of major NGOs in the West Bank and Gaza, Shu'fat, December 12, 1995.

16. Lots vary by number, so West Bank solution (sold for 6 NIS) can be distinguished from Gazan batches (sold at 4 NIS because of the subsidy). Two doctors confirmed this account. They preferred to remain anonymous.

17. CPRS data, cited in Shikaki, "The Peace Process," p. 7.

18. *Yedi'ot Ahronat*, September 7, 1993. Cited in Usher, "The Politics of Internal Security," p. 28.

19. Hamas claimed responsibility for three of the four bombings; Islamic Jihad claimed the fourth.

20. *Middle East International*, March 31, 1996, p. 6.

21. Usher, "The Politics of Internal Security," p. 30.

22. This debate also was held within the PFLP, with activists living in Gaza arguing for participation in the elections while those on the outside and to a lesser degree in the West Bank argued for boycotting the elections. The boycott vote won the day.

23. *Jerusalem Post*, December 15, 1995.

24. *New York Times*, March 4, 1996.

25. The Council and Executive Authority technically replaced the PA, which was an interim body established to manage affairs until the elections could be held. For simplicity's sake, I continue to use the term PA to represent the political regime in Gaza and the West Bank, headed by Yasir Arafat.

26. Interview with Khalil Shikaki, Nablus, December 13, 1995. According to Shikaki, the commission's plan also included a direct vote for the "Ra'is" as well, which Arafat also rejected for fear that he might not win. He changed his mind later on this issue when it became clear he would win easily.

27. Interview, Bayt Sahur, December 20, 1995.

28. Six seats were set aside for Christian candidates and one for the small Jewish Samaritan sect near Nablus which, proportionately, considerably over-represented these two communities.

29. There was some discussion of a quota representation for women as well (up to 30 percent of the seats), but this was ultimately rejected.

30. From a speech given by Shibley Telhami to the United Nations Conference on Palestine, Paris, June 30, 1995.

31. The map was displayed in the Knesset prior to its vote on Oslo II. When a picture of the map was subsequently reproduced in Israeli and Palestinian newspapers, it created a firestorm of criticism, much to Arafat's embarrassment. The map was not included in the Oslo II document distributed to the public (as had been promised), probably to avoid further embarrassment of Arafat.

INDEX

GLENN E. ROBINSON is Assistant Professor at the Naval Post-graduate School in Monterey, California, where he teaches courses on the Middle East and on political violence. He is also affiliated with the Center for Middle Eastern Studies at the University of California, Berkeley.